ARCTIC CIRCLE
ICELAND
(Den.)
Diupivogr
Mt. Hecla
FAROE
VIGTEN
Levanger
Hernosand
Umea
Gefle
CHRISTIANIA
Stavanger
Drammen
Gothenburg
Norrkoping
GOTHLAND
BALTIC SEA
Wick
SCOTLAND
COPENHAGEN
DENMARK
Glasgow
Edinburgh
Belfast
Newcastle
Hamburg
Bremen
Stettin
Danzig
IRELAND
Dublin
Cork
Liverpool
ENGLAND
LONDON
BERLIN
Dresden
Frankfort
Prague
Breslau
POLAND
Munich
STREAM
Havre
PARIS
Strasburg
BERNE
Budapest
Nantes
FRANCE
VIENNA
Bay of Biscay
Trieste
Milan
Belgrade
Bordeaux
Marseilles
Adriatic Sea
SERVIA
Corunna
Toulouse
Leghorn
Vigo
Pyrenees
CORSICA
ROME
Cetinje
MONTE NEGRO
Oporto
MADRID
Barcelona
SARDINIA
Naples
Salonica
LISBON
SPAIN
Valencia
Palermo
PORT.
Cordova
Cadiz
Constantine
SICILY
Gibraltar
Algiers
Tunis
TUNIS
MALTA
Oran
ALGERIA
Tangier
Fez
C. Blanco
MOROCCO
Cabes
Tripoli
G. of Sidra
Wargla
Mogador
Morocco
Ghadames
TRIPOLI
Sella
Anjila
Ainsalah
Aksabi
Ghat
Murzuk
Bel Abbas
RIO DE ORO
Rio de Oro
C. Blanco
Wadan
Jebado
Bardai
Dirko
Walata
Timbuktu
Agades
St. Louis
CURRENTS OF THE NORTH ATLANTIC

EX LIBRIS
Jones Collection
MADE IN USA

SOUTHEASTERN BRANCH LIBRARY—UNIVERSITY OF CONNECTICUT—GROTON, CONN.—
JUL 30 1981

WILD OCEAN

Books by Alan Villiers

WILD OCEAN
THE CORAL SEA
MONSOON SEAS
FALMOUTH FOR ORDERS
BY WAY OF CAPE HORN
CRUISE OF THE *CONRAD*
GRAIN RACE
SONS OF SINDBAD
WHALING IN THE FROZEN SOUTH
LAST OF THE WINDSHIPS
THE MAKING OF A SAILOR
THE SET OF THE SAILS
QUEST OF THE SCHOONER *ARGUS*
POSTED MISSING
JOEY GOES TO SEA
PILOT PETE
THE SAILING EAGLE
WAY OF THE SHIP
WHALERS OF THE MIDNIGHT SUN
NOT TO YIELD

McGRAW-HILL BOOK COMPANY, INC.

WILD OCEAN

THE STORY OF THE NORTH ATLANTIC AND THE MEN WHO SAILED IT

ALAN VILLIERS

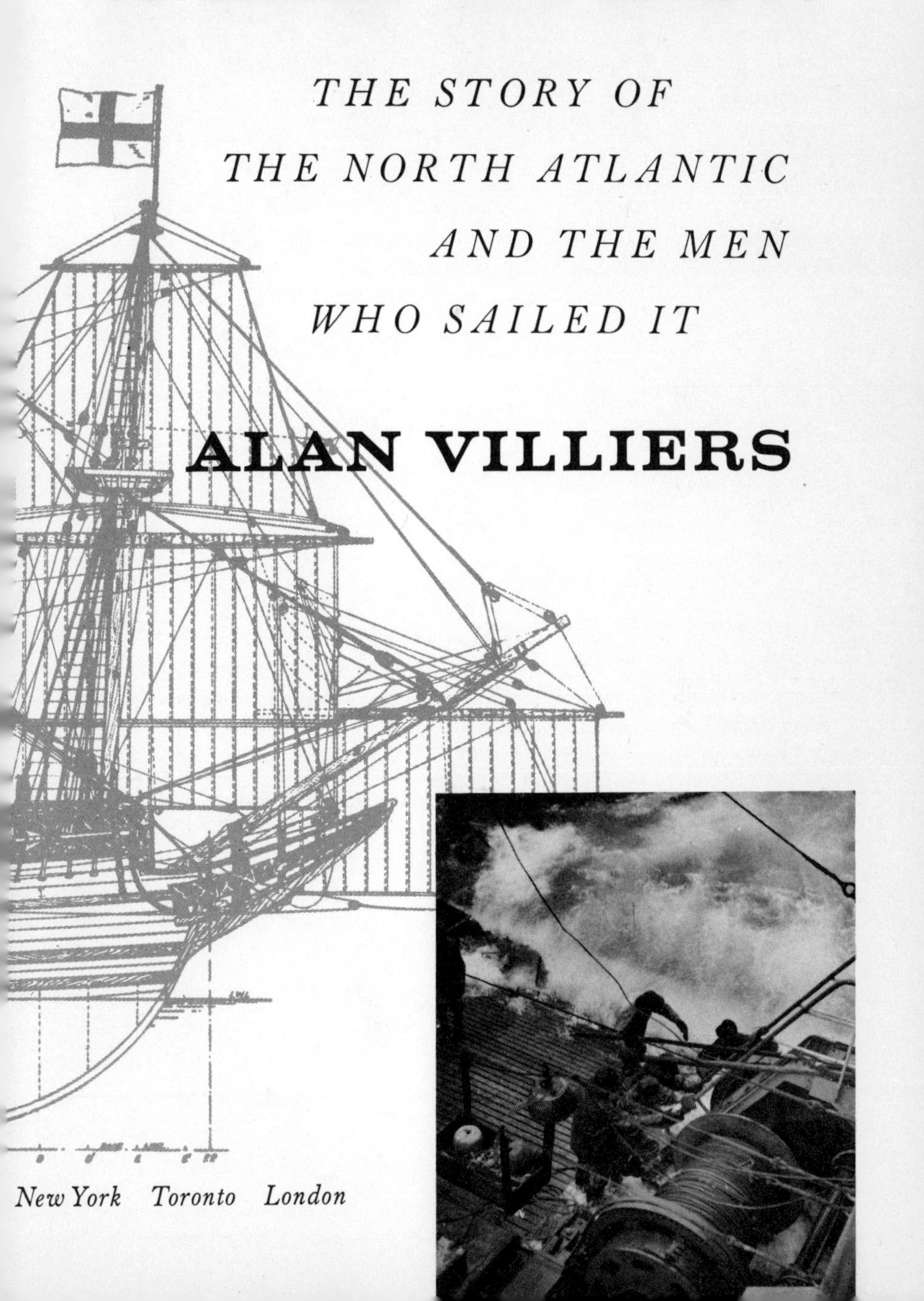

New York Toronto London

WILD OCEAN

Library of Congress Catalog Card Number: 57-9440

Published by the McGraw-Hill Book Company, Inc.
Printed in the United States of America

PREFACE

On almost every aspect of the story of the North Atlantic Ocean, there is not just a book or two but a large shelf of them or a regular library. I have done my best to read most of them. In adding a book which is an attempt to give a concise and straightforward picture of the whole ocean, I can only offer the apology that this is not just another book about the Atlantic. Such as it is, it is my story of that great and storied sea.

I have sailed the Atlantic, perhaps, as much as most men, in peace and war, in all sorts of craft, from a full-rigged ship (which I sailed westward the way Columbus went, and made his landfall on San Salvador) to the liner *Queen Elizabeth;* I have known the ocean from the decks of an aircraft carrier in wartime and from the frail thwarts of a Banker's dory, tossing in the stormy sea off Newfoundland where there is no peace, ever. I have read, and I have been. I have studied, and I have seen. I have looked dispassionately at the records of the great explorers and have discussed their endeavors and their achievements with scholars, seamen, adventurers. Where I could, I have sailed in their tracks myself. At the moment, I am supervising the preparations for a new *Mayflower* to sail in the tracks of the old, from Plymouth, England, toward Plymouth in what is now Massachusetts in the United States. And so I have made such endeavors as I could to know whereof I write: having done what I could to see and to learn. The result is in this book.

As for my sources, they are legion—all those books, mostly culled from the shelves of the National Maritime Museum at Greenwich, London, and I thank the director, Mr. Frank Carr, C.B.E., and his librarian, Mr. John Munday. Those two most interesting sources of original material, the *Mariners' Mirror* (which is the journal of the Society for Nautical Research) and the *American Neptune*, have been invaluable.

For the illustrations, again I am much in debt to the National Maritime Museum (for most of those which are not my own) and, in this department, I thank especially Mr. Michael Robinson, of the Museum staff. I am grateful also to Plimouth Plantation, and to the National Celebration Commission for Jamestown, Williamsburg, and Yorktown, Virginia, for their good cooperation, and for permission to use the photographs which are credited to them.

Alan Villiers

CONTENTS

CHAPTER		PAGE
	Preface	v
1	Wild Ocean	1
2	The Wonderful Gulf Stream	18
3	Before Columbus: Phoenicians and Vikings	35
4	The Pioneers from Portugal	51
5	Christopher Columbus	69
6	The Spanish Main	88
7	The Roanoke Mystery	105
8	The Jamestown Story	121
9	God Works a "Mirakle"	142
10	The New *Mayflower*	156
11	The Struggle for Power	169
12	Privateers, Pirates, Slavers	185
13	Whalemen and Fishermen	204
14	The Wonderful Record of the Packet Ships	219
15	The Atlantic Ferry	232
16	"Drowned from Our Brig, *Mary Celeste*"	248
17	Some Adventurers	265
18	Two World Wars	278
19	Conquest by Air	293
20	Today	305
	Index	313

ILLUSTRATIONS

Elevation of the original *Mayflower* (from Dr. R. C. Anderson's and Mr. Pritchard's drawing of a contemporary ship of same size and rig, courtesy of *Mariner's Mirror*); the *Royal William* crossing the North Atlantic (courtesy of the Trustees of the National Maritime Museum [N.M.M.]); passenger ship in an Atlantic blow; fishing in the North Atlantic *title page*

following page 10

Sailing ships opened the trade routes of the world

Viking ship preserved at Oslo (Photograph courtesy of Science Museum, London); Henry, Prince of Portugal (N.M.M.); the Armada off Fowey, 1588 (N.M.M.); Sir Francis Drake (N.M.M.); model of a Portuguese caravel

Columbus (N.M.M.); model of the *Santa María* (Photograph courtesy of Science Museum, London)

following page 122

Mayflower model at Pilgrim Hall, Plymouth; Construction of *Mayflower II*, at Upham's Shipyard, Brixham, England; Launching of the new *Mayflower*, Brixham

Ship close-hauled on the starboard tack, 1565 (N.M.M.); New England, from Mercator's *Historia Mundi*, 1635 (N.M.M.)

Virginia, from DeBry (N.M.M.); the *Susan Constant*, *God Speed*, and *Discovery* (from a painting by Griffith Baily Coale)

The battle of Trafalgar, 1805 (N.M.M.); the *Serapis* and *Bonhomme Richard* (N.M.M.)

following page 250

Anne Bonney, woman pirate (N.M.M.); the *Prince Frederick* and *Duke*, privateers (N.M.M.)

Sailing the *Joseph Conrad* in Columbus's tracks; the *Red Jacket*, American clipper (N.M.M.); the American whaler *California;* the *Clermont* (N.M.M.); typical West Indiamen (N.M.M.); Donald McKay (N.M.M.); model of the *Sirius; Great Eastern*

Portuguese fishermen; becalmed in the Sargasso Sea; whaling (N.M.M.)

WILD OCEAN

1

WHAT ARE the seven seas? I don't know. It seems to me that I have sailed in at least seventeen—Yellow, Red, White, Black, Timor, Arafura, Adriatic, Java, China, Arabian, Baltic, Mediterranean, Caribbean, Coral, Tasman, Greenland, and North Seas—and that is only the beginning. Maybe "seven" refers to the oceans, for there are in fact seven of them—the North and South Atlantics, North and South Pacifics, the Indian, the Arctic, and Antarctic oceans.

Of these, the North Atlantic is the smallest, but it has been of greater importance to man than all the others put together. The proportionate length of its vast coastline, the tremendous area drained by the rivers flowing into it from the long slopes of the two broad continents which form its western and eastern boundaries, the great inland bays and seas which open from it on both sides to give ready access to all the Western world, the wealth and power of its continental islands and bordering lands, the profusion of good harbors which surround it, the richness of its long-exploited fisheries—it is no wonder that the North Atlantic is the most colorful, most used, most fought over, and the richest in history of all the sea areas in the modern world.

Yet, in its confines from the Arctic Circle in the north to the Equator in the south, its waters cover less than a tenth the area of the oceans of the world. Its coastlines, not counting those on the inland seas to which it is connected, extend over more than 70,000 miles. Its area, again not reckoning those inland seas, is some 10½ million square miles. Its average depth is just over 2,000 fathoms, and its mid-Atlantic ridge, following roughly the line of Western Europe and the bulge of Africa, may be the ancient backbone of the Western world, the former dividing line between what we know now as the Old World and the New. It has long been noted that the western seaboard of Europe-Africa fits roughly into the eastern seaboard of the Americas, allowing for a few million years of weathering. Did the two drift apart from some ancient cataclysm, millions of years ago? Many scientists consider it probable that they did, and they are accumulating new evidence and arguments to support the theory. At the meeting of the British Association held in Sheffield, England, in September, 1956, scientists agreed that the gap between Europe and America had widened by at least a thousand miles during the past 150 million years—a few yesterdays in the story of the earth.

This question of the crustal movement of the earth was discussed at length. Modern methods of investigation have opened up a wide range of probabilities in this fascinating field of the drift of continents and the movement of poles. There is no doubt that there have been large movements of the continents during the history of the earth. England, said the president of the association, Prof. P. M. S. Blackett, F.R.S., had moved a long way northward during the past 150 million years, from a previous position near the Equator, and North America had made the same kind of movement. It looked as if the land masses of the Northern Hemisphere had moved collectively some 40 degrees relative to the poles, although with smaller, but considerable, relative motions of the parts—for instance, the widening of the gap between Europe and America.

How old the North Atlantic (more or less as we know it now) may be, how it all began—these are matters for further investigation. But it is a curious fact that the apparent wandering of the North Pole, as ascertained by scientists using a system based on the magnetic measurements of rocks, follows a different course depending on whether the course is calculated from measurements made in Britain or in the United States. This inconsistency can be removed if the distance between the two countries is taken to have increased by 2,000 miles during the past 170 million years, with the movement largely completed 30 million years ago. There can be little doubt that the Atlantic *has* widened.

It must have been something of a ditch when it all began, because even now it is not wide, as oceans go. From western Ireland to eastern Newfoundland, the distance across is 1,750 miles—about two days' run in a 35-knot steamer and two hours in a fast jet aircraft—and in the south, from Cape Palmas in West Africa to Cape São Roque in South America, the width is 1,600 miles. (Cape São Roque is actually washed by the waters of the South Atlantic, just below the Equator.) At its widest, which is on latitude 25 degrees north, the North Atlantic is 4,500 miles across. Even at that, it is wider than the South Atlantic, for the greatest breadth of that ocean, land to land, is 3,700 miles.

The South Atlantic is a very different division of the ocean from its old and bad-tempered brother in the north. By comparison, its coastline is simple. Its fronting continents are narrow, jutting into it lengthwise. It has no inland seas, while in the north there are the Mediterranean, Baltic, Gulf of St. Lawrence, Hudson Bay, Gulf of Mexico, Caribbean. Many more rivers flow into the North Atlantic—the great St. Lawrence, Mississippi, and Hudson in North America; the Amazon and Orinoco from South America; the Elbe, Rhine, Loire, Tagus, Rhone in Europe; the Niger and Senegal in West Africa. Geographers estimate that 20 million square miles of rich territory drain into the North Atlantic, some four times the area draining into all the Pacific. And yet the water of the North Atlantic, despite the influx of all this fresh water and the vast quantities of melted ice which drift southward from the Arctic Ocean, is the saltiest of all oceans.

The tremendous land masses both to the west and to the east, the frozen sea in the north, and its comparatively narrow entrance in the south, to some extent upset the more normal weather patterns which make, by comparison, the South Atlantic a more placid ocean. Whatever else it might be, no one would call the North

Atlantic peaceful. From Norway's grim western seaboard, round by the west of Scotland and the Western Isles, all down the west of Ireland and of Cornwall, of Devon, and of Wales, across the wild Bay of Biscay and past Cape Finisterre, southward down Portugal's high, rugged, and lovely coast, the waters of the North Atlantic beat at Europe. They do not "wash" the coasts: they thrash them violently, turbulently, without end. From the Point of Sagres near St. Vincent to the North Cape of Norway, the wild challenge of Atlantic gales has screamed for a billion years, and the coastline that survives the onslaught is harsh and strewn with offshore rocks, over which the sea boils in fury.

In Europe, seamen have always known the North Atlantic as the Western Ocean. In the early days the untamable and little-sailed sea, which sent its violent storms to lash at them and beset their seaports and their beaches with the noisy, fearful challenge of its gales, seemed unconquerable. The march of these wild Atlantic gales against all Europe is most severe in those areas where men are the best seamen, and yet seafaring progress here was slow at first, as compared with that made in kinder seas. Arab, Persian, and Indian dhows crisscrossed the monsoonal waters of the Indian Ocean at least two thousand years before European seamen could manage anything other than coastwise passages in the open waters of the North Atlantic, and the Mediterranean was at least a galley-filled sea while only the Sargasso weed drifted on the surface of the broad Atlantic. The conditions were very different. In the tropic waters of the Indian Ocean there were clearly defined seasons which brought their own winds—the good northeaster, with clear visibility and ideal sailing conditions; the turbulent southwester, which could blow hard but at least provided easy means to sail home again. There was a wind to go out with and another to return with, and, in the northeast season, there was a reasonable assurance of continued good weather. Fishermen working from open beaches could develop craft suited to their purpose, and mariners could learn to extend coastwise passages to ocean wanderings as far as the monsoon blew. Primitive ships could suffice, in such conditions, and did. Even in 1956, many such ships continue to sail the Eastern seas.

But in Europe it was not so. The North Atlantic, beyond the tropic's edge, could blow home gales at any season, and there were no seasonal winds, obligingly changing direction twice a year, to help mariners on their way.

On their way to what? What lay in the West, beyond all that bitter sea? In the Asian East, there was trade. In the East were ancient civilizations. In the East were silks, spices, jewels, gold. The Old World turned east. The long spice and the rich silk roads led there, and the European emporiums for both centered on the Mediterranean. India, Persia, Araby "the Blest," were the sources of riches and of trade. What point was there then in sailing out into the Atlantic, bound for nowhere? European seamen had no incentive to make bold transoceanic voyages. So the Atlantic was not crossed by ships for centuries and, in the end, its opening was a chance by-product of the quest for a sea route to the East. Scholars had long theorized that to sail west would bring ships east, if they sailed far enough, and it was the East they sought. Until the day he died, the great Columbus appears to have had no slightest idea that he had in fact stumbled upon a new world. The continents of the two Americas blocked the sea route westward toward the East, and the idea was too big, too stunning, even for him to grasp.

To sail the North Atlantic, to conduct the rich sailing commerce which grew to flourish there, it was essential first to gain a knowledge of its wind and weather system, of its currents, and its sailing secrets. In the Indian Ocean the matter was much easier. But there was a way to turn the North Atlantic winds to the use of sailing ships, too—even primitive ones. For the winds and surface waters of the Western Ocean went round and round, not in seasons but more or less all the time. To Western Europe's mariners, looking at it from their ancient ports, the ocean's wind system seemed too prone to hard west winds for their puny square-rigged ships to face and fight. They could make coasting passages along the Atlantic's western length, from the Straits of Gibraltar to France, Britain, northwest Europe, and as far as Iceland. They could sail that way in the summer months because there was the shelter of the land, though they had to use great care when crossing the Bay of Biscay and weathering the stormy northwestern promontory of France.

For them no gentle monsoon blew. Across that tumbling Western sea was no route to valued trade, as far as the ordinary mariner could be aware. Ocean of myths and a thousand challenges, ocean of drowned islands and lost peoples, ocean of fabled isles and furious storms, ocean of violent seas and tempests, of raging tides and implacable sets and eddies to sweep a ship toward its rock-strewn bordering land—the North Atlantic was a very different proposition from the Indian Ocean, the Eastern seas, or the trade-wind zone of the Pacific. Men fought it, of course. Brave fishermen—Portuguese, Basques, Spaniards, French, Welsh, Britons, Irish, Scandinavians—fought it at its wild edge, to wrest some part of the harvest of the sea; and in the long nights men spoke of ancient fables of voyagers from long ago who knew its secrets—its lost island of Atlantis, almost of continental size, its "Island of the Seven Cities," its Brazil, its lost land of Lyonnesse, its mysterious "Ilha Verde."

There was a trade wind blowing from the east—from northeast and east-northeast—in the Western Ocean, too, for the use of westbound ships, as soon as seamen understood it and merchants saw reason to send ships that way. But the trade-wind zone lay off western Africa, and there was no commerce there. Neither was there any sailing fleet operating in that area to discover the way to use the Atlantic winds. True, northerlies blowing off the coast of Portugal in the summer months would waft ships down to the trade-wind zone, whence they could make westing or southing as they wished. But it was a long, long time before questing seamen saw any need to sail that way. It took a genius to inspire them, a great man—not a seaman himself at all—to strike boldly out to a new idea. Seamen were conservative then as now, as the sea taught them to be. But when at last European seafarers began to master the sailing secrets of their Western Ocean, it was with better ships, better hearts, and better skills than their predecessors of the Eastern seas had known the need to develop. All these things were essential before they could conquer their sea at all. Therefore, when the Portuguese burst into the Indian Ocean, led by the great Dias and da Gama, at the end of the fifteenth century, they brought ships which were immeasurably superior to those they found already sailing there. It was not only that their ships were much stronger and better. They were also larger and more stable gun platforms, and so could fight better, too. The Eastern navigators got such a shock and took the lesson so much to heart that it has never been forgotten: a ship, called a *baggala,* which I sailed in during 1956 from Colombo to the Maldive Islands, was still built to the modified hull form which Indian mariners first copied from the galleons of the Portuguese.

It was the Portuguese who found the way to make Atlantic voyages, below the west-wind zone. To the north, beyond the west winds on their northern side, there was another area where favoring winds could often be found. These were the east winds of the sub-Arctic north—no trade winds, these! A "trade" wind is a wind so reliable in strength and direction that trade can be built upon its sure help in shifting goods, and the trades are the constant winds of the tropics which blow inward toward the Equator from north and south in both the Pacific and Atlantic oceans, given a helpful easterly slant by the rotation of the earth. The northern easterlies were different and far from constant, but they were enough to take tough Vikings to their distant fishing grounds and to blow them to Iceland, to Greenland, Labrador, Newfoundland, and Nova Scotia, if they wished. The Vikings initiated no commerce along that route, save salt cod from Iceland. It was a long time after they had first crossed the narrow Atlantic westward that other mariners in the south learned the ocean's secret—that it could be conquered by sailing west before the northeast trades and returning with the westerlies, farther north, for the ocean winds went round and round. So did the currents. There was a rough but usable circulatory system which, once understood, made possible an infinite variety of voyaging.

It took time to find that out, a great deal of time and courage and infinite perseverance. There were grave difficulties. If the wind system and the surface waters went round and round, the constant million-years-old drift of the waters to the west, banking up in the bottleneck of the Gulf of Mexico where the hot summer's sun played upon them month after month, built up ideal conditions for hurricanes. The maddened air, beginning a wild and violent circulatory movement within itself, swept round and round, gyrating at a hundred knots and more, shrieking and screaming, an unlashed and frightful primeval force hell-bent for destruction. There was a season for these violent and most dangerous winds, and it took seamen time to find that out, too.

July, stand by.
August, you must.
September, remember.
October, all over.

So runs the seaman's rhyme, to remind him of the season of the West Indian hurricanes. Before he made that rhyme he had lost many ships and many men, and he continued to lose ships and men afterward—up to today.

Added to the hazard of hurricanes was the even worse hazard of the Sargasso Sea and its deadly calms. A sailing ship could at least go somewhere so long as she had wind. In a calm, she could go nowhere. If the calm continued too long, she would use up her food and her stores. The legend of lost ships adrift in the weed-strewn waters of the windless Sargasso Sea is based upon reality. An ancient galleon, becalmed in there, would grow long grass and barnacles until she became virtually unable to sail at all, and the borer worm of tropic waters would riddle her under sides until, a rotted and putrid mess manned by skeletons, she slipped at last with her threadbare sails and her besotted rigging, below the heated surface of the calm and relentless sea. Ships *were* swallowed up in the depths, though they were not swallowed by serpents nor by giant whales, nor dragged under by the enormous tentacles of some colossal octopus. It was more simple and less dramatic than that, but each ship which solved the mystery added yet another mystery herself, and no man came back to reveal how she had met her end.

So the cartographers continued to sprinkle their rough charts with frightful sea beasts, adding for good measure a scene or two showing a sea serpent swallowing a three-master whole.

Such representations were on a general par with the other information in those "charts." It was not until the middle of the eighteenth century that the first large-scale chart of the North Atlantic was published for shipboard use. This was a representation, reasonably accurate in parts, of the Western Ocean under the general title "Spanish or West Indian Seas," and it was put out by the house of Van Keulen in Amsterdam. Before that, there had been portolanos, which were very much the property of the pilots who had bought them from cartographers or perhaps prepared them themselves. The second Atlantic chart was published in London, and it was not a great deal better than the Amsterdam effort. Cartographers thought nothing in those days of adding a few extra islands here and there, large and small. After all, the islands *might* be there, and it was better to have mariners keeping a sharp lookout for what was not there than take the risk of being wrecked on what was. A couple of extra islands in the Cape Verde group, a mysterious island called "Brazil," which seemed to flit about the Atlantic almost at will (and was still on a chart published by J. Purdy in the nineteenth century, allegedly corrected to the year 1830, showing "Brazil Rock [high]" on 51 degrees 10 north latitude, 15 degrees 50 west longitude, where no rock or islet was, high or low). In those days additional hazards to navigation like this were regarded as minor matters.

Navigation was an approximate art anyway, and few mariners seriously tried to keep track of their precise positions at all stages of a passage. It was sufficient to make the passage safely at all and to arrive whole, more or less where the ship was bound. There were real islands enough and to spare, what with the coral keys and the high mountainous islands of the West Indies, the Azores group, the reef-protected Bermudas, the Cape Verde Islands, the Canaries, Madeira, St. Paul Rocks on the Line, to say nothing of the continental-shelf group of the United Kingdom and Eire, the vast island of Greenland, rocky and fogbound Newfoundland, fish-rich Iceland, and the barrier of the Shetlands and the Faeroes strung across the arm of the Atlantic which seamen called the Norwegian Sea. There are as lovely islands, in their way, in the North Atlantic Ocean as any in the fabled South Seas—the garden of Madeira, for example, hilly, luscious, fertile, grand; the sun-drenched Canaries, with the massive cone of Teneriffe; St. Michael in the Azores, where the most flavorful pineapples in all the world are grown and the fabulous soft waters at Furnas are a beautician's dream (for they would put a soft skin on a rhinoceros, if he bathed there long enough); Bermuda, the happy holiday isle; and all the galaxy of the heterogeneous West Indies, so vast and rich in story that they must have a book of their own. Greenland, which is not green; Iceland, where there are more hot springs than icebergs; Newfoundland, which was probably the first land seen across the North Atlantic by any voyager from Europe—these are great Atlantic islands.

The mountainous Azores may be the surviving peaks of lost Atlantis, that fabled island continent of the ancient Greeks. Is it all fable, this ancient yarn? *Was* there ever any Atlantis? It would be effrontery to say categorically that there was never such a place, but it is impossible to bring forward any real evidence of its existence. If the continents bordering the Atlantic Ocean have drifted a couple of thousand miles apart in a mere 150 million years or so, what might have been between them, even 25,000 years ago? What lacerations of the earth's crust, what drifts of what excrescences on the fluid core of its own burning interior might once have thrown up a lost island, peopled by a race now swept away as completely and irrevocably as the dodo? We simply don't know.

The case for Atlantis—or Atalanta, or Atlantica—is considered generally to rest on the references to it first made by Plato, who reported stories of a large island, "larger than Asia Minor and Libya together," somewhere out in the sea to the west of the Pillars of Hercules. Beyond it lay an archipelago of lesser islands. Atlantis was a wonderful place, an ideal commonwealth, peopled by a race of able warriors—according to Plato—who overran the Mediterranean and were withstood by Athens alone. Nine thousand years

Sailing ships opened the trade routes of the world

Henry, Prince of Portugal

Viking ship preserved at Oslo

Sir Francis Drake

The Armada off Fowey, 1588

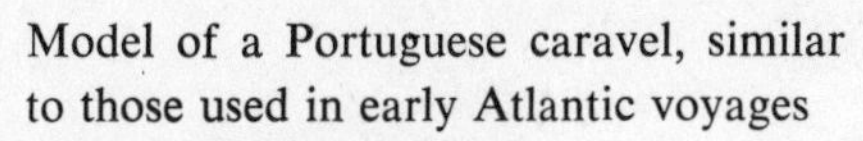

Model of a Portuguese caravel, similar to those used in early Atlantic voyages

Columbus

Model of the *Santa Maria*

before the birth of Solon this Atlantis was a powerful kingdom. But the sea rose and destroyed it utterly.

Well, maybe. It is possible that Plato's own enthusiasm for an "ideal commonwealth" led to some invention of details. But it is probable that there *was* some such ancient island, or knowledge of the mainland across the sea. There are numerous traditions of "lost" islands in the Atlantic sea and of voyages made to them long ago. The Greek "Islands of the Blest," or the "Fortunate Isles," the Welsh lost land of Avalon, the old Portuguese Antilia and "Island of the Seven Cities" are only a few of these legendary lands lost in the sea mists of Atlantic antiquity. Were they all myths? It is hard to say: I don't think they were. It is certain that there were plenty of real islands in that ocean, and the reasonable assumption is that some knowledge must have survived of some of them from voyages made and now unrecorded. The Atlantic, or any other ocean, can rise and drown land. That much is certain, but it is usually small-scale activity only. There are stories in the west of Wales of ancient church bells that can be heard tolling beneath the sea upon occasion, and of drowned farms and castles, and great holdings. In the Scilly Islands, in the North Sea by the treacherous Goodwin Sands, and elsewhere round the British coasts there are definite traces of drowned areas. But the probable truth about many of the legendary islands of the North Atlantic is that they are not legendary at all, but real. Knowledge of them became so old that it was lost again, perhaps, and reality became apparent myth. When it was difficult to establish with certainty the positions of discovered lands, there could be but poor record of them. The establishment, with accuracy, of the exact positions of places anywhere is a comparatively modern accomplishment: to this day navigation charts contain many references to such and such a place or reef or rock, in such unprecise terms as "reported three miles westward of this position."

The tradition of transatlantic islands is altogether too general and too strong for the whole thing to be dismissed as a series of imaginations. The Arab geographer Idrisi, writing in the twelfth century, recorded that a group of nine islands lay out in the Atlantic far to the west of the Pillars of Hercules. There *are* nine islands in the Azores. What did Idrisi know of them? Had he been there? The Azores were "discovered" in 1437. Perhaps we should say rediscovered. A hoard of Carthaginian coins was found on the island of Corvo, one of the outermost of the Azores Islands. Who brought them there, and for what? If Carthaginians landed on Corvo, either they had found someone worth trading with there, or they were shipwrecked on their voyage to lands farther to the west. There certainly were peoples in the Americas with whom they could have traded, and profitably. There was no one on the Azores—at least, as far as we can say now. There was supposed to be nothing there but birds.

It is all most mysterious, and rather likely to remain so.

The North Atlantic is the highroad to all the oceans and all the seas. Sailed by Columbus, Cook, Cabral, Cabot, da Gama, Magellan, Dias, Drake—not just some of the great discoverers but *all* of them, the scene of a thousand sea fights great and small, ocean of the speeding Down East clippers and the glorious white-winged flying yachts of the tea trade and wool, sea road of the slavers, hunting ground of the pirates and privateers, used by the greatest ships of the past and the greatest ships of the present, crossed and crisscrossed by the busiest sea routes of the world, hurried over by a million sea passengers in 1956 with another million hurrying even faster in the air—how stirring a sea this is! How great its story!

I entered this ocean first at the age of sixteen, an ordinary seaman in a lime-juice four-masted bark, bound up from Australia toward France. I came in at the proper threshold—in the doldrums of the equatorial calms—and my four-master paused there for three weeks, as befitted a true ship of sails entering so great an ocean. Day after day the sea lay stagnant all around us and the sails slatted and banged, useless and fretful, against the great steel masts, while the mariners hauled the ponderous yards about to every catspaw that came whispering deceitfully across the oily sea. None grew into usable wind. Some days we moved not at all; on others, backward. Our captain had misjudged the best place to cross the zone of calms which guards the Atlantic sea to ships coming from the south. There were better places to cross, where the northeast trade winds of the Northern Hemisphere could be trusted to dip nearer to the southeast of the Southern, and a few days of catspaw catching would suffice to get a ship across. I did not know that then, but the captain should have known it. I thought three weeks of doldrums was the usual ration with which all sailing ships must contend, and when later we came also into the Sargasso Sea and languished there, I thought that normal too.

We were two months from the Equator to the Bay of Biscay—a longish passage. Day after day in the burning doldrums the sun beat down and the wind, when it came at all, played useless tricks, like coming at the ship suddenly from ahead to blow her backward and then, by the time we had all the yards hauled round and the sails properly trimmed, dying at once, so suddenly and thoroughly that it was hard to believe it had ever blown. All the while the Equatorial Current bore us westward, away from our destination, and I began to understand all too well the fears of the ancient mariners who, drifting into these windless zones and observing the current's stealthy, silent thwarting of their every effort to gain ground, held that their ships never could return to the ports whence they had sailed, never could progress again but in one way and that way hopeless. We drifted to the area of the St. Paul Rocks, and almost upon them, for the ship had no steerage way to answer her helm nor wind to fill the sails and blow her off those five steep, craggy rocks. Our anchors, as in all deep-sea sailing ships, were long since secured on the forecastle head and the cables unshipped and stowed below, but even had we tried to use them there was no anchorage there.

We looked upon those five rocks for five consecutive days, near and far, expecting almost momentarily to be set upon them, and we came close enough to confirm the description in the pilot book that there was no good place there to land. That daring and perhaps unscrupulous navigator, Capt. Amasa Delano—ancestor of Franklin

D. Roosevelt—*had* landed there, but saw nothing but a lot of booby birds whose guano whitened all the rocks, while the sea roared and surged everywhere, even on a day of calm. There were plenty of fish there, said Captain Delano. We caught a good number too, in our four-master, and they made a welcome change from the monotony of our salt-horse and pea-soup diet.

If Amasa Delano dared to land on the St. Paul Rocks, our captain desired nothing but to be away from them, and at last a breeze came which developed into the northeast trades. We were still not finished with windless zones, and after a few days or a week of tolerable sailing, the grass-covered bottom of that steel four-master again languished in almost continual calm. Unlike the dolorous doldrums on the Line, now it was at least dry. Day after day, that 3,000-ton four-master stood upright and idle, mirrored in the blue and slothful water where the lines of golden weed spread out as far as the eye could see, to the right and to the left, in great straight lengths of unblemished perfection which spoke of windless days lasting for weeks, for the slightest ripple on the surface would set the weed to dancing and break the lines.

In our free watches, we boys hauled up bucket after bucket of the warm water, full of weed, and sieved it through or flung it on the warm deck planking to shake the tiny sea horses out and the minute crabs. That weed was no dead, dull, brown stuff. It was pure golden, afloat on its own profusion of nodules, and it was alive with small sea beasts. We bottled the sea horses, and I wondered that so tiny a thing could be called a "horse." We varnished the wings of flying fish which skimmed aboard by the colored side lights at night, and I kept a sharp lookout for ancient galleons and other derelicts lying unmanned upon the sea. I had a great belief in these, for I had read all the sea books and I knew this was the place, if ever there were one, where the archaic weed-imprisoned and barnacle-encrusted timbers of long-lost ships could momentarily be expected to drift into our view. But we saw nothing of such things, not as much as a barnacled plank.

There was a tremendous area of this weed-strewn Sargasso Sea, in the backwash between trades and antitrades. At that time, there were derelicts to be encountered in the waters of the North Atlantic—waterlogged and abandoned schooners, drifting about sometimes for years, small wooden ships driven off from some stormy coast and picked up in the waters of the Gulf Stream Drift, to be eddied somewhere into the immense and silent stagnation of the Sargasso Sea. We saw nothing of these except one burning ship, which became a drifting and abandoned hulk through our captain's failure to run down to her. Her crew took to their boats, and our lime-juice four-masted bark wallowed there for many days in the waters of the Sargasso Sea. It was a punishment, said the older sailors, who told queer yarns to "explain" the place. Some said that the waters were raised above the level of the surrounding ocean there and that the stagnant sea was a great watery plateau; others that the Sargasso water was on a lower level, so holding the weed drifted into it from the Gulf Stream. But I could detect no difference in the level anywhere. Sargasso weed, unlike most seaweed, grows and flourishes when adrift from its parent stem, and often we saw patches which were as large as a city block. At no time was there any accumulation through which the slightest movement in the air could not set the ship a-sailing, though the old sailors declared that ships *could* be stopped by this weed. It was lack of wind that stopped us. All the weed was freely adrift, afloat on or near the surface. If only we had not stayed there to admire the view for so long, the wonderful panorama of the lines of golden weed alternating with the brilliant blue of the too-calm sea would have been entrancing.

As it was, our captain took to his bunk sick after a week of it, and after a while the sea was so still that scarcely a block creaked in all the maze of our tremendous rigging and the sails hung lifeless, with not even a gentle heave of the ship to send them slatting against the masts. There was not the slightest movement in the oppressive air, and the surface of the sea lay panting quietly, like a great heat-tormented beast. Day after day, we drifted in calm, while the ship stood upright mirrored in her own stagnant image, and cans we threw overboard glinted in the blue depths, down and down and down, a hundred fathoms down, it seemed, where the light still caught them. And our garbage littered our unseen wake, until the sharks came, and the sailors were afraid to swim, and the pitch bubbled in the seams of our wooden deck. Our passage became a drifting match.

We were more than four months at sea before we sighted the island of Flores in the Azores. There we were becalmed again and were another month before we arrived at last at our destination, which was St. Nazaire. This was in May and June, which can be windless months in the North Atlantic when an area of high pressure settles in the neighborhood of the Azores. We lay in sight of Corvo for four days, and then, in the end, the wind came from the east out of Biscay and we had to beat into the mouth of the Loire.

In such a manner I came first to the wonders of the North Atlantic Ocean. Though I was from the other end of the world, I was to get to know that ocean well—to sail my own full-rigged ship there, across from Harwich to New York and outward again toward Rio, and home two years later up from the Horn. I was to cross and recross that ocean and to sail its length and breadth time after time, from the Channel to Panama, from the Arctic Circle to the Line; from Lisbon to St. John's, New York to London. I was to know that ocean from warships and from liners, from tramps both steam and sail, from a Coast Guard training bark, a destroyer, an aircraft carrier, a hospital ship. In more than a score of great liners, including both the *Queens* and the *United States* and other historic vessels, and by air, I crossed that ocean time and time again. Upon the sea and over the sea—but never, praise the Lord, under the sea—I wandered.

From the beautiful Point of Sagres in southern Portugal, from the lovely bay of Funchal in Madeira, from the great mole-protected anchorage off Las Palmas in the Canary Islands, from the naval base in Bermuda, from Seydisfjordur in eastern Iceland to the Arctic Circle west of Greenland, from Watling Island (where Columbus first glimpsed the New World) to the Western Isles off Scotland, from St. Vincent in the Cape Verdes to Havana in Cuba, from St. John's in Newfoundland to Ponta Delgada in the Azores—over all these areas and into all these places I was to sail the Western Ocean.

I was to get to know this ocean in many moods and all weathers, from many varied types of ships in war and peace—the sea and the islands. Never have I found it without absorbing interest. Never have I lost the sense of wonder with which I first gazed upon the blue immensity of its storied breadth, from that clumsy big four-masted sailing ship away back in 1921.

THE WONDERFUL GULF STREAM

2

THOSE WHO COMPLAIN of the British climate might reflect that in the same latitudes, westward across the North Atlantic, lies Labrador. It is the eastern half of the Atlantic Ocean that enjoys the better climatic conditions. Over almost the whole of the easterly part of the North American continent, north of about the latitude of Philadelphia, the climate is harsh. The roaring hot summers alternate with frequently savage winters, when the northwest winds blow straight off the ice wastes of the Arctic. These winds, funneled southward between the two great mountain systems of the Rockies in the west and the Appalachians in the east, are further nourished by the ice-littered Labrador Current setting southward with its cargo of icebergs and the floe ice from Baffin Island and all Hudson Bay. This intense cold frequently blocks great rivers like the St. Lawrence and the Hudson, impeding navigation and all communications, freezing the land.

In comparable latitudes on the open coasts of Western Europe, no rivers freeze and navigation is not impeded. The North Cape of Norway is in about the same latitude as the northern point of Baffin Island, but it is ice-free the year round. So distinctive is this warmth in the eastern half of the North Atlantic that a theory was long held (and argued at length by the great authority A. G. Findlay, whose directories of the oceans were the standard works at sea for many years and even now may be found in some old ships) that the *whole* of the sea water in the eastern Atlantic was on the move toward the north, bringing life-giving warmth along with it. The effects were so tremendous and enduring that it was felt they could not be due merely to the efforts of the Gulf Stream Drift, no matter how immense or powerful the Stream itself might be.

Where the open Atlantic does not freely penetrate, European winters can be cold enough. The Baltic can freeze up and often does, while palm trees grow on the west coast of Scotland. When an east wind whips across the gray North Sea to flail the east coasts of Britain it can bring intensely bitter weather, and outmoded plumbing, festooning the houses with steel pipes outdoors, freezes and bursts. But no one pays much real attention. Freeze-ups are regarded as temporary. The water pipes remain outdoors. The houses remain unwarmed. It will soon blow from the southwest again, and be wet and humid and warm.

It is the mighty current system known generally as the Gulf Stream which warms the winds which make northwest Europe habitable, drifts tropic seeds to the rock-strewn beaches of the Faeroe Isles, and keeps the inland waterway which is Norway's Arctic highway free from serious ice the year round. It is the Gulf Stream winds which keep the climate of Devon and Cornwall mild, just as it is the Gulf Stream's drifted water which brings the nutrient salts that help nourish the fish-rich waters of the Norwegian Sea, and keep the ice from Iceland's coasts and Scotland's Western Isles.

The Gulf Stream, sometimes called the Florida Stream, more properly known as the Gulf Stream system—for it is not just one simple current, a sort of river flowing in the sea—has probably been the subject of more speculation than any other movement of water anywhere in the world. Mariner, oceanographer, and philosopher alike have added their laborious investigations into its behavior and its idiosyncrasies. More drift bottles, oceanographers' nets, scientific instruments, and thermometers have been thrown into it than into any other current anywhere. It has been the subject of the most intensive and long-continued investigation ever lavished on a marine subject. To a great extent, it is still shrouded in mystery. Old theories are disproved or found to be unsatisfactory, without any better theory to take their places, and the Gulf Stream goes merrily on.

The Stream was first encountered, at strength, by a Spanish navigator named Ponce de León, who tried to sail southward through the Straits of Florida in the year 1512 or 1513 and found that, despite the fact that his ships enjoyed a fresh favoring wind, the current against them was so strong that they actually were sailing backward. Columbus himself noticed the northern equatorial drift, which may be regarded as the southern arm of the Gulf Stream system. On September 13, 1492, the great discoverer noted the effect of this drift, when his ships were in 27 degrees north, 40 degrees west (more or less). According to Findlay, this is the first record of a mariner's ocean-current observation anywhere.

Within a year or two of Ponce de León's encounter with the full force of the current in the Florida Straits, the first theorist was at work. This was a man named Peter Martyr, who, with only the data then available, came forward with a good theory. He knew of the east-to-west flow of the north equatorial winds; he knew of the east-northeast and northeast wind system which Columbus had used, with the wind banking up the water always to the west. What happened, he asked, to all this water? It did not pile up against the coast of the Americas, for that much was evident. It had no way through to the farther west, or ships could get through too. So it must be deflected by the configuration of the American mainland and be forced to flow north, concentrating for its outlet on the only really usable spot there was—the Straits of Florida.

Peter Martyr was the first of the many Gulf Stream theorists. Over the years they have come up with some truly astonishing ideas, working out complicated and impossible systems based on evaporation, or stacked-up waters which then flow downhill, or different water densities nearer the Equator which cause the

Atlantic sea to begin its clockwise drift. There was a theory seriously put forward that the north-flowing water disappeared into a hole in the earth somewhere in the north polar regions.

Like all forces in nature, the Gulf Stream is not tidy. It is no constant, measurable, and confined flow, to be transferred to a series of pretty graphs or expressed in neat diagrams. It is a free movement of warmed-up waters, which twist and turn and eddy and meander in all sorts of directions across the whole face of the Atlantic, in a great area, and, to some degree, below the surface too.

It sloughs off great sections of itself. It seems to split, and hold streams of colder water within itself. In places it flows eastward accompanied by a similar but apparently unrelated stream which comes from nowhere and goes east, especially in about the parallel of 41 north, while the main Stream itself is farther south, on latitude 39. It seems to disperse just west of the Azores, only to pick up again and drift warm waters north toward Norway, toward Iceland, recurving there to flow westward again by Cape Farewell. It contains swift inner currents, like jets. It fluctuates unpredictably and for unknown causes. It marks itself with the golden Sargasso weed, yet the drifting weed is by no means to be found everywhere it flows and is no certain indication of its range of influence. The older mariners dreaded it for its vile effect on contrary gales, for when the wind blew against its direction, so great a sea rose, violently and quickly, as could overwhelm their ships and drown them. Where it met the cold water off the Newfoundland Banks, it caused fogs of alarming length and density. The Gulf Stream system might make northwest Europe habitable and might help eastbound ships, but to ships westbound it was a curse.

"The Gulf Stream has had from very early times a very bad reputation among shipmasters for its dangerous character, and the hundreds of wrecks and millions of property which have bestrewed its margin have given good occasion for such a character. For not only is it to be dreaded for its storms, but also its violent stream can render a ship quite unmanageable during a calm. . . ." So wrote A. G. Findlay in his *North Atlantic Memoir*, a fat directory of some 900 well-filled pages meant primarily for captains of sailing ships. Westbound ships he advises—very rightly—to keep out of the Stream altogether, either by keeping north of it or sailing down to the edge of the northeast trades and making their westing there, as Columbus did. That encyclopedic volume, *Ocean Passages for the World*, published by Her Majesty's Stationery Office for the Hydrographic Department of Admiralty, was still giving sailing-ship captains much the same advice in the 1950s, although there were no sailing-ship captains left by then.

The general zone where the Gulf Stream can be expected to operate is well known, and there are sections which can be defined, like the Florida Current, where the Stream first comes tumbling northward out of the Gulf of Mexico. It is what it gets up to in its wonderful, day-by-day distribution of the radiated energy of the life-giving sun that is not exactly known, and possibly never will be. Does it change? Of course it does. It has no strictly defined "banks." Do its changes affect the weather? Of course they do. (In a sense, its changes *are* the weather. And how fickle is that!) How? We just don't know. As yet, we do not have data enough to find out. Oceanographical and climatological data gathered up to the mid-1950s are enough only to show how vastly much more is needed, before scientists can safely theorize in these matters or laymen have a hope of understanding them.

But some facts stand out. Instead of regarding the Gulf Stream, for instance, as a sort of Old Man River of warm water in a cold Atlantic sea, flowing always between more or less defined "banks," modern investigation indicates that the Stream system is a great ambling mass of warmed-up water, emerging from the Caribbean by way of the Straits of Florida and then, after sweeping northward along part of the Atlantic seaboard of the United States, meandering toward Europe on a broadening, weakening front, sloughing off great chunks of itself as it goes, mixing at the edges and in the middle too, containing within itself both a powerful current—a sort of jet stream—and a countercurrent (sometimes more than one) going the opposite way. The whole of this gigantic and vastly complex system is only part of a greater circulatory movement which pushes a large part of the North Atlantic round and round in a clockwise and ceaseless flood.

The Gulf Stream system—consisting of the Florida Current, the Gulf Stream proper, and, farther east and north, the Gulf Stream or North Atlantic Drift—forms the western and northern edge of the main circulation. The eastern edge is known as the Canaries Current, which swings down the Portuguese coast southward to link up with the west-setting North Equatorial Drift, to complete the circle. But all this water definitely does not circulate in a tidy, predictable, and orderly manner. Water left to its own devices is far from orderly when it flows through the harder confines of the land, bursting from its banks on the slightest provocation, constantly seeking to break down the land. Why should it flow more easily in the open sea, where it has no banks?

There are circulatory movements of the ocean water like this in the other oceans—the Indian, the North and South Pacifics, the South Atlantic.

But the Gulf Stream is known best, maybe because it was the first met. The North Atlantic was the first ocean that European man sailed across, and it has carried the bulk of his shipping ever since. In the North Atlantic or any other ocean, you don't just have a lot of sea and some fretful winds, blowing as they "listeth." You have moving, living waters and a great circulatory system of surface currents and ocean winds. In the North Atlantic the trade winds—masses of swiftly moving air always hustling toward the equatorial belt and diverted eastward by the earth's rotation —pile up Atlantic waters toward the west. Those trade winds drive the sea before them toward the bight of the Gulf of Mexico and the bottleneck of the Caribbean. They pull down the Atlantic level in the east by measurable inches, stack up the waters ceaselessly toward the west where the hot sun warms them and sends them tumbling north (as Peter Martyr noted), out into the open sea by the only escape route possible. Here the warm waters sweep inexorably northward over a front 40 miles wide, at the rate of 4 knots, and sometimes more.

The whole vast body of the ever-flowing sea, sweeping up the eastern seaboard off the Carolinas and Virginia, widening on a front of more than 100 miles off Cape Hatteras—sometimes close inshore, sometimes with a cold countercurrent setting southward inside—swings across in a broader and ever broader zone toward the Azores. No continuous flow of water anywhere, salt or fresh, approaches anything like the Gulf Stream's mighty volume, strength, or length. Compared with it, the Mississippi, Amazon, Indus, Congo, Volga, and Yellow rivers, rolled into one, would look like the Harlem River flowing into Long Island Sound. Much Gulf Stream water drifts the best part of 6,000 miles across the North Atlantic, from the Caribbean to the Arctic. If the world's best engineers were asked to design a means of making eastern Atlantic lands habitable, they could not possibly have done a better job. If they had to produce the heat the waters of the Gulf Stream system bring to Western and Northern Europe daily, they would have to use all the oil resources of the United States and all the coal in England to produce anything like the same heat energy. Yet this tremendous plant has been at work for millions of years, consuming no natural resources but adding to them.

Blue, clear, warm, the Gulf Stream is at the same time the greatest ocean-current system and the decisive factor in the climate of the most densely inhabited areas of the Western world. Only today, when it is no longer such a vital factor in the voyages of ships, is its full significance as a vital factor in Atlantic weather, sea and land, beginning to be understood. Scientists now know that the last Ice Age is steadily receding. Hydrographers are aware that the North Sea is warming, for their records of average temperatures tell them so. What effect may such a warming, if it goes on long, have on the sea wealth of this fish-prolific stretch of gray and hitherto cold water? May it affect one of Europe's principal sources of sea food?

The herring has long been the most important fish on the North Sea grounds, but the herring schools have been doing odd things in recent years. Sometimes they have been missing altogether. Overfishing could have something to do with that, just as it has thinned out the fish on many offshore banks along the eastern seaboard of the United States. It seems that a greater volume of warm water from the ubiquitous Gulf Stream is somehow percolating into the North Sea. Fish are conservative creatures. They will not tolerate temperature or salinity changes in the water they frequent. If there is too great a change of any kind, they die. A good fisherman fishes by thermometer and salinity indicator, if he wants to find fish in these days. Of course, if the colder-water fish go, others may come to take their places, and both tuna fish and sardines, warm-water fish, are now being found in the North Sea in increasing numbers.

The Gulf Stream was formerly regarded as the most clearly defined of ocean currents. In 1922, for instance, the Coast Guard cutter *Tampa* lay stopped athwart the edge of the Stream to experiment, with her stern in the warm current and her bows in the cold water at the side of it. A thermometer immersed by the stern read 58 degrees while that dropped at the bows, 240 feet away, read 34. Where could you get a cleaner cut than that? But the area of the cut had shifted by the following day. There was still a clear "wall" between cold water (from the Arctic Current) and warm, but it was in a different place.

On both sides of the North Atlantic, oceanographers are doing their best to probe the secrets of the Gulf Stream's vagaries and their connection with the weather. One of the primary objectives of the Woods Hole Oceanographic Institution in Massachusetts, when it was founded in 1930, was to investigate the Gulf Stream. Similar studies are being carried on in Britain, Germany, and France, for Western Europe is on the downwind side—the leeward, or receiving end—of Gulf Stream weather. It is not the water but the nature of the winds blowing off the water which is the main climatic concern. If the Florida Current swept nearer inshore or passed farther north than it does today, it is unlikely that the Gulf Stream would have any more effect on the climate of the United States than it does now. Continental winds matter more to America's eastern seaboard than does the proximity of the Gulf

Stream. If by any means the current were diverted, the winds would also have to alter and blow from south or southeast before they could have any noticeable effect on American weather.

It is not so in northwest Europe. There the winds come mainly from the west, blowing in from the warmed-up water. It is that fact which affects the climate there above all else. If the Stream did come nearer to the Atlantic seaboard on the American side, its most probable effect there would be to make the harsh northwest winds of winter stronger, and the cooling sea breezes of summer weaker. The winter winds would rush in to fill the low-pressure area caused by the warmer rising air, and the summer sea breezes would blow the less as the offshore air grew warmer. It is the possible effect on the path of hurricanes which causes the average citizen to fear changes in the Gulf Stream—just why, he is not quite certain. It is a fact that the hurricane belt has turned inward on the eastern seaboard, which once it passed harmlessly. Until 1938, a hurricane was regarded in New York and New England as a tropic curse which bothered the Southern states and ships at sea. Now, unfortunately, they seem to have become regular summer visitors.

Why? The most logical explanation, and that generally accepted, is that it is because of some change in the course of the mysterious Gulf Stream. If this continues, it may lead to increased winds and decreased rains in all the Eastern part of the United States and much of Western Europe too. Tendencies in both directions are already noticeable. If such changes continue, they must lead eventually to a realignment of populations around the Atlantic basin, with Siberia and Canada increasing in power and importance.

And yet, meteorologists think that the noticeable warming of the North American climate is at least an important factor in causing more hurricanes to curve toward the Atlantic coast. In addition to the circulatory movements of the surface water and the sea-level air, there is also what is known as a "planetary air current" high in the sky, and knowledge of this increases with the greater use of high-flying fast aircraft. This planetary current is a sort of river of high-altitude wind, sweeping round the earth's temperate zones from west to east. Scientists know that it flows in waves, and how those waves behave has a lot to do with Atlantic weather. Nowadays this "planetary air current" is bringing more air from the Gulf Stream zone of the Atlantic toward the United States. This ocean air is warmer than the flow of air from Canada. Hence the milder winters—and the summer hurricanes.

Curiously, while these changes have been going on in the United States, more typhoons than usual have been blowing in Japan. (A typhoon is another name for hurricane.) Meanwhile droughts increase throughout much of the United States and even in parts of Britain. Ice shrinks back from the Greenland icecap. Glaciers disappear. Ships which could approach the Greenland coast only during a few summer months now trade there the year round. Why is all this? All these matters are linked in some way which is not yet clearly understood. Climatology is a most complicated and difficult subject. Does the Gulf Stream affect the weather, or the weather affect the Gulf Stream? The fact seems to be that they affect each other. As Henry Charnock, of the staff of the British National Institute of Oceanography, pointed out in a recent broadcast talk,* all the factors of climate are interlocked and linked together in such a way that none is dominant:

> Tides apart, all the motion in atmosphere and ocean alike is due to the radiation from the sun, which provides the energy. The atmosphere is transparent to most of the sun's energy, so the bulk of it is absorbed in the top few feet of the ocean, ignoring the land which, after all, covers only about a fifth of the earth's surface. The transfer of heat energy from the sea into the air above it is mainly due to small-scale eddies in the wind near the surface, but once it is in the air the energy creates density differences which combine with the force due to the rotation of the earth to form much larger flow patterns, varying in size from the cumulus clouds associated with showers to the vast wind systems we recognise as depressions and anticyclones. These wind systems react both with each other and with the ocean. They modify the heat-transfer from sea to air, and they produce ocean currents. The ocean currents, of which the

* Published in the B.B.C.'s *Listener*, November 4, 1954.

Gulf Stream is only one example, carry vast amounts of heat with them and so they determine where the sun's energy is fed back into the atmosphere. By changing the pattern of weather and cloudiness they modify the radiation into the system. In this way the process is modified countless times until all the motions of the atmosphere and ocean, on every scale, are mutually adjusted so as to transport the sun's energy from the tropics to reradiate it nearer the poles.

We can hardly hope to make long-term forecasts by taking a thermometer into the Atlantic. What we must do is slowly, and we hope steadily, investigate the mechanism of energy transfer between the ocean and atmosphere; it will be a long and a difficult but a fascinating and rewarding task.

To get a picture of just what and where the Gulf Stream *is*, at any one time, is difficult enough, even with modern resources. For years, drift bottles have been tossed into the Stream by the thousand. Those which turn up again indicate how far they have traveled, but not how they may have meandered. The direct distance is only part of the picture. Ships like the Woods Hole ketch *Atlantis*, recording data for years, are only nibbling at the major problem, no matter how hard they may work, or how well they are manned. Data accumulated slowly and painfully in this way would take many, many years to grow to anything of real value. So the oceanographers thought of a better idea—the instantaneous multiple-ship survey. Instead of sending one ship to drift about in the Gulf Stream area for weeks or months, measuring velocities, chasing meanders, taking temperatures, and so on, why not use six ships, or ten ships and some aircraft too, and make a cut through the Stream—a clean cut, a precise cross section—first one, then two, then twenty, fifty, a hundred such cross sections?

Older sea surveyors had no such facilities, but they exist today. Old-time surveyors of the ocean sea, if the truth be told, very often did not know just exactly where their ships were. No matter how good or how experienced navigators they might be by the old astronomical methods, in moving waters like those of the Gulf Stream, their plots of where they thought their ships had been must often have been approximations—intelligent guesses, fortified by mathematics. This naturally affected the value of their data.

The multiple-ship survey of 1950 was carried out by better methods. Modern electronics have made a new, and a much more accurate, science of navigation. The development of the wartime facility for fixing the positions of ships by precise and dependable radio beams, known as Loran, made really accurate ocean plotting possible for the first time. The development of two other electronic instruments made precise observations possible, too. These were a remarkable instrument called a bathythermograph (which makes an accurate and continuous record of subsurface temperatures while a ship is under way), and another device called a geomagnetic electrokinetograph, which does the same thing for water velocities. In 1950 a fleet of six ships steamed into the waters of the Gulf Stream armed with this highly specialized equipment, and manned by scientists and technicians who knew both how to maintain it and to use it. This survey was given the code name of Operation Cabot, and half a dozen scientific bodies, both in the United States and Canada, cooperated to make it a success.

To provide further data and even greater accuracy, aircraft were called in. For these, special instruments were devised which made possible the precise plotting of an ocean current from low-flying airplanes. An airborne radiation thermometer helped in this. Visual observation from the air was also useful. The Loran system gave air crews pinpointed positions. The principal objective of Operation Cabot was, by means of this first cooperative simultaneous survey, to obtain a synoptic plot of the Gulf Stream's path from Cape Hatteras to the Grand Banks, to measure its surface velocities and its rate of change, to observe its effect on the lower atmosphere, and to see what happened when large meanders of the warm water in the Stream were separated from the parent drift.

This was a large order, even for six ships full of scientists and several aircraft similarly manned. Operation Cabot was the most thorough and comprehensive piece of applied oceanography ever attempted. The six ships, zigzagging into the Stream and out of it, and through and back again, under way continuously about 100 miles apart, taking simultaneous observations every half hour the whole way from Hatteras to the Banks, amassed an enormous amount of precise data the evaluation of which took years. Nor was this all. Every so often, after their first general run, the six ships got together and made a systematic cross-section plot of the Stream waters. Every ship kept continuous sonic depth records, and an accurate track chart. For extra measure, the six got together again, with the aircraft, and all fell upon one small area of the Stream to make the most thorough survey of what it was and how it moved that had ever been attempted.

The whole project worked splendidly. Communications between the ships were excellent. All the instruments worked as expected. The survey went on for seventeen days during June, 1950. But there were limits to what even six ships could do. The upshot of the whole operation was to convince the scientists that the Gulf Stream was a current system of far greater complexity than had been thought even a few years before.

They found themselves nearer, perhaps, to the solution of some Gulf Stream and weather problems—at least they could state the equations. But they could get no further, at the moment, for the simple reason that the ocean and its circulatory system are altogether too complicated. The complexity is not considered insoluble, but it will take time to get anything like final answers —perhaps a great deal of time. Meanwhile, hurricanes continue to curve into New Jersey, New York, and all New England, the tendency to drought increases both in the United States and Europe, and the seasons seem less clearly defined than they have been since weather records were begun.

During Operation Cabot it was noted that off Hatteras the Stream shifted toward the southeast at a rate between four and five miles a day. It was computed that the Stream shifted position by as much as eleven miles a day, and this affects the water for a thousand fathoms down. As for the cutoff eddies, it had been noted for years that large cyclonic eddies were frequently met to the southward of the Stream. The *Atlantis* had met one 200 miles long. The theory was that these eddies were formed by the lopping off of meanders in the main Stream. Operation Cabot proved the correctness of this idea. It showed, too, a surprising degree of similarity between the oceanic and the atmospheric circulation of the North Atlantic, so far as each is known. It showed that the Stream, instead of being hundreds of miles across, may be in places —sometimes, at any rate—only 20 or 30 miles wide.*

All this is a long way from the days when knowledge of the Gulf Stream consisted in the main of sailors' yarns based upon approximate observations indifferently kept, or when, in 1770, the knowledgeable Benjamin Franklin caused a heavy representation of the "Gulph Stream" to be etched on the Atlantic map, like a broad and confined Mississippi. His cartographer showed British ships, westbound, bucking the Stream, and American ships, eastbound, sailing with it. Franklin was at the time deputy postmaster for the North American Colonies, and the story is that, being consulted by the British Treasury as to why the British Post Office packets always took a fortnight or so longer to reach New York than the London merchantmen took to sail to Boston and Providence, Rhode Island, he consulted a relative named Folger, a Nantucket whaling man, who declared that the Britishers sailed against the Gulf Stream because they were ignorant of it. Whaleman Folger laid down the course of the Stream on the map, and it was this which Franklin had copied.

This yarn is incredible. Almost a hundred years earlier, the British mariner William Dampier had noted the behavior of the Stream in a book he wrote called *Discourses on the Trade Winds*. The Post Office packets sometimes got up to curious dodges, and during Franklin's time it was common for their appointed commanders to stay ashore comfortably in Falmouth, their English base, while the sailing master or one of the mates took the ship across. The commander was paid anyway, and there was no bonus for speed. There is at least one recorded case where a packet commander handed over his ship for an American voyage to a crony who was a

* The interested reader is referred to papers written by Drs. F. C. Fuglister, L. V. Worthington, and others, of the Woods Hole Oceanographic Institution.

Cornish lawyer with some slight coastwise experience in yachts. Even the lawyer did not try to sail his ship against the Stream, for he was involved in a bloody battle with a privateer close to Madeira, near which island he passed to make the southward passage. Falmouth packet commanders might at times have been successful and accomplished smugglers and leaders in illicit trade (which paid much better than any postal contract: they owned the ships, which were merely chartered for Post Office use) but they were highly experienced seamen who were scarcely likely to be ignorant of the Gulf Stream. The packet service was founded in 1680; by 1770, surely, they knew what they were at, even in a government service.

Whaleman Folger had a seagoing naturalist's interest in the Stream, which he had studied because he took sperm whales at its edge. The whales seemed to know the Stream very well. Not only were its waters rich in food but its drift was very useful for their navigation. There is no doubt that whales must have a tremendous knowledge of the abundant life of the sea and movement of the waters. Even in these days, when the last of the world stock of whales is being slaughtered as rapidly as possible, the occasional "pod" of sperm turns up among the Azores, coming from the west, doubtless with the Gulf Stream. But the creatures to which the Stream is most important may be the eels, at the other end of the scale. For a long time, many curious features about eels puzzled scientists and naturalists alike. The elongated, cylindrical form of the eel occurs in all the rivers and fresh waters of Europe, except those draining toward the Arctic Ocean, the Black Sea, and the Caspian. It is also found in abundance on the Atlantic side of North America.

For years and years, where eels came from was a complete mystery, and no eel larvae was ever found. Where were eels spawned? Finally a Danish scientist, Dr. Johannes Schmidt, discovered that the European eels, when they became fully matured adults, swam off to a part of the Sargasso Sea to the west of the Azores, and here spawned, and the baby eels took a couple of years to make the passage east again with the Gulf Stream Drift, coming back to the rivers and wells and ditches their parents had left. The North American eels, at the same time, migrated eastward to the same part of the North Atlantic and, for a while, there was a sort of international convention of all the eels there below the silent, deep, and dark blue waters of the rim of the Sargasso Sea. The adult eels died there: only the babies returned, which they did in such vast numbers that, in many French, English, and Dutch rivers, they could be taken almost by the bucketful, a solid jellied mass of tiny eels. The European babies swam east again, and the American baby eels swam west. Why? Why should so small a creature swim such immense distances, and always in the same directions, toward the same destinations? To these questions no one yet can give an answer. The waters of the Gulf Stream Drift and of the Stream itself abound with such problems.

The advance of knowledge goes on apace, on both sides of the Atlantic. Techniques for investigation are advancing rapidly. Wonderful electronic devices which can plot the Stream and record data from low-flying aircraft are being developed in America. Scientists and oceanographers like the Iselins, Fuglister, Stommel, Worthington, and many others at Woods Hole, at leading universities, in the Navy and the Coast Guard, are working on rich accumulations of precise data on a scale thought impossible not long ago. In Britain, Dr. J. C. Swallow, oceanographer, has developed an ingenious device for recording currents at all depths with precision. His instrument is a sort of neutrally buoyant float, set for a predetermined depth, which can be followed for days by means of the acoustic signals it transmits. Already this instrument has shown that, even in mid-Atlantic, tidal currents can be considerable, and there is a continual movement of the waters. The International Geophysical Year of 1957 is the occasion for a large-scale use of this device in order to find out whether there is a countercurrent in the depths below the Stream.

All this can be very important for many reasons, not the least of which is the problem of the disposal of radioactive waste in the sea.

Daily the accumulation of knowledge quickens, yet there is still a great way to go. When a hundred racing yachts gathered for a race from Newport, Rhode Island, to Bermuda, the Woods Hole

Institute was called in to provide briefing data on how best to cross the Gulf Stream—the principal hazard in the race. Even with all the data from Operation Cabot and everything else, the little booklet provided for the racing yachts was entitled *A Prediction of the Unpredictable*, and the advice to the yachtsmen was to do the best they could, as their sailing forerunners had had to do for centuries before them.

A Prediction of the Unpredictable—that is the way of it. The vagaries of the immense, powerful, and still largely mysterious Gulf Stream are too little known for any accurate plotting or ambitious graphing on a chart. The ramifications of this greatest single factor in the whole Atlantic scene—its power to affect climate on both sides of the ocean, its capacity for change, its importance in the migrations and the life cycles of the food fish of the sea—are not yet fully understood.

BEFORE COLUMBUS: PHOENICIANS AND VIKINGS

3

IT WOULD be odd if the story of discovery in the North Atlantic were the other way round. Instead of Europeans sailing to "discover" the new world across the sea, why did not the inhabitants of that new world sail across to have a look at the old? There was a time when their civilization, in places, was far ahead of Europe's. In their temperate zone, they had the westerly winds and the Gulf Stream Drift to help them, but it seems that they had neither navigators nor ships. Indians built only canoes. There was land enough for all, an unexploited continent to roam in and fight over, and there was no occasion for them to venture by sea. Farther to the south, in the tropic belt, the trade wind blew home to make an onshore wind the year round and pin down frail craft, and there was also the scourge of the hurricane to point the dangers of the sea. There were no mariners there, and no ships. The good land they occupied was good enough for them, which, perhaps, is as it should be.

On the European side it was different. From the harsh coast of Norway in the north, round all the west of Ireland and down to the coast of Portugal, there was not good land enough to go round. Pressure of population growth, clashes of leadership, the fierce urge of freedom however imperfectly understood, and the necessity to sail the seas in quest of food forced the tough fair Vikings and the enterprising dark Portuguese alike to take to the sea and, in time, to venture upon great voyages. The industrious Basques, the adventurous Irish, and the other Celts in Wales were not far behind them.

Yet the first discoverers in the North Atlantic of whom we have any sort of knowledge came from none of these lands, and were not trying to sail across the North Atlantic at all. They were Phoenicians, and they entered the Atlantic from the south, having just sailed round the whole of the rest of Africa. The casual manner in which we are informed about this voyage—there is a brief reference in the writings of the Greek historian Herodotus, and that is all—makes one wonder what records of what other voyages may have been lost altogether. Herodotus himself, while recording it, expresses some skepticism about the Phoenicians' jaunt around Africa:

> As for Libya (Africa) we know it to be washed on all sides by the sea, except where it is attached to Asia. The discovery was first made by Necho the Egyptian King who, on desisting from the canal which he had begun between the Nile and the Arabian Gulf, sent to sea a number of ships manned by Phoenicians, with orders to make for the Pillars of Hercules, and to return to Egypt through them and through the Mediterranean. The Phoenicians took their departure from Egypt by way of the Erythraean Sea and so sailed into the Southern Ocean. When autumn came they went ashore, wherever they might happen to be, and having sown a tract of land with corn, waited until the grain was fit to cut. Having reaped it, they again set sail; and thus it came to pass that two whole years went by, and it was not until the third year that they doubled the Pillars of Hercules and made good their voyage home. On their return they declared (I for my part do not believe them, but perhaps others may) that in sailing round Libya they got the sun on their right hand. In this way was the extent of Libya first discovered.

Being the only reference to a remarkable voyage, this story has been scoffed at by some academic shore-side critics. Let us take a sailor's look at it. For myself, I find it wholly credible. For one thing, the academics are in agreement that the Phoenicians were able seamen and traders who knew how to build ships good enough to sail from the Mediterranean as far as the Scilly Islands, which meant crossing the Bay of Biscay. If they could sail across the Bay of Biscay with heavy cargoes, they could also round the Cape of Good Hope; there is no doubt of that. What were the real problems of such a circumnavigation, allowing that the ships were fit to make it? (In recent years, surely there has been evidence enough of how extraordinarily unseaworthy craft can survive for long voyages at sea. Dr. Bombard's rubber raft *L'Hérétique* is an example. Why then query the capabilities of the ancient Phoenicians, who were perfectly competent professional seamen?) Their problems, firstly, were wind and weather.

In that matter, the whole 13,000-mile-long coasts of Africa were peculiarly suited to a *westward* circumnavigation, as opposed to a voyage which might be tried the other way. First, from Egypt, there were fresh northerly winds to blow the Phoenicians down half the length of the Red Sea. After that, in the fine weather season which they would have to use, it is true that they must contend with southerlies in most of the lower half of that sea. Sailing the Red Sea was old stuff to them, and its problems were well understood. It is a landlubber's idea that sailing ships had to have favoring winds to make their passages. Fair winds were a help, of course, but they were not essential. The ancient Phoenicians, beating down the southern half of the Red Sea, would also have to beat past Cape Guardafui. Well, they could do that too: Arab dhows are at it by the score to this day.

Another argument frequently put forward by the dry-land critics against such voyages seems to me equally groundless. That is the assumption, or the inference, that they could not go to windward. How do they think, then, that the commerce of the Old World was carried on? A Portuguese Grand Banks fisherman can make his flat-bottomed dory go to windward on the Banks by the simple process of using *one oar* as a leeboard. It is his skill that does it. What a doryman can do in a boat, surely a Phoenician could manage in a ship.

There were three problems in oceanic voyages: first, to evolve a reasonably seaworthy ship; secondly, to work out an understanding of the oceanic wind systems; and thirdly, to be able to make to windward, to sail against the wind. These three things the Phoenicians, hired by Pharaoh Necho to sail round Africa, well understood. One reads statements that since their ships had one sail only, large numbers of oarsmen must have been carried as the main power. Nonsense! Most Arab dhows, deep-sea and coastal, get along very well with one sail to this day. It is not the number of the sails that affects their ability to make a voyage but the *efficiency* of the sail. Oarsmen and sweeps were a Mediterranean idea, very useful there in the narrow-gutted craft which passed for ships over much of that area. The underwater shape of the hull and the ability to trim the sail—one sail, two sails, square sails, fore-and-aft sails, lateen or lug or any other variety—were the factors which mattered. A one-masted square-rigger, with one big yard, could adjust her sail to the fore-and-aft with the same ease that a properly fore-and-aft rigged ship could. What impedes square sails for windward working is rigging—*standing* rigging, permanently fixed to support the mast. A single-sparred mast required no permanent standing rigging. The lee rigging would not be needed at all, just as it is never used even in large dhows, and so the yard could lie as much in the fore-and-aft line of the ship as the captain might wish, and the ship be made to point as close to the wind as any other, by the manner of setting the sail. A lateen-rigged Arab dhow is as much square-rigged as she is fore-and-aft, from a practical point of view, for her great single yard will swing across the ship with the same ease and controlled by the same unimpeding minimum of rigging as will cause it to lie fore-and-aft. And so the dhow will run as well as beat, always providing that her hull form has a sufficient grip of the water and good sailing lines. As for that, look at any dhow, hauled out at Aden or Zanzibar, Djibouti or Mukalla. Such dhows have been sailing a long, long time. Those circumnavigating Phoenicians required no large hordes of oarsmen. What were the wind and weather conditions they could expect to meet? After getting past Cape Guardafui (which took a big dhow I sailed in two days from Aden and put her to no trouble at all), the whole of the East African coast could be run along with a fine fair wind and favoring current. Good visibility, clear water, a sufficiency of useful natural harbors, and the absence of rain make this ideal sailing. As for food, there are plenty of fish in the sea to be salted or dried or eaten fresh. The Arab dhows take their fresh water from coastal wells and carry it aboard in skins, and a single skinful of water can last a long time among mariners who know how to use it sparingly. Fish, a little rice, a bit of flavoring stuff, some coffee beans from Mocha, a handful of chilis, some Persian tea, a jar or two of clarified goat's butter—these were the provisions. My big dhow had a crew of thirty men but the provisions were all stored in one small space, and we did not go hungry. What the Arabs can do the Phoenicians could do likewise. The northeast monsoon blows the Arabs down as far as the Comoro Islands, if they want to go that distance, and gives them ample time to make the run, trade a cargo outward, haul out the ship at least twice and "repay" the unprotected bottom against the teredo worm, and sail back again to Arabia in the one season, with plenty of wayside stops whenever the spirit moves them, and no kind of hurry at all.

Beyond the monsoon zone there are favoring currents which would help the Phoenicians to sail toward the south—the Mozambique Current, setting obligingly toward the south in the Mozambique Channel, to bring them down to the Agulhas Current, setting with equal good will and assured service westward round the Cape, and then the Benguela Current, to drift them north again once they were round. The currents and the winds were helpful the whole way (granted an avoidance of the Cape storms: as for that, they could beach, if they could shelter no other way, but they had a nasty piece of open coast to work past from Durban almost to Cape Agulhas and, if a fresh wind got up against the current, the seaworthiness of their ships would be tested pretty thoroughly). The same thing applied in the South Atlantic Ocean. There the wind sets in very nicely from the southward, right from the Cape, with a bit of luck.

It was off the bulge of West Africa, in the North Atlantic, that the Phoenicians would know their really rough time. There the northeast trade wind, the Guinea Current, and the Canary Current would all be against them. But they had weatherly ships. They could make progress, even against this combination of conditions, which was no worse than the beat through a good part of the Red Sea. They might have been forced off the land (and so come upon the Cape Verde Islands, the Canaries, Madeira?), and had to fight head winds, in the end, to fetch the Pillars of Hercules. But the proof that they did so is surely in the sting in the last line of Herodotus' story. He infers that the idea of having the sun on their right hand was impossible, and he thinks that because, like all his contemporaries in the world that was known to him, he was a child of the Northern Hemisphere and the sun for him always came from the south, on his left hand. Yet those who sailed round Africa equally *must* have had the sun in their north, on their right hand. They had to get down well to the south, while Herodotus imagined that his "Libya" was a short continent, nowhere extending any great distance south of the Mediterranean.

His disbelief of that reported bearing of the sun is, in a way, good evidence that the Phoenicians' story was right and that they did sail round Africa. Why not? Necho, at the time, may have felt that he needed some such achievement to bolster his arrogance, as later-day Egyptian dictators have also found. It was Necho's cherished ambition to restore the old Suez Canal by recutting the ditch from the Nile to the Gulf of Aqaba, but his oracles, pointing out that a way through Egypt might also become a way in for Egypt's enemies, put him off that enterprise. And so, maybe, he hired that group of seagoing Phoenicians instead, to go off on the spectacular jaunt of a sail right round all Africa as a popular diversion.

Nobody signed up those Phoenicians to write a book. They made the voyage as ordered, reported to the overlord who sent them, and that was that. The vast and everworking machinery of publicity, to which we are so accustomed, is a modern idea. Shouting about voyages and all manner of discoveries is new. As for that, the Phoenicians appear to have been a particularly secretive race of seafarers. They have left us no historians and, though they controlled the known seas for a thousand years or more, they have not left behind as much as a single chart, or the log of one voyage. They sailed in the days when voyages were trading voyages, and, like the deep-sea Arab dhows of today, they sold their own cargoes and did not use ships to earn freights. Ships were their warehouses, as well as their mode of transport. That sort of trade was personal and restricted: competition was not welcome, as it is not to this day, when the date dhows are outward bound from the Basra River to peddle their fresh-season dates round the coasts of Arabia. A dhow master has to find a good market and ready sales, as well as to sail, navigate, and maintain his ship. To the Phoenicians, what they learned on their voyagings was their good will, their source of income and hope of profit, not to be parted with lightly.

A Phoenician shipmaster, bound with a cargo to sell in Britain somewhere and then to lift a cargo of Cornish tin for home, was once followed by a Roman ship eager to find the source of tin cargoes. So the Phoenician sailed deliberately into shallow ground off Ushant and was wrecked. The Roman, following him, was likewise wrecked, and discovered nothing. The Phoenician shipmaster, we are told, was recompensed by his fellow merchants for the value of the cargo which he lost, but the Roman drowned.

Voyages such as the circumnavigation of Africa had to pay, and it is doubtful whether that particular excursion could have done so. Another group of Phoenicians tried sailing down Africa the other way, setting out in the North Atlantic, which made at least an easier beginning since the trade winds and the Canary Current helped them there. But there is no record and no evidence that they rounded Africa. The combination of circumstances which so favored the other way was against them. There was a tremendous lot of Africa to sail past when the conditions were adverse, as Prince Henry's captains discovered.

These other Phoenicians were sent by Hanno, a Carthaginian. How far they may have sailed no one can say, but the discovery (or rediscovery) of a route round the Cape of Good Hope from the Atlantic to the Indian Ocean had to wait more than another thousand years, until those able successors of the Phoenicians, the

Portuguese, led by Prince Henry the Navigator, finally found the way to make southing against winds and current by leaving the coast of Africa altogether and standing boldly out to sea.

The Phoenicians traded down the west coast of Africa, and relics of them have been found at ancient marketplaces there. Where else they might have sailed we cannot say. To the Azores? To mysterious Antilia, over the sea? If they sailed much backward and forward between their port of Tarshish and emporiums anywhere along the west coast of Africa, it could scarcely be long before they came upon the Canary Islands. You can see Teneriffe a hundred miles away on a clear day. Are these the "Islands of the Blest," the "Fortunate Isles" of mythology? Knowledge of what the Phoenicians did and the voyages they made, the islands they knew, died with them. Just how much they knew of the world they sailed we are very unlikely to find out now. But this much seems certain—it was a Semitic people known as the Phoenicians, sent out by an Egyptian monarch peeved by the situation over the Suez Canal, who began the long story of Atlantic discovery. It is at least possible that the "myths" of Atlantis and the legendary transatlantic islands began with real voyages, and those voyages were made by Phoenicians.

Who followed them? Greeks? Romans? Irish? Neither Greeks nor Romans were as keen traders, nor as able seafarers, as the Phoenicians had been. *Somebody* was wandering about the North Atlantic Ocean long before Columbus set out to cross that ocean, or the Vikings had sailed to Newfoundland. In Cardiff Museum, there are fragments of ancient Roman pottery dredged up from a shallow fishing bank called the Porcupine, far out in the North Atlantic beyond the coast of Ireland. Who dropped such pottery there? We have no idea. But the very discovery rips apart the notion that Atlantic voyaging began with Columbus, or with the Vikings, and that before that there was nothing but sea—plain, bad, endless sea, off which one would go sliding into a bottomless abyss if one sailed too far and reached the edge.

Irish monks were in Iceland in the sixth century. St. Brandan, or St. Brendan, probably knew the Azores. In all the legends of Atlantic islands and lands beyond the sea, few are more persistent than the stories of this St. Brandan and his Isle. St. Brandan's Isle appears on early representations of the sea we now know as the North Atlantic with the regularity and the variety of that other mysterious land, Brazil. The early *Imrama*—the Irish sea legends—lose nothing in the telling, but unfortunately it is impossible to sift through to what is fact where there is obviously also so much fiction. The first Vikings to arrive found the Irish already in Iceland. Irish bishops, we know from Vatican records, went to Greenland. Irish fishermen were, and still are, fearless and competent seamen. They had not far to sail, if they felt inclined, to reach Iceland, and the Atlantic's westerlies were a beam wind for both the outward and the homeward passages. Irish monks were famous and inspired wanderers. There was early intercourse with Norway, not all to the advantage of the Irish. The connection of Ireland with Iceland was an ancient one. An early settler there (and troublemaker) was one Queen Aud, called the "Deep-minded," who was the widow of a Norwegian king of Dublin named Oluf the White.

Those who could carry on a regular sailing trade between Ireland and Iceland would be forced to develop ships seaworthy enough to voyage farther, if there were any point in making long passages—if they knew anywhere to go. Did they? That wandering island of Brazil persistently haunts the seas to the west of Ireland. What basis was there for the place? We don't know and are unlikely to find out: whatever contribution the Irish might have made to the solving of Atlantic mysteries is now lost.

We are on firmer ground when we come to those fierce, courageous, and frequently lawless types, the Vikings—firmer, but not as solid as it might be. There is no doubt that the Vikings did sail right across the North Atlantic by stages, but there is a great deal of doubt as to where they went. The famous sagas, which are the main—if not the only—source of accounts of their voyages, are contradictory in many ways and vague in others, and the view of most modern academics (to whom I willingly leave that field) is that of all the so-called relics found in the United States and Canada, from the alleged Viking tower near Newport, Rhode Island, to a cache of weapons recently unearthed in Canada, not a single one is really acceptable—not even the runic stone of Minnesota, with its story of the twenty-two Norwegians and eight Swedes who walked or perhaps rowed there from Vinland in 1362.

Where was this Vinland? We don't know, and we are very unlikely to find that out, either. It is sufficient that the Vikings did sail across the Atlantic. They were competent and courageous enough to do that, and they had some incentive. That was their difficulty in getting on with one another. The very word "viking" means pirate in Old Norse, and pirates were no more popular then than later. Even among their own kind, they quarreled violently. In the view of those they plundered, Vikings were thoroughly horrible fellows, murderous robbers and rapists, who had become good seamen because the harshness of their homeland, offset in some degree by the richness of its coastal waters, forced them to take to the water and to develop seaworthy ships.

The conditions which bred their individual toughness and immense courage and endurance also offered little future for many ambitious and able men. In Norway, hardheaded leaders were constantly arising who threw out those who had had the courage to oppose them while they were on the way up. Submit or flee was the rule, and many Vikings fled. Submission, real or pretended, was not in their disposition. They sailed off in their long ships to Ireland, Britain, France, Russia, even as far as the Mediterranean. Hordes of them sailed up the river Shannon, in Ireland, and took over much of the country. Others raided the east coasts of England and Scotland, or founded Normandy in France, and in general made themselves such bloody and continual nuisances all over the ports of Christian Europe that, in England at any rate, the only welcome kept for them was the permanent occupation of "seven feet of English earth." This, far too often, they refused to lie down on: the Irish, when they took them, flayed them alive, for their depredations were brutal and intolerable.

When an especially tough leader of the race known as Harald Harfagre—Harold with the Fair Hair—fought his way to the leadership of most of Norway, many prominent families who had opposed him fled forthwith to Iceland, where they took the best land and put the Irish to work for them. Very soon they were quarreling among themselves and proceeded to throw out the more violent, or the less successful, of their own number, who then sailed farther west. One of these was the now famed Eric the Red, a hairy and loathsome fellow who appears to have distinguished himself by committing more than the usual number of local murders. Among Vikings, excess of murder was for export only. Eric was thrown out. He had a ship, as all those wild chieftains had. He could handle that ship, as well as a battle-ax or an iron-studded knobkerrie. His story is handed down to us in a saga which is more a catalogue of embarkations, quarrels, battles, and plunderings than a serious piece of documented history.

It seems that, long before Eric the Red made himself so unpopular, a fellow Viking named Gunnbjorn had been driven away by a violent easterly wind when approaching Iceland on a voyage from Norway, and had run before this wind until he sighted some land far to the west. No one had since visited this land. Therefore Eric decided, since he had to go somewhere, that he would look for the place and make what he could of it. In this way he came to the coast of Greenland which, indeed, was not very far from Iceland—a mere 250 miles away. (We are so familiar with the distorted Mercator's projection of the North Atlantic that we are brought up with a wholly wrong idea of these distances. Iceland's coast is not much more than 400 miles from Norway with the Faeroes as useful wayside stops: from Greenland's west coast, it is a comparatively short hop of a few hundred miles to Labrador, with the southgoing Labrador Current to assist ships to sail toward more kindly areas. From Iceland toward the southern tip of Greenland, too, the currents help.)

The east coast of Greenland is inhospitable and frequently jammed with icebergs. Eric wisely continued toward the west, rounding Cape Farewell with the current to help him. He continued up the west coast until he came to an ice-free fiord, where he settled for a period, said to have been three years. It was Eric who called Greenland by that name, with an eye on its propaganda value.

Having established himself, he sailed back to Iceland to lead another group of Vikings in his wake. This time twenty-four ships made the difficult passage, or tried to: we are told that only a dozen or so arrived. That kind of voyaging in Viking craft was particularly dangerous, even for tough mariners as used to hardship and the cold enmity of the sea as they were. Eric the Red was a great seaman, whatever else he may have been. He possessed also a genius for organization and reasonable government, as he showed very well in the development of his Greenland settlement, and as many other Vikings showed, too, when they got the chance.

Eric's migratory voyage from Iceland to Greenland is given the date of 985, and in the course of time the colony grew to support a community of several thousand persons—ten thousand, we are told. To do that anywhere in Greenland was a considerable accomplishment. Eric was a pagan, but his community was, or soon became, Christian. There were sixteen churches, a monastery, a nunnery, and a cathedral. There also very probably was still the occasional, fiercely individualistic character who had to be thrown out, and there also certainly was the enmity of the original Eskimos, who finally seem to have overthrown the place, or more probably, its decaying remnants.

There is no doubt about these Norwegian settlements in Greenland. The ruins are still there. There can equally be no doubt that a considerable amount of seafaring went on between the parent state of Norway and its offshoots in Iceland and Greenland. The doubt is where else these Vikings sailed. In West Greenland, they were very close to Canada. What, if anything, did they get to know about America? The son of Eric, one Leif, sailed there in the early years of the eleventh century. The remnants of the various sagas which refer to his voyages, and to those of Thorfinn Karlsefni, record three separate places where they landed in America. The names of these are given as "Helluland, Markland, and Vinland." In Vinland there were grapes. In Helluland there were flat stones. In Markland there were forests and good salmon. What else there may have been in these places we don't know.

And we don't know where any of these three named places really was. Academic argument has raged about them for a hundred years and more, but the problem remains. Judging by the distances said to have been sailed, it seems probable that they were the places we now call Labrador, Newfoundland, and Nova Scotia; but the descriptions given of them are so sketchy and the details so vague that they could all have been sections of the same coastline—parts of Newfoundland. Various "authorities" have identified at least one of them as Maine, Massachusetts, and even Virginia. At any rate, the Vikings left them all, and in due course they were gone from Greenland as well. One can understand their desertion of Greenland but not, perhaps, the mentality which could prefer such a place after knowing Virginia, or Maine, or even Newfoundland. The great ice-capped island slipped back into the mists again and had to be rediscovered over 400 years later, and "Vinland, Helluland, and Markland" likewise disappeared—the more thoroughly and mysteriously since they never had appeared on any recognizable maps or other records and cannot be identified now. The Vikings navigated by the stars and their knowledge of bird migrations: such methods leave no charts. And so the Viking contribution to solving the Atlantic mystery was not permanent.

If we are vague about the Phoenicians' vessels, at any rate we are well informed about the Norwegian ships, for some excellent examples of them survive. They have been dug up from the grave mounds of long-dead leaders, and the actual ships, or in some cases reconstructions built on them, still remain. Two examples, known as the Oseberg and the Gokstad ships, are especially noteworthy. One glance at them shows the idea that the Vikings braved the Atlantic in cockleshells to be quite wrong. The Oseberg ship is a perfect example of harmony of line, 71 feet 6 inches in length with a beam of 17 feet. The height amidships is just over 33 inches, but this could easily be built up at sea in the manner used by the Arabs (who build up their bulwarks with loose planking, or with mats in the smaller ships, to prevent the sprays from driving in). The Gokstad ship is a little smaller, and much more strongly built. Both ships are open boats, with high prows and sterns and a tremendous flare to give their low hulls good stability as they listed to the weight of the great single sail. The hull would sail well and could be rowed comparatively easily, for it would move lightly through the water. Its shape gave it capacity and seaworthiness without bulk, and the big single sail had power enough to drive it at nine or ten knots without the sea's spilling in over the low sides. There was plenty of stowage space aboard and space, too, for a big open cooking place, where caldrons holding enough for a thirty- or forty-man crew could be boiled.

Viking ships were roomy and manageable. They were light, fast, and strong, yet flexible in the sea in a way which eliminated many of the stresses of big wooden ships. Those Viking ships were real "clippers." The planks overlap each other, being joined in the "clinker" pattern. The rudder is strong, and well secured to the side of the ship in an efficient manner. All the Viking ships were double-enders—alike at bow and stern. Their beauty of line and wonderfully symmetrical proportions seem to have been universal. Upwards of a hundred examples have now been found, large and small, in Norway and in Denmark: all follow much the same general pattern.

If there ever was any doubt that such a ship could safely sail across the North Atlantic, it has long since been dispelled. A reproduction of the Gokstad Viking ship was sailed across to the Chicago Exhibition in 1893. Built at Sandefjord in southern Norway, the idea was to demonstrate the feasibility of Leif Ericson's voyage to an American "Vinland" by sailing the vessel across more or less in his tracks, without, however, any deviation to Iceland or Greenland. The Chicago Exhibition was held to commemorate the 400th anniversary of the discovery of America by Christopher Columbus, and Spain was sending replicas of his three ships. Captain Magnus Andersen, a Norwegian who was both seaman and writer, thought it was time Americans learned that Columbus had had predecessors.

Captain Andersen sailed from Marstein, near Bergen, on the thirtieth of April, 1893, and was in Newfoundland on the twenty-seventh of May. Much bad weather was experienced but the ship showed that she could behave very well, in spite of her low freeboard midships and her single great mast and sail. The replica's bottom planking, as in the real ship, was fastened to the ribs with withy (a primitive lashing) and nothing else—no bolts or nails. In this way, the whole bottom could work in a seaway, and at first this alarmed the Chicago-bound new Vikings. But the ship made no water, in spite of her curious working, and they were quickly reassured. The gunwale could twist half a foot out of true but this, too, seemed in order. Her elasticity helped the ship's speed, and "we often had the pleasure of darting through the water at speeds of ten and sometimes even eleven knots," said Captain Andersen. "And this in spite of a primitive and relatively small rig."

The captain was particularly impressed with the efficiency of the side rudder, the "steer board." The rudder, said the captain, was "nothing short of brilliant and, from the experience I have now had, I consider it greatly preferable to a stern rudder for a ship of this kind. A man can stand at the helm for hours in all kinds of weather without the slightest trouble, steering only with a small stick." This Viking ship was presented to the Field Museum in Chicago after the exhibition, but—as is too often the way with old ships—it was neglected for years. Finally, after being restored, it finished up its days in a Chicago park.

It had proved its worth. If Leif Ericson discovered America in a ship like that, his discovery came to little at the time, but at any rate Chicago rediscovered Norway through the new Vikings and their vessel. The point was well made, too, that a westbound transatlantic voyage in a true Viking ship was a perfectly straightforward feat of seamanship.

Just where the original idea for the Vikings' ships came from it is not possible to say. Some historians hold that its origin was in the Mediterranean, pointing to the circumstance that the word for sail used in all the northern countries—*sejl, segel,* sail—probably originated in the Latin word, which was *sagulum,* and noting also the points of similarity between the long ship and the Mediterranean galley. But in March, 1956, I admired the beautiful lines of what looked like a true Viking ship, with its high prow and stern, its magnificent symmetry of grace in sheer and flare and hull form generally, its ultra-low freeboard midships, its easiness of handling and speed under its one great single sail. This ship was not in Norway, or anywhere in the Mediterranean. It was fishing in the lagoon at Malê in the Maldive Islands, along with a dozen others of its kind, and the local seamen told me it was a common Maldivian type. The manner of its evolution was unknown to them. How comes it that the Viking type of ten centuries ago should be found in that remote group of the Indian Ocean now?

Whatever the answers to these puzzles may be, there is no doubt of one factor in the story of discovery. Transatlantic voyages had to pay. There had to be a reason for making such expensive ventures, and there was no future in trade with the Eskimos either of Greenland or of Labrador, and poor hope of profit in wresting a cargo of salt cod from Davis Straits when there was cod enough in Norway's own home waters. The magnificent achievements of the Vikings came to little, on the North Atlantic run. It was left to others to appreciate just how the solution of the riddle of the Atlantic could be made to pay or, at any rate, lead to voyages which ought to show a handsome profit. The theory had long been put forward, by the Greeks and others, that the world was a sphere and could be sailed round. It followed, then, that to sail far enough westward over the great ocean should bring a seaman to the East—to the other side of the sphere. It was known that there were great riches in Asian lands, for the land routes from the East were very old, and emporiums in Italy and elsewhere in the Mediterranean had been handling the trade profitably for ages.

Maybe the Vikings knew their Atlantic well enough to be aware that the quest of the East that way, by sailing either north or west, was futile, for the way was blocked in both directions—in the one, by ice, and in the other, by the great land, parts of which they knew as Helluland, Markland, and Vinland.

It was almost five centuries after the Vikings first knew these things that others began painfully to find them out for themselves. This time they retained the knowledge.

THE PIONEERS FROM PORTUGAL

4

THE BROODING FIGURE of a long-dead Portuguese prince who never commanded a ship at sea at all, yet was called the Navigator—Henry the Navigator—is the next Atlantic figure. There is little doubt that he deserves to rank as the greatest of them all. Without the driving force of his unflagging genius, there would have been no Columbus, no Cabot, no Corte-Real, no Cabral, and the age of discovery might well have been put back for centuries. Prince Henry made exploratory voyages possible for Western Europeans. He fostered the development of the science of navigation, and he developed the ships. His country had the seamen. He was the inspiration and the fountainhead of all the great Atlantic voyages of the fifteenth and sixteenth centuries, though he never voyaged farther from his homeland than to Ceuta, which is in Morocco, immediately south of the headland of Gibraltar. He was the "originator, the organiser and the leader of the state-controlled systematic voyages of discovery, made according to plan and scientifically carried out," * which opened up not only the great New World but also the sea route to the Old, and founded the Modern Age.

Yet he spent a great deal of his time in meditation and in learning, surrounded by scholars—mathematicians, astronomers, cartographers, students of geography, history. Particularly did he study the stories of voyages.

* These are the words of the historian Armando Cortesão.

He lived upon a windy, stony point in the remote southwestern corner of his small country. Here the Point of Sagres turns its back on Europe to jut bleakly out into the often stormy sea, standing guard—with its sister promontory of St. Vincent—against the inroads of the westerly storms. The storms blow hard upon the Point of Sagres, so hard that the vegetation cowers from them, nowhere rising more than a foot from the stony earth. Spray dashes at the vertical cliffs and breaks over them at the least provocation. Even in the quietest weather, the beat and surge of the surf is rough and ceaseless, and the Atlantic waves roar and thunder into the great caverns which a million years of their savage onslaught have cut into the hard, gray rock. The muffled growling of their ceaseless anger can be heard a mile out to sea.

Here is a place to contemplate the immensities of nature and the power of God! There is a wild and a stimulating grandeur at the Point of Sagres. On three sides the sea beats and rolls, and pulsates, and tosses restlessly, beneath the unimpeded dome of the cloud-flecked sky. On the fourth side, inland, the distant mountains of the beautiful district of Algarve are in direct contrast. Flowers rear their small heads, to add a further note of comfort. Sagres is no show place, even today. There is no large town near, no imposing monument, no shrine. But something of the inspired spirit of the Prince of Portugal called Navigator still haunts the place, and it is very moving.

Henry the Navigator—Knight of the Garter, Grand Master of the Order of Christ, Prince of Portugal—born in 1394 at Oporto, was dead for more than thirty years before the magnificent decade in which Columbus crossed the Western Ocean and da Gama sailed to India. The son of King John I of Portugal and Philippa, daughter of England's John of Gaunt, he became quite early in his life inspired with the great ideal which proved the incentive of really effective European voyages. He lived in stirring times. The Moslem hordes, fanatic and merciless, threatened to overrun all Europe, and the Crusades against them had been, too often, incompetently led and expensive failures. The Moors had laid waste to southern Italy. They held all North Africa and much of southern Europe. Their inroads threatened to overturn Christianity and destroy European civilization. There seemed, at the time, not a great deal of hope of being able to stop them by force of arms.

The idea which came to Prince Henry was the bold one of attacking their power at its source, and the way for Europeans to do that was to sail to the Indian Ocean, to find the sea route to the East. The Moors then dominated the Eastern trade, which was the principal source of their wealth. By turning their flank, their power could be destroyed, and the way to turn their flank was to sail round Africa or, if that proved impractical, to sail westward over the unknown sea until the East was reached—putting into effect the old idea of the Greeks.

The Prince fostered the dual arts of navigation and of naval architecture. The methods by which the Vikings had been able to cross the misty Northern seas, where distances were comparatively short, would not suffice for lengthier voyages. The Norsemen used knowledge of bird migrations and even birds themselves, which they released to look for land. They reckoned distance in terms of sailing days, which was vague and inaccurate, and were unable to fix the positions of their discoveries, so that we have no real idea of where they might have been. Astronomy and mathematics were the true basis of navigation, then as now, and there were Semitic peoples, and Egyptians, Italians, and others who had studied these things. The clear night skies of harsh Arabia and of the Egyptian desert were ideal for noting the ordered regularity of the movement of the heavenly bodies and the division of time—the root of position fixing. Sumerians, Babylonians, Assyrians, Phoenicians, and Egyptians had accumulated considerable knowledge, and worked out the wonderful means of establishing position on earth or sea by means of calculations based on the observation of heavenly bodies and knowledge of how those bodies moved.

For proof of their wonderful prowess in these fields, it is necessary only to look at the mathematic precision with which their ancient cities were laid out, their temples planned and built, or the Egyptian Pyramids. The Great Pyramid of Khufu, which was built at Gizeh about 3,000 years before the birth of Christ, is planned in such a way that the rays of Sirius—the propitious star to the Egyptians—shone directly through a long air shaft into the king's chamber at its every transit across the meridian, in this way bringing its eerie illumination precisely to the head of the Pharaoh's mummy. Through another shaft, planned with the same skill, shone the rays of the Polar Star at its lower transit. A people who could manage these things possessed a remarkable knowledge of the movements of the heavenly bodies. If they could devise instruments to survey with that degree of precision ashore, the same alert abilities could equally be turned to the use of astronomical data for fixing the position of ships at sea, and to the accumulation of the necessary data to be set down in tables for the use of navigation. It might take time, but they had both the idea and the ability.

A Jewish mathematician named Zacuto, an instrument and map maker named Master Jacome from Majorca, a cartographer named Peter, together with certain Italians, Portuguese, Arabs, and others, worked together at the Observatory of Sagres. There was a school there for the better instruction of shipmasters and pilots in the principles and the practice of ocean passage making. Intensive study was made of all matters bearing on discovery and maritime geography. Legends, ancient references (including probably some which have since been lost), theories and arguments put forward by philosophers, geographers, and historians down the ages, were all carefully sifted and examined. The old stories of the Western Islands were studied especially, and it appears from the early gropings of his captains in the Western Ocean that Prince Henry first favored the quest of a sea route to the East that way. His captain João Gonçalves Zarco had rediscovered Porto Santo and Madeira by 1418.

"Madeira" is the Portuguese word for wood, and the timber trade from Madeira was of early importance. The island was colonized, and soon produced exportable quantities of sugar, corn, honey, and excellent wines made from grapes introduced there from Crete. There is a lovely story of a runaway English couple who are said to have sailed to Madeira in the 1370s. A fellow whose name is given as Robert Machin or Macham—possibly MacKean or even McLean—ran off with his girl, Anna d'Arfet, or Anna Dorset. As they attempted to elope to France, the story goes, the ship was forced away by a storm which drove them to Madeira. This must indeed have been a remarkable storm, but, at any rate, the romantic couple reached Madeira safely. There they perished pitifully, still devoted to each other but unmarried, and their crew were carried off to be sold into slavery on the Barbary Coast.

The story comes, apparently, from one of the crew, named Pedro Morales, who was later ransomed and told Zarco about the island. Whatever basis in fact there may be for this yarn is impossible to discover now, but it is a typical story of early Atlantic voyages. If any Robert Machin, or McLean, and Anna d'Arfet, or Dorset, ever sailed from the English Channel to Madeira, it must have been with prior knowledge of the island: ships cannot be blown that far off course in those regions. It was then and still is a good spot to choose for a romantic adventure, and the two lovers showed good judgment in their choice of island. In the stories of discovery of so many of these Atlantic islands, it is a rare navigator whose claims are not disputed by somebody, but it is refreshingly rare to come across a story of lovers as the pioneers.

By 1427, Prince Henry's ships were familiar with Azorian waters. The westernmost Azorian island is little more than a thousand miles from Cape Race in Newfoundland, and the islands were useful bases for further voyages either due west across the Atlantic, or toward Davis Straits, where the Vikings had been. The Portuguese sent ships to look there for a route north about or westward to India and the Spice Islands. The investigators of the School of Sagres knew of the Viking voyages, and the names of several mysterious Danes are mentioned in their sparse chronicles. The systematic plan conceived by Prince Henry included the proper investigation of transatlantic possibilities.

A ship able, strong, and seaworthy enough for extended exploratory voyaging had been developed. This was the caravel, described by Cadamosto as the "most seaworthy vessel of her time"—a three- or sometimes four-masted barkentine. The barkentine rig combined the best advantages of the fore-and-aft sail, for pointing up to the wind, and the permanently square sail, for running; and it is curious that the rig should have been one of the last to survive in the sailing world. The same rig (improved with gaff-and-boom sails set abaft the fore-and-aft-rigged masts, and a full mast setting a square course, two topsails, topgallant, and royal on the fore) became one of the standard rigs for use in the Pacific Ocean, where big wooden four-masted, five-masted, and even a few steel six-masted barkentines survived almost to the end of the sailing era. Because it was so useful, economic, and efficient, the barkentine rig survived a long time in such a tough trade as the Grand Banks cod fishing, and the last working square-rigged ship out of all Western Europe today is still a barkentine, the Portuguese *Gazela Primeiro*, a true successor to Prince Henry's wonderful ships. In the Baltic, round the coasts of Britain, in the Tasman Sea, on the Pacific slope of North America, the barkentine was a very successful rig.

Prince Henry's captains, then—seamen with illustrious but too little honored names such as Gil Eannes, Diego Gomes, Diniz Dias, Nuño Tristán, Cadamosto the Italian—slowly extended European knowledge down the baffling west coast of Africa, right round all the "bulge" and almost to the Line, making voyage after voyage in that long and difficult quest which led, in the end, to Bartolomeo Dias's rounding of the Cape and da Gama's triumphant voyage to India.

Where else these early captains of Prince Henry may have taken their questing caravels into the wide area of the North Atlantic we do not know with certainty. They wrote no books and, often, only the scrappiest of reports, many of which are lost. The policy of secrecy was essential, if the advance of knowledge (and the reasons for seeking it) were to be kept from the warlike "Moors," to say nothing of rival schools of seamen-discoverers in the Mediterranean. There were ports and merchants with cause to be well satisfied with things as they were, since they profited from them. The distributive trade of Eastern products, brought by the ancient routes, was in their hands. Why look for means to destroy this trade, or—from the Portuguese point of view—publicize them when found?

Nor did the serious, plodding, and heartbreaking business of oceanic discovery often yield any sudden, triumphant achievement, to be announced with fanfare and noise. Rather was it a slow and painstaking process, built up over many years of effort on the part of countless men whose contributions and very names are now unknown. It was the "discoverer," riding on the combined achievements of all the others, fortunate enough to come back from some moment of dramatic triumph like the rounding of Good Hope or the first sighting of the West Indies, who took the glory, then and now. Equal glory should reflect on those who paved the way—not that much contemporary glory was allowed to any of them, from Dias (about whom next to nothing is really known) to Columbus, who was dragged back to his adopted and well-served Spain finally in chains.

As for the early Atlantic voyagers, we know a few names. We have a few odd references on maps and in old writings. Some such references may still remain to be found, though students have made diligent search for them. The great Lisbon earthquake of 1755; the sixty years of Spanish occupation of Portugal (when the two countries shared the same king, to the infinite loss of the smaller partner); the French invasions of Portugal; the fire which burned down Lisbon's India House and destroyed its treasured archives—all these have helped to impoverish sources of documentation. But some facts have been established. A paper unearthed in Portuguese archives only last century about the voyages of João Fagundes Lavrador; the writings of the Azorian chronicler Fructuosa; a Venetian North Atlantic chart brought to light from the famous collection of the late Sir Thomas Phillips, who died at Cheltenham in England in 1872—these throw a little further light on what was going on. We know, for instance, of the voyage of a mariner named Diogo de Teive in 1452, made in quest of the mysterious "Island of the Seven Cities," which brought him to the Newfoundland Banks and under the very lee of Newfoundland itself, 500 years ago. This Diogo de Teive, of whom otherwise little is known, brought back the news that the Newfoundland waters teemed with cod. This was interesting to the Portuguese, for the catching, drying, and salting of cod were businesses well understood by their fishermen, who had held rights to fish the North Sea since 1353.

When fishermen first ventured to sail across the Atlantic from Europe in quest of cod, we do not know precisely. They were silent men who kept their sources of supply a trade secret, if they could. But we have a record, not so many years after de Teive's voyage, of a king of Portugal establishing a tax on codfish brought from the banks off Terra Nova. We see the name "*Terra Nova da Bacalhau*"—the New Land of the Codfish—beginning to appear on the charts, sometimes marked as the "domain of the King of Portugal," sometimes as the "Land of the Corte Reals."

João Vaz Corte Real was another of those shadowy navigators, a nobleman who set out in his caravel from Fayal in the Azores, bound west, and possibly reached Terra Nova—Newfoundland. In the year 1473, Corte Real was given a royal grant of the transatlantic lands which he had discovered. He might have been the first to colonize Newfoundland, but what point was there then in establishing a costly base in that island? It was obviously no post of succor for ships bound farther west. Indeed, the land blocked their way. As for the cod, ships could base on Europe and catch all the fish they wanted off Newfoundland, bringing back the salted cargoes where they could be sold. Portugal was a small country, and not rich. The entire population then numbered some million and a half souls. They were not interested in colonies, nor in colonization. The Portuguese purpose, and that of Prince Henry, was to find the sea route to the East and so prevent the too successful "Moor" from destroying the Christian faith. So rich a trade could be expected to repay the costs of its establishment.

These early transatlantic voyagers—de Teive, and Corte Reals (João Vaz was followed by his sons Gaspar and Miguel, who were lost with their ships somewhere along the North American coastline), João Alvares Fagundes, Fernandes Lavrador, Pedro de Barcelos, Alvaro Martins Homem, David Melgueiro—found what Prince Henry wanted to know, that there was no usable Northwest Passage for sailing ships round Canada to the Eastern seas, that a great land stood in the way of westward voyages, but that there was a useful industry in catching and salting codfish on the Newfoundland Banks. After that, like the practical seamen they were, Portuguese navigators concentrated on discovering the way to India where it was to be found—round the Cape of Good Hope.

The fishermen got on with catching the cod. They have been doing that successfully ever since, and still send a fleet of seventy ships annually to fill with salt cod on the Grand Banks. The names the pioneers gave to many Newfoundland bays and headlands still survive, Anglicized perhaps, but still obviously Portuguese. Cape Race on the old charts is Cabo Raço—the bare cape, the shaven cape, named so by the Portuguese. The Cantino map of 1502 shows this. The Portuguese word for codfish—*bacalhau*—occurs as a place name more than once in Newfoundland, to this day. Conception Bay, Fogo, Boavista, Trinity, Portugal Cove—the names are eloquent. The very name of Labrador is Portuguese—*lavrador*, a farmer—named for the *lavrador* who first sighted it. As early as 1501, there was a Guild of Codfishing Shipowners of Aveiro, Viana do Castelo, and Angra in the Azores—ports which still send out their transatlantic fishermen.

Doubt has been cast on these earlier fifteenth-century voyages, and some scholars have wondered whether they were ever made. Their documentation is frequently vague, and sometimes nonexistent. This is scarcely to be wondered at, when knowledge of all such voyagings was kept as a strict royal secret. It was Portuguese policy deliberately to suppress all navigational and geographical information discovered by them which was likely to excite the jealousy of other powers. There was good reason for this. One stimulant, in making the earlier West African voyages, was knowledge of the profitable trade carried on by the Moors by land caravan across the bulge of Africa. What could be done by land by others the Portuguese could do by sea, but there was apt to be plenty of resentment of those who upset old trade practices, then as now. The Portuguese followed a careful policy, strictly applied, of prohibiting the export of maps, charts, pilot's reports, nautical instruments, and tables. Of all the maps and charts produced at

Sagres, almost nothing now remains. No example of the work of the industrious Master Jacome, no copy of the charts issued to Dias or da Gama, or any of the other discoverers, survives. Yet there was then a Director of the Royal Depot of Sea Charts at Lisbon, and he must have had charts by the hundred.

Some of the discoveries of Prince Henry's seamen are shown on foreign maps, including the Andrea Bianco map of 1448 (which shows the African coast to the south of Cape Verde); Fra Mauro's planisphere, dating from 1457 (which shows the discoveries of Cadamosto); and the 1471 atlas of Benincasa, which records something of the work of another famous pilot named Pedro de Sintra. It is quite likely that these foreign maps are copies of a now lost Portuguese original, for there was a minor industry in ferreting out and copying information, conducted on the part both of private pilots (whose *personal* sea knowledge was their salable stock in trade) and foreign powers, who at least felt that they liked to know what was going on. As time went on and the Guinea trade, for instance, was shown to be profitable, Portuguese pilots were in demand in all the maritime nations. When they were so much in demand, some went—to Spain, England, France, Holland. It was Portuguese information (and at least in the French case, also Portuguese pilots) which allowed French, British, and Dutch ships to sail, in due course, to the Indian Ocean.

To a seaman, looking dispassionately at the known facts, realizing how much sailing commerce was being freely conducted in the North Atlantic—not only on coastal passages along Africa (where in any event it was impossible to sail both ways by coasting, for the wind and current would not allow that: quite early, returning ships were making a leg out first toward the Azores, and calling there), but across to the Grand Banks off Newfoundland for fish, and backward and forward to the Azores, Madeira, the Canaries, the Cape Verde Islands—it is reasonable to accept as a fact that these seamen already understood the sailing winds, and to some extent also the currents, of the Western Ocean. They could learn these things only in the hard way, by sailing there. Nautical tables could be compiled ashore, but knowledge of how to take small sailing ships constantly on useful voyages could be learned only in one way—by making the voyages, and plenty of them. The excellence of the sailing directions given the discoverer Cabral for his voyage down the Atlantic (which led to the official discovery of Brazil, said to have been known at least a decade earlier) could only have been achieved by men who already had discovered the proper way to sail there, both with and against the trade winds.

The remarkable knowledge which went into the preparation of these directions cannot be accounted for only from the known voyages. The refusal to entertain the curious proposals of Columbus; the long and inexplicable (in history) pause between the voyages of Bartolomeo Dias and Vasco da Gama (for Dias had found the way more than ten years before da Gama sailed it); the satisfaction with the Pope's division of the world between Portugal and Spain at the Treaty of Tordesillas; the remarkable statement of the accomplished seaman and navigator Duarte Pacheco, made in 1498, that he knew *even then* of a great continent in the west of the Atlantic which stretched from 70 degrees north almost to 30 degrees south (though there are now no records of voyages which could account for this certain knowledge, at that time or for years afterward)—for all these things there can be only one explanation. That is that the Portuguese policy of secrecy was all too successful, and records of not just one but a whole series of Atlantic voyages have been spirited away.

As good seamen, it was quite feasible to make those voyages, such as de Teive's and Corte Real's, and David Melgueiro's in search of a Northwest Passage, and all the others. Their ships, though not ideal, were adequate. Ferdinand Magellan—yet another Portuguese—was taking such little ships round the world at the turn of the sixteenth century. The sails, the cordage rigging, the cumbersome and complicated array of blocks and tackles necessary to maneuver, set, and secure the big, simple sails, were perhaps not as efficient as they might be. But they worked. Indeed, to a large extent one may say that they still do work, in Arab, Indian, and Maldivian dhows, which make long voyages. The Portuguese shipbuilders well understood the art of constructing seaworthy hulls which could move quite well through the water, without becoming half-tide rocks (as many of their successors did) whenever it came on to blow. Their apparently clumsy appearance is only in the above-water hull. They were buoyant, husky, able little ships, balancing well with their sails, the spritsail forward and the lateen aft helping to trim the ship and keep her on a good course with a minimum of assistance from the helmsman.

There was nothing slipshod or lackadaisical about either the ships or the seamen. If the sails appear cumbersome to us now, it should be remembered that all the large sails lowered to the deck, where they could be manhandled with comparative ease, and the lighter topsails (of which there never was any profusion) could be handled aloft very simply. They were small and of light canvas. A few boys sufficed to pull the bunt of a light main topsail—or fore topsail on a barkentine-caravel—into the roomy top, where they had a good place to work—a better place by far than the slippery, swaying, often ice-infested footropes of some big square-rigger trying to round Cape Horn. The area set in a big sail could be reduced by removing its lower third, for this was laced on, and could be unlaced again by the simple process of lowering the yard while the men stayed on deck. There were plenty of men, and the Portuguese were then and have ever since remained excellent seamen. Watch-keeping, turns at helm and lookout, the maintenance of the reckoning—all these were well understood and thoroughly regulated duties, most efficiently carried out. Helmsmen watched the course with meticulous accuracy, which they could do in a ship that was balanced by her sails and had no problems from the thrust or torque of floundering propellers to confuse her. They were under the constant supervision of an officer who never left his bridge to go into any chartroom, or peer into a radar screen. The whole of the works of the ship, and the whole of the work of the ship, were in the open where all could see. A watch-keeping officer had instant and complete control and supervision of everything.

"They kept a mariner's compass set always against the mast, besides another on the poop by which a lantern burned at night; and when they were at sea they never took their eyes off the latter;

there was always someone watching it, and from time to time he sang out sweetly and melodiously, an indication that the voyage was going prosperously," wrote Brother Felix about a passage he made in a Mediterranean galley in 1483. Time was kept by sandglasses made to measure half an hour, and there were ship's boys whose duty, day and night, was to watch these, striking the bell (or gong) each time they turned the glass—one strike for the first turning, two for the second, and so on up to eight, which was a watch. These four-hour watches were of great antiquity, and the sailing night was divided into three of them by the Egyptians and Phoenicians and, apparently, all the old seamen. A time measurer was essential to see that the watches were properly regulated, and the sandglass was the answer. The crew must divide the labor and the rest equally, in order that they might "take their turnes at the Helme, trim sailes, pumpe, and do all duties . . . for eight Glasses or four houres, which is a Watch . . ."

When the watch was changed, a psalm was sung and a short prayer recited, for the seamen were aware that they sailed under God, and never forgot that they were in His power. In Spanish ships, the boy who tended the sandglass (keeping the binnacle candle trimmed was added to his duties) was required to sing a little ditty of his own on taking over from his shipmate of the other watch. It went like this: *

The Watch is changed
The glass is running:
We shall make a good voyage
As God may will . . .

In the Portuguese four-masted schooner *Argus*, sailing to the Grand Banks from Lisbon in the spring of 1950, very similar little hymns were still being chanted at the changing of the watch, though the time was no longer kept by sandglass. The same bells were struck, the same hymns sung, the same brief but meaningful prayers offered as the fresh watch of mariners took over the helm and the

* I quote from an interesting paper, "Early Time and Distance Measurement at Sea," written by Comdr. D. W. Waters, R.N., and published originally in the *Journal of the Institute of Navigation*, April, 1955.

deck. In British sailing ships, almost to the very end of the sailing era, the principal duty of the ship's apprentices by night was to watch the time and strike the half-hourly bells, to which was added the duty of tending the binnacle light, and seeing that the helmsman could properly see the compass. (The coming of oil lamps made his task no easier, for they were an abomination in a fresh wind and frequently went out.) Ways of the sea change slowly, or did so under sail. There are still men serving at sea, in 1957, who kept the time aboard some hard-case Cape Horner when they began their careers.

The sandglass, in the Portuguese caravels, was housed in the binnacle with the compass. This was the only light allowed to be lit in the ship. In wooden ships, the light was a serious fire risk and it had to be watched. Compasses had been used by Mediterranean seamen since the twelfth century. As for the timekeeping, ship's boys then were no different from ship's boys today, and sleepy lads, apparently, soon learned the trick of shortening their watches by keeping the sandglass tucked inside their shirts where the warmth of their bodies slightly increased the neck, so that the sand ran out more quickly. To be detected in this sin of "warming the glass" meant a good beating, stripped naked and lashed to the capstan, but the habit persisted.

Rough charts, compasses, hourglasses, a traverse board, lead lines—these were the equipment, with possibly an astrolabe, a cross-staff, and a book of tables of the sun's declination north of the Line. It was the custom to use Route Books (just as it became again in World War II, when ships in the Channel and North Sea had to buoy-hop from darkened buoy to darkened buoy when the E-boats and the marauding German aircraft were after them). Route Books gave routes, positions, courses, distances. They described headlands and harbors roughly, but accurately enough for a seaman's use. The Arabs used them (and were still using them when I was a year in a Kuwait dhow, 1938–1939). Quite early, European mariners understood how to use the heavenly bodies for their guidance (when they could see them), and after Prince Henry's School of Navigation had provided proper tables of declination they could establish their latitude with sufficient accuracy. Duarte Pacheco states the problem and gives rules for its solution quite clearly in his large Route Book which is called the *Esmeraldo de Situ Orbis*,* issued for the guidance of Portuguese sea captains and pilots in the fifteenth century.

Solution of the problem of finding a ship's distance north or south of the Equator was a comparatively simple matter, once the range of the sun's movements was understood and tabulated. By measuring the altitude of his noonday sun, and knowing from his tables where—in what latitude—the sun was then overhead, the navigator need discover only his angular distance from that latitude to be aware of his own. The sun, of course, was always moving; but his tables recorded this movement. That was their whole point. Working out the latitude was a matter of common sense and simple arithmetic (given an instrument which could accurately take a meridian altitude from a moving ship, as the cross-staff could). Once aware of his latitude, and knowing from his Route Book the latitude of the destination which he sought, the pilot need only sail to that latitude and run down the parallel until he reached his port. There are yachtsmen and others who go to sea today with no better equipment for a transoceanic voyage, and they usually arrive. Longitude, though useful, was of less importance in the days when ships moved slowly (and hove to by night, practically stopped, if there were danger about or they were unaware of their position). The establishment of ship's longitude had to await the perfection of the chronometer.

The ship's reckoning was very important, and was kept as accurately as possible. Sailing-ship sailors had a good idea of the speed of their ships, under varying conditions. After all, they had to know their ships very well, and they had time to get to know them. They were much more *sea*men—men of the sea—than the mariners in the powered ships of today. A method of gauging the speed, or checking their estimate of it, was to throw a chip overboard forward and time its passage along the ship's side—a rough method, but I have seen it used many a time and used it myself. Deepwater sailing ships lost the rotators of their patent logs very easily, and what we knew

* Published by the Hakluyt Society, London, in a translation by George H. T. Kimble, M.A., in 1936.

as the "Dutchman's log"—our name for this chip method—was used when there were no patent logs left aboard. We had stop watches, which helped. The whole basis of the calculation was accurate timing.

In the fifteenth century there were no stop watches and the method must have been somewhat approximate, but a strict plot of the ship's movements and probable position was kept on a chart. The time and distance spent on all courses was carefully recorded, sometimes on a specially prepared board, and the ship's position was worked out as accurately as it could be. The whole point of Prince Henry's work was to ensure that this was so. There was to be an end to the legends, whatever their basis, and so long as each groping mariner continued to come back without precise knowledge of where he had been, obviously nothing real could be added to the sum of knowledge. Each generation of seafarers would remain as ignorant as those which had gone before. The importance attached to careful and precise navigation (in so far as that was possible in ships dependent on the wind) by Prince Henry's pilots, and all who followed that great tradition, and the proper recording of what was done, and found, on charts, were new ideas.

And so Diogo de Teive, João Vaz Corte Real, David Melgueiro, and all the rest of those shadowy figures from the insufficiently chronicled past are likely to have had tolerable ships, good mariners properly imbued with a sense of duty toward the ship and one another, skillful pilots meticulous and able in the performance of their duties as they knew them, and sufficient instruments to do better than just grope their way blindly and hopefully about. But how did they keep the seas? What about food, living conditions, water, and so forth? The short answer to those questions is that a well-found sailing ship was well able to keep the seas then for four, five, or six months, just as she could do to the end of her days.

As for food, it was surprisingly varied and good for the gentlemen of the afterguard, and abundant and good (but not varied) for the mariners. Abundant, nourishing food was a luxury for the poorer people of those days as, unfortunately, it still is in some countries. The sailors had the staples of bread, wine, dried fish, and salt meat. Most of their bread was biscuit. There were royal ovens for baking ship's biscuits at Lisbon in the time of Prince Henry, and there is a record (quoted by Professor Prestage *) that they turned out over a thousand tons of the stuff a year. The output was 1,070 tons, which was enough to allow three large biscuits a day to 300,000 men, but even this supply was not enough. Ship's biscuit had also to be imported from Spain. More royal bakeries were established as the Portuguese sea power grew, and the daily ration is recorded as two pounds to each man. These were no pallid compounds of flour and water, but real ship's biscuits with something to bite on and a bit of nourishment to offer. They kept well and they served well. In 1497, Vasco da Gama's seamen were allowed, in addition to the biscuit (cut to one and one-half pounds on his very long voyage) daily rations of one pound of beef or one-half pound of pork, two and one-half pints of water, one and one-half pints of wine, with olive oil and vinegar to cook with and to swamp their victuals with too, which they doubtless did. On fast days, fish or cheese were issued instead of meat. The fish was dried fish, probably *bacalhau* from the Grand Banks, or bought from Norway or from Iceland.

When Sir Humphrey Gilbert came to the crater harbor of St. John's, Newfoundland, to claim Terra Nova on behalf of Queen Elizabeth I of England, he was received by the Portuguese, who had then been using the place, in all probability, for a hundred years or so. "The good Portuguese," wrote Sir Humphrey, "put aboard our provision, which was wines, bread or rusk, fish wette and drie, sweet oyles, besides many other, as marmalades, figs, lymmons barrelled, and such-like." Except the fish, all this had been brought from Portugal. With provender of that kind, a sea cook worth his salt could turn out good meals. There was abundance of fish on the Grand Banks, to be eaten fresh, and there were albacore, bonito, dolphin, and flying fish enough in the deep sea which a sailing ship had time to catch. Olive oil was used for cooking. Good hams, bacon made into sausages and rolled into tough sausage skins (as it is in Portugal today), dried and smoked meats, pickled, salted, dried, and smoked fish, honey, olives prepared and preserved in

* Edgar Prestage, *The Portuguese Pioneers,* A. & C. Black, London, 1933.

many different manners, added variety to the diet, at least for the officers. They could live well if the voyage were not too long, and there is no reason to believe that they did not do so.

As for wines, these were not taken for the sake of their alcoholic content, to drink as diversion. Wine was a product of the country and had its part in the diet of all classes, as it still has today. It was drunk sparingly at sea, where it helped to keep the scurvy away. Wine and water were carried in barrels, which were strongly made and well looked after, an artisan being carried for that purpose. Simple medicines were carried. The commander's "great cabin" was a fine place with stern windows, commodious, well furnished, light, and airy. Its big stern windows brought in light and air and gave a view such as cannot now be equaled or even approached in the largest transatlantic liner. Officers had at least satisfactory though small cabins, and were no worse off than their counterparts of the earlier years of the twentieth century in some Welsh and North-of-England tramps. Mariners knew at least the same standards then acceptable ashore. They lived rough, sleeping in their cloaks where they could lie down, but they were used to that.

Instead of a poor old lumbering "galleon," sailing slowly and painfully upon her pioneer ways with her crew untidy, ill-fed, ill-kempt, and probably mutinous, her officers unaware of the ship's position and unable to establish it, her sails in ribbons and her rigging festooned with bights and broken strands, I think instead of a sweet and noble little vessel with the underwater lines of a swan, the efficient sail plan of an Arab dhow, an orderly and well-disciplined crew of men and boys all knowing their business and content to serve, sailing across a sunlit sea (or a gray and tumbling one), with the great Cross of Christ emblazoned on her sails where Prince Henry had ordered it to be.

These were the ships of destiny, the pioneer discoverers of the New World and the founders of our modern age, and their achievement was magnificent.

After them came Columbus.

CHRISTOPHER COLUMBUS

5

THERE ARE many mysteries about the North Atlantic Ocean, but in some ways the personality of Christopher Columbus is the biggest mystery of all. Who was he? We are not even sure of the name he gave himself, for he did not use an ordinary signature but a hopelessly puzzling cipher. *What* was he? Miraculous discoverer and superb navigator, leader of men, magnificent seaman and great explorer? Or just a plain and somewhat ignorant fanatic with one idea, upon whom God briefly smiled? That idea of his, which opened up the New World—just what *was* it? To sail to Asia, or to discover America? Historians, seamen, philosophers, and scholars of all kinds have argued about the enigma of this great discoverer, all down the centuries since he made his famous voyage. They seem likely to go on arguing the louder as the sources become more remote from them, and the consequences of his voyage the more important.

There is a tremendous library on the subject, in many languages, but it contains no book written by Columbus himself. His first biographers—his son Ferdinand and Bishop Las Casas—are regarded as questionable authorities. He himself seems deliberately to have created obscurity about not only his antecedents and his early life. Why? It is sufficient for the school children of five continents to be taught that, in 1492, Christopher Columbus discovered America.

Discovered? Or was it rediscovery, or a mere and largely fortuitous stumbling upon the fringing islands of a continent which he thought was Asia? The majority of his contemporaries did not look upon him in any sort of kindly light. To them, his wonderful voyage was either to some islands which were already vaguely known to be there, or else the fringing islands off part of Asia. Their attitude was, let the fellow who demands so much make profitable contact with the great markets of Asia, and then we shall be interested. But he did not; and the fact that he had found a whole great and wonderful New World dawned slowly upon his fellow citizens after he was dead.

There is evidence that, until the day he died, such an idea never once occurred to Columbus. The excitement of his real discovery Columbus never knew. He must have been a severe trial to those who tried to understand what it was he sought to do, at first, and then, afterward, when he had made his voyage, to those who tried to support and help him. For Columbus came champing to the courts of Portugal and Spain with his project for a westbound Atlantic voyage as a modern, with no previous experience of interplanetary travel, might come along demanding finance for a jaunt to Mars, declaring that he would and could go to Mars but failing ever to explain how, and demanding to be Viceroy and Governor of Mars in advance, with a 10 per cent cut on any profits arising from any sort of trade, or revenues, or source of income which arose from his one voyage.

To extend the comparison, the Mars-bound Columbus would fail ever to explain satisfactorily that he even knew what he was talking about. "*I* am greater than other men. *I* can go. I *will* go. I, and I alone, shall do this thing. It is ordained that I accomplish what I set out to do."

Those are hard beliefs to accept, or to live with. Yet that substantially was what Columbus said to the contemporaries who would listen to him, and he had to go on saying something of the kind for seventeen years. If this sort of behavior gives a real picture of the man, the wonder is not the magnificence of his voyage but that so astonishing a figure ever made the voyage at all. But there was more to it all than that. Everything was against Columbus and, according to himself, just about everyone. Not quite everyone, nor everything either, or he would never have gone; but even those few who had believed in him turned against him toward the end. His extravagant claims of material reward, the self-asserting zeal with which he pursued what he regarded as his sublime purpose (to reveal a "New Heaven and a New Earth"), his at least questionable competence as cosmographer, navigator, and seaman—these things were difficult for his contemporaries to accept, and the theorists and the practical men alike have been taking sides ever since.

Yet the fact remains, in all the arguments, that Columbus is the central figure. In the short space of half a year or less, he achieved an immortal voyage which was to transform the world. It might be fair to regard this more properly as the culmination of Prince Henry's efforts, the logical conclusion toward which the great Portuguese genius had always striven. It is logical to assume that such a discovery was inevitable anyway (and may already have been quietly made) when so many Portuguese were questing about the North Atlantic. The fact remains that Columbus blew away the mists of legend from the West Indies in the backwind of the *Santa María's* spritsail, and put the mystic islands of the Western Ocean once and for all where they belonged. In so doing, he blazed the way to the wonderful New World which was neither a New Heaven nor a New Earth, but wonderful nevertheless.

The facts of Columbus's life, and the amount of credit due to him personally for the accomplishment of his discovery, may be in dispute. But the broad facts of his voyages are well enough established. He was born in Genoa (even this has been questioned but is generally accepted) in 1451, the son of a citizen named Domenico Colombo, said to have been a weaver, or a tavernkeeper—possibly at different times, both. He received little or no schooling (this is disputed, too). He never once wrote in the Italian language, which would appear to indicate that he learned to write after leaving Italy. His son Ferdinand says that his father was educated at the University of Pavia—a statement quite unacceptable to modern scholars who have investigated the claim, and in variance with Columbus's own account that he went to sea at the age of fourteen. In later life Columbus appears to have gone to considerable trouble to obscure the circumstances of his humble youth, and he was by no means the first or the last to do that. He was a sailor at fourteen, he says; but there is other evidence that he did not go to sea before 1475, and was settled in Lisbon by 1477, when he was twenty-six years old. He certainly knew some service in ships as a young man, but it is thought that this was more probably as a trader than as a seaman. He was probably a sort of assistant supercargo on trading voyages to the Levant and round the Mediterranean, possibly also to England and—more unlikely—Iceland.

In those days, supercargoes were important men in ships, and, as an assistant in that department, a young fellow with the sharp natural intelligence of Columbus would have a good opportunity to observe the seafaring life. But he would not become a practical seaman, or navigator. Columbus himself, in reporting on his first transatlantic voyage, refers to his method of fixing the ship's position on one important occasion as a "prophetic vision." To any practical seaman, this was nonsense. If Columbus ever were a seaman sailing long voyages in ships, he certainly spent the greater part of his life ashore, for he was settled in Lisbon in 1477, was in Spain by 1484, and remained there—except for his voyages—for the rest of his life. He is supposed also to have lived in Madeira (which is probable) and the Azores. In both these island groups he would hear stories of the lost islands, of lands dimly seen in ocean mists far to the west, of the bodies of strange men of no known race which drifted up on the islands, bits of strangely carved wood and other transoceanic flotsam washed up by the Atlantic currents and winds. He married a Perestrello, of Porto Santo and Madeira (though there is doubt as to this, too, and the name of his wife is never mentioned by him).

His father-in-law—if he did marry into this family, which some students doubt—had been one of Prince Henry's captains and was first governor of the island of Porto Santo. It is thought more likely that Columbus spent his time in Madeira as the representative of an Italian business house rather than as son-in-law of the governor.

Whether he did or not, Funchal was a good place to hear Atlantic legends, and perhaps to meet seamen who had been blown far off on its wide surface.

When Columbus first conceived his idea of making a great voyage is not known. He broached the project in Portugal, where he was received in audience by the King, who refused to back him. This possibly was for the reason that his advisers were well aware that Columbus's plan was based on three known errors. He overestimated the extent of the Asian continent and thought that its easternmost coast could not be far from southwestern Europe; he underestimated seriously the proportionate size of the oceans (and so thought that his Atlantic crossing would be comparatively short—which in fact it was, for he was right in that surmise but not for the reasons he gave); and he underestimated the size of the globe itself. The fact that he made these errors, and clung tenaciously to them, was Columbus's own good fortune. If he had not clung to them with such determination, it is highly probable that he would never have sailed to the West Indies at all.

He acted like a man inspired, a man with a constant and indestructible belief in his own destiny. The rebuffs of counselors and even of kings bounced off him. Rejected once, he tried again, and went on trying. Turned down by the Portuguese court, he went to Spain. Here he did no better, and the story of his vicissitudes there has been often told. Living in penury, often publicly derided and scorned by the very children in the streets (who thought him mad), scoffed at as a foreign upstart with a stupid and impossible idea, he seems to have supported himself in part on a few miserable grants from the royal purse, by the help of some friendly clerics, and by his efforts as an itinerant bookseller and trader.

He had left his wife and home, he said, to devote his life to the divine call which rang in his willing ears always: but he had not left ambition. The price of his services he set high—inordinately and even stupidly high. He demanded, as the price of his voyage, that he be made a Don of Spain (though he had no Spanish blood), Admiral of the Ocean Sea (though he had never even served as the modern equivalent of a reserve sublieutenant), and Viceroy and

Governor of the Indies with, as his personal revenue, one-tenth of all the profits secured for himself and his heirs forever. These demands were more than the court of Spain could accept, even when at last it was disposed to back Columbus: but he would not revise his proposition. Ferdinand and Isabella could take it or leave it.

In the meantime, he had been again to Portugal (precisely why, we do not know) and had been present when Bartolomeo Dias returned from the first rounding of the Cape of Good Hope. (The picture of the obscure, derided, and poverty-stricken Columbus, standing unnoticed in the crowd which watched the Dias caravel come up the sunlit Tagus with banners flying, trumpets blaring, and beat of drums—back at long last from the culmination of Prince Henry's efforts to discover the way round Africa to the East—is a scene charged with drama. Yet if we know little of Columbus, we know next to nothing of poor Dias, not even for certain the date of his voyage—nothing but the fact that he was drowned at sea. Not even an alleged likeness of him is to be found anywhere.)

Whatever Columbus did then in Portugal—his visit might have been connected only with his private business—he was soon back in Spain. Queen Isabella and King Ferdinand were well disposed on his behalf, but a tribunal they appointed to investigate his proposition had turned him down. In all fairness, it must be admitted that the tribunal, on the evidence put before it and after examining Columbus at length, had no other choice. The Italian's demands were put very definitely before them, but there is no real evidence as to what he based them on, for he sought state finance for a scheme which he would not or could not explain. His idea of reward was, to say the least, extravagant, and the list of his qualifications was remarkably short. It is true that, if he were not a seaman, that was nothing against him. It was not usual for professional seamen, as such, to count for much in those days (or indeed, since) and expeditions were entrusted much more readily to courtiers, fidalgos, anyone with noble blood. Poor Columbus had no claims in that direction either. Moreover, the royal house was impoverished by its long battle with the Moors, and Columbus's expedition was bound to be costly. It is no cause for wonder that he was temporarily turned down. The wonder is really that he was ever accepted.

His sublime self-confidence sustained him. Again and again, Columbus was turned down—not over a period of weeks or months, but for years. Yet he never lost either patience or his indomitable will to succeed. Sustained by the unshakable belief in his own selection by the Almighty to perform this wonderful task (whatever it was), he could afford to wait until mere mortals came to their senses, and provided the material wants without which he could not perform God's will for them. In due course, they did; and the act must be put down to the divine will, too. It was only at the last moment that Ferdinand and Isabella agreed, not so much to finance the expedition, but to enforce the port of Palos to provide ships and men under duress. The port of Palos was in trouble with the court, and this was the royal punishment.

It could scarcely be expected that either ships or men provided under duress in such a way would be the best available, and Columbus had to fight until the last moment, indeed, to get off on his voyage at all. If a tribunal of the best brains in Spain had been so dubious about his claims and apparently far-fetched ideas, the common seaman could hardly be expected to be enthusiastic about them. At last he managed to get hold of a fleet of three little ships, the famous *Santa María*, *Niña*, and *Pinta* (and here again, though "models" and paintings of all three and especially of the *Santa María* exist in abundance, we have no certain knowledge about any of the ships except that they were small—very small—which was really no disadvantage). If the ships were indifferent and the crews, in the main, recruited from the waterfront toughs, Columbus was well served by the sailing master of his flagship and the two pilots who went in the smaller vessels.

This trio—Juan de la Cosa and the Pinzón brothers—were competent seamen and navigators, and were a source of great strength to the expedition. These men were real seamen, with their own ideas as to how oceanic voyages should be conducted, and all three had great difficulties with the impractical visionary who was leading them to immortality. Almost the last place where any visionary could expect a welcome—then or now—is in a sailing ship at sea, and Columbus must have been a difficult man to serve, or even to put up with.

As for the crews, one authority mentions that they included an Irishman named William Ires, from Galway, and an Englishman whose name is given as "Tallarte de Lajes." These men are mentioned later as among those left behind in the West Indies when the *Santa María* was wrecked there, and it would be in keeping with the cosmopolitan character of the crews of deep-sea sailing ships that seamen of many nationalities would be aboard. Seamen were never particular as to nationality. If a man knew his work, that was enough. It took a later age to insist that seafarers should stay in ships of their own nation, and go about the world documented and visaed like passengers. One would love to read that Galwayman's account of the Columbus voyage: but Seaman Ires was killed at La Navidad and probably could not write, anyway.

Columbus sailed from Palos (which is near Huelva, on the Gulf of Cadiz, on Spain's southern Atlantic coastline) on the third of August, 1492, having confessed himself and his crews and committed them all to the care of the Almighty, Whose efforts would have to be the greater both because of the indifferent manner in which the ships had been prepared and because it was already then the West Indies hurricane season. They all well knew the poor state of the ships, but they were spared the grimmer knowledge of the impending storms.

As for the ships, the shipowners of Palos parted with them with a very bad grace: calkers, shipwrights, and riggers alike had scamped their work, as if it was their deliberate intent that the ships would be unable to sail very far and would have to return. They reckoned without the strength of character and single-mindedness of Columbus. He had to put into the Canary Islands and was delayed for three weeks there, repairing the *Pinta* which had lost her rudder, and seeing that the other ships were better fit for the voyage. It was not until the sixth of September that the lonely little fleet sailed from the Canaries, bound west: and now they headed toward the middle of the hurricane season. No hurricane hit them, and here indeed the divine guidance not only helped them but made their survival possible. If those poor ships had struck the outermost edge of any of the hurricanes which habitually arise in the Caribbean, late summer after late summer, and bring up so tremendous a sea and so violent a raging wind that even the mightiest and most powerful steamships of today can be overwhelmed by them, the whole Columbus fleet would surely have foundered.

But they set off from the Canaries in good weather, and the good weather stayed with them. Whatever else he knew or did not know, Columbus knew the route to sail, and his run down to the Canaries and then westward before the northeast trade wind was the ideal way to make a passage westward in the North Atlantic. Day after day, the three little ships skimmed along beneath their white sails toward the mysteries beyond the setting sun; day after day the fair wind followed them, until the more fearful among the sailors began to cry out that they never would come back again, for sure, for the unchanging wind could blow them only westward and they were lost men. The seamen were most superstitious men, ready to see an evil portent in anything—the spilling of salt, the crossing of knives, the presence of a dark-robed cleric, whistling when a wind was already blowing (though perhaps allowable in a calm), above all sailing from a safe harbor to begin a voyage on a Friday—these were all dreadful things, from the forecastle's point of view.

The Columbus ships *had* sailed on a Friday, perhaps because the harassed discoverer was so sick of the delays and exasperations of the land that he sailed the instant that the ships were ready, regardless of what day it was. Perhaps there were some among his mariners in the *Santa María* who declared they had heard women sneezing on their left as they boarded the ship, on sailing day: and that was fatal. If only the sneezing had been from the right! To hear sneezing from the right was a good omen. They recalled, too, that when they began to put her provisions aboard, the *Santa María* had taken an instant list to starboard. The older sailors regarded that as fatal, and were quite sure from that moment that the *Santa María* would never return. These old men likewise regarded it as a very bad thing to cut their hair or nails when the weather was fine, for such unnecessary operations, they held, would bring on a gale. If the gale were already blowing, why, then you could pare your nails—but more likely the fighting, wind-stiffened canvas would break them off for you then, anyway.

Theirs was a strange world, riddled with superstition. They were following a strange leader, whose personal inspiration did not extend to many of his officers or any of his crews. Regarding them as instruments divinely sent for the furtherance of his great endeavors, he paid little attention to the crew at all, though he consulted with his experienced pilots upon occasion. It was as well that he did so, for it was the advice of Martín Alonzo Pinzón to alter course toward the west-southwest, when the ships were almost across—very close to 70 degrees west longitude—which made his West Indies landfall possible. If he had continued to sail due west, it is highly probable that Columbus would have sailed into the full force of the Gulf Stream and have been pushed away to the northward, out of sight of the American coast, and been quite unable to work the ships back again. But they saw birds—the usual migratory flight down to the West Indies by way of Bermuda—and so they altered course, and it was as well that they did so! Here, too, was evidence of the divine ordination of that voyage: that Gulf Stream swept northward at the rate of knots, and if the little *Santa María, Niña,* and *Pinta* had been caught in that, further westward voyaging would have been made very difficult if not impossible until they were swept past Hatteras. There they were in Viking territory, and brief knowledge of that area had failed to open the New World. But Columbus, advised by Pinzón, made the necessary alteration of course, and sailed on more to the southwestward where he could scarcely go wrong.

Day after day now his crews railed at him, and there was everything but open mutiny. It is obvious that they had no confidence in their leader. The unreliability of the compass (caused by the increasing variation as the ships sailed west) alarmed the professional pilots, too, and they began to fear, with the crews, that they would be lost in the wastes of the trackless ocean if they continued the voyage. It is fallacious to think that these men—officers or seamen

—feared that they might sail over the world's edge if they continued too far, for the sphericity of the world was then well accepted. There were dangers without that—dangers real and dangers imaginary. Indeed, the real danger of hurricanes was much greater than any imaginary evil, such as the prospect of being swallowed by some outsize sea serpent, or lured to destruction by sirens, or simply caught in a downhill stream (caused by some protuberance of the earth) and unable to go back again. If the earth's sphericity were accepted, it was not yet known—could not be known—what imperfections there might be in the global shape. These problems had all to be solved, and it was a fearsome thing to be led by a "madman" and condemned to take an active share in their solution.

As the days passed, and the weeks, the crews became the more convinced that they were sailing under a lunatic to death, and they made a plot to throw Columbus overboard, to sail then northward out of the easterly winds, and go back to Spain with a report that the visionary had fallen over the side. Had they managed to do this they would probably have been believed. But the divine aid—or his wonderful good fortune—did not desert Columbus. Signs of approaching land—fresh weed on the water, those migrating birds, a piece of a tree with fresh berries on it—convinced even the most fearful that some sort of land could not be far away. On the thirty-fourth day out from the Canaries, the island of "Guanahani" was sighted (and there is controversy as to just which island this was, though it is accepted generally that it must be Watling Island, sometimes called San Salvador).

The island showed itself barely in time. There had been false landfalls before this: this was real. Guanahani was a small place and obviously not of much importance, but it was land and there were people living on it—real people, not monsters. There were no cities and there was no slightest sign of the wonderful civilization they had been led to expect. But it was solid, friendly, sun-warmed earth. Coconuts grew upon it, and it was a reasonable supposition that it might prove to be one of the outermost islands of the great continent they sought. Columbus fell upon his knees and thanked God; but the poor man's real troubles were just beginning. Guanahani was an off-lying island right enough, but it was off the wrong continent. There was another 9,000 miles to go to India, and all the breadth of America and the Pacific lay between.

Columbus dressed himself magnificently and went ashore, but there was no one of like magnificence to receive him. The natives were all naked, and they thought the ships and the clothed men in them had come from heaven. In due course, Columbus passed on, to find no emissary of the Grand Khan with whom he could leave the letters he was carrying addressed to that monarch. He sailed among the islands now called the Bahamas; he touched at Cuba, Haiti, and Hispaniola; he lost the *Santa María* on a sandbank, left some forty-odd men behind (including the Irishman) at a fortified point which he called La Navidad, and sailed back home again in the small *Niña.*

There were two extraordinary things about that homeward passage—more mysteries in the story of this most extraordinary of discoverers. The first striking feature was the route chosen, for this was the perfect sailing route which one would expect could only have been followed from preknowledge; the second was that, if Spain were "home"—as it should have been—Columbus did not make for home at all. Instead of going back directly to Spain, which sent him and paid for the voyage, he went into the Tagus to report himself at the Portuguese capital of Lisbon, which had refused to send him and paid for nothing. Why on earth should he do that? He says that he was driven into the Tagus, because of a storm: we will come to that.

First, that homeward passage. Columbus sailed to the northward from Hispaniola, making more than 600 miles in that direction, with the northeast trade wind on his little ship's starboard beam. After that, he continued toward the northeast until well north of the latitude of 35 degrees, where the westerly antitrades, and the Gulf Stream Drift, could be relied upon to give him a good passage home. Relied upon? How could he know that reliance could be placed upon such features if he did not know already of their existence? If he did know, who told him? What vague, unchronicled figure of the illustrious past had really first sailed there? As a sailor, one is reminded of those yarns of the deathbed pilot at Madeira who had already crossed the Atlantic, and is said to have told Columbus all about it; of the prior knowledge that he must have gained in some way from his access in Lisbon to whatever the Portuguese there knew; of the excessive secretiveness he always showed, for the excellent reason—perhaps—that he dared not disclose the true sources of his knowledge. God knows. God alone knows the answers to many of the riddles of Christopher Columbus, called (but only once, and then allegedly in his own writing) Cristobal Colón, and also, on occasion, Colomo, Colonus, and other things.

Perhaps it was merely fortuitous that he chose the best sailing route and, finding the trade winds persist, stood northward with them on his starboard beam because that was the most sensible thing to do, and then, with further good fortune, found the anti-trades ready and blowing nicely for him. It was the northern winter—a good time for Atlantic winds. But if I were to bring a sailing ship from Hispaniola to Lisbon now, I could not follow a better route than Columbus did that historic voyage, and I probably would not make any better time. Thirty-three days outward, back in forty-two—these were good West Indies passages, and the *Santa María* was not a fast ship, nor the *Niña* much more than a 40-ton launch. A further odd feature about this homeward passage is that Columbus did not follow quite the same route on his subsequent voyages, though he always made first toward the north. He did not again go far enough, as he did in 1493. Perhaps the Pinzóns told him the way to go. Or perhaps, after all, it was just luck.

On his first voyage, Columbus had indeed done well, even for one who had made such extravagant claims. But why had he gone into Lisbon and not returned to a port in Spain? He says that it was because of a heavy south-southwest gale: but such a wind was perfect to blow him into the Spanish port of Vigo, or round the corner to Ferrol, if he had wished to go there. His own track shows a leg to the southward from his apparent landfall off Cape Roca, to make the entrance to the Tagus. If he could have sailed to the southward against the wind that far, it is common sense that he could have continued and weathered Cape St. Vincent, to stand along the Algarve shore toward Palos, or Cadiz. Martín Pinzón did it, with the *Pinta*. Columbus did not try, but came bounding into Lisbon with banners flying. At the very least, this was a piece of flagrant discourtesy toward Ferdinand and Isabella: there were many who regarded the act as plain treachery.

Columbus was well received in Lisbon, and feted and honored there, which was a change for him. Having arrived at Lisbon, Columbus dallied there a week, which was not the act of a great discoverer anxious to report to the sovereigns who had sent him. He was full of himself, and the exaggerated, lavish, and inaccurate descriptions which he gave of his discoveries, to say the least, must brand him as a man who had no great regard or perhaps capacity for precision either of observation or of thought. There were some at the Portuguese court who are alleged to have suggested his assassination forthwith; indeed, if Columbus had had no secret reason for going into Lisbon and was therefore sure of a welcome, it is most extraordinary that he should have gone there. Here he came, happily publicizing the apparent triumph of his easy run to the "Indies," which the Portuguese navigators had been doing their utmost to reach, then, for the best part of a century—the hard way, right down the length of both Atlantics and round Good Hope. And now here came this salesman bouncing in to tell them that he was right and they were all wrong! It has also been suggested that it was good Portuguese policy to let the King of Spain imagine that his servant had found the Indies, and Columbus had in fact put in to receive instructions on how he was to present the "news." Those who sailed west would never come that way to Asia, and the Portuguese knew that. More mysteries, indeed!

No matter. He had made his voyage. The divine will was carried out: his work was done. Or was it done? When, at last, he arrived back in Spain, and the "Indians" he had captured and the "spices" and bit of gold and so forth which he had brought had been displayed in triumph, and there was time for stocktaking, there were many who asked: What is it all about? Even in Lisbon, the Admiral of the Ocean Sea—said the chroniclers—"was somewhat elevated above his condition, and in telling his tale always exceeded the bounds of truth, and made the tally of gold, silver and other riches much greater than it was." It did not take long to wonder at the amount of substance there might or might not be in these discoveries.

After all, discovery was no new thing in the Iberian Peninsula. Just what had the fellow found? Japan, he said. Antilia, said the Portuguese—their old name for the West Indies. What offered there, in the way of trade? Riches, gold, spices, valued timber, dyestuffs, said the discoverer. A mess of unexploited islands inhabited by a race of naked savages with whom there could be no trade and who could not be made even to work, said the critics.

Poor Columbus! He sailed off again—three times again. He came upon Dominica, Guadeloupe, Antigua, Puerto Rico, the Virgin Islands, Jamaica, Trinidad, Tobago, San Domingo, the American mainland of South America, and the Isthmus of Panama, in quest always of evidence—apparently—that this was Asia, that somehow, somewhere near at hand, a race of civilized and wealthy Asiatics would appear with whom Spain could quickly establish a profitable trade. He found no such race, and it was left to his successors to exploit the wealth of the Incas and ravage the golden land of Mexico.

Plenty of "colonists" sailed on the later expeditions, anxious to stake an early claim to some share in the promised riches. When there proved to be no riches there for them and in fact little but fever, hard work, starvation, and pestilence, these turned against the Admiral who, they said, had grossly misled them. The early settlements were in unhealthy places, and there was a lot of fever. The lovely, fertile islands of the West Indies were indeed a paradise, or could easily have been made so, but the "colonists" were after quick returns. They wanted what they had been promised—gold, silver, precious stones, pearls, and the quick profits of trade with a developed and exploitable civilization. Such things, indeed, were just round the corner: but they were there first and they wanted them at once. They were not forthcoming. Fifteen hundred rushed westward with the first colonizing expedition, toward the end of 1493. It was not long before five hundred were rushing back to Spain again, howling.

From his third voyage, Columbus (who appears not to have been a genius as administrator) was brought back to Spain as a prisoner in irons, for the court sent a Spaniard named Bobadilla to supersede him. It was a bitter and an undeserved fate for one who had never spared himself, and who had achieved much. However, back in Spain the moving story of his efforts which Columbus told swayed the court again in his favor: but he was allowed to make only one more voyage. It was left to others to find just how wonderful a discovery the unfortunate Genoese had really made.

His fourth voyage was made difficult by a mutinous crew and more recalcitrant "colonists." He spent a year in Jamaica, but misfortune dogged him and he achieved little. He returned to Spain in November, 1504, a sick and disillusioned man. From that time onward, for the few years that were left to him, he spent much of his time urging his case, demanding the just reward of his labors. It was in vain. Queen Isabella died not long after he returned, toward the end of 1504, and that was his last powerful friend gone. His titles remained unconfirmed, and his old age, though far from poverty-stricken, was embittered by his constantly reiterated demands for the share of the West Indies and Central American profits which he regarded as rightly his.

Rightly his they may have been, but he did not get them. His demands had never been modest—one-tenth of all the net products of all the lands he had discovered, all the profits of his own ventures carried in outward voyages, and a 33⅓ per cent rake-off on the trade of all the ports in his jurisdiction as Admiral of the Ocean Sea. What he received was a tenth of the sovereigns' share of this gold, which was a fifth, so that Columbus's real share was one-fiftieth. This was a substantial amount, but it was far from the sum agreed. Out of it, Columbus not only maintained his household, but looked after a large number of impoverished sailors who had survived his difficult fourth voyage. Looking after old sailors was an expensive matter, then and now, and Columbus was not a rich man.

Though all his letters to redress his grievances brought him nothing, he was at least allowed the royal permission to ride a mule—a privilege not granted to everyone, not on the grounds that mule riding was in any sense an aristocratic means of conveyance, but because the horse breeders of Andalusia were strong enough to prevent the practice, lest it interfere with the profits of their trade. This seems to have been the only privilege granted the now elderly and gout-stricken Admiral. On his mule he rode at last to court, but the effort did him no real good. On May 20, 1506, the Admiral of the Ocean Sea and Viceroy and Governor of all its islands died in his Spanish bed, not wholly without honor and not without some small reward. But his funeral was a modest one, and many generations passed before one-tenth the far-reaching importance of his achievement was even begun to be understood. He appears to have been at least dimly aware of the real nature of the work that he had done, by God's will and with His infinite help, though not without an undue and really appalling share of man-made difficulties and unnecessary obstacles, some of which he had certainly brought upon himself.

Shortly after his death, the arguments started. If he had set out deliberately to obscure the issue and to create such arguments, Columbus could scarcely have done a more thorough job. No copy of his journal or of his reports exists now in the original. The accounts we have are edited. Contradictory and improbable statements are found in what he said, or is alleged to have said. Some of his papers have been lost. It seems certain that the traditional account of his first voyage is something wide of the facts, but just what the full facts are nobody now can say. His reputation has been attacked by some historians, while he has been almost deified by others. If his shortcomings were as serious as some historians have argued, surely the Genoese was the greater man for overcoming them. He was a man of deep religious convictions. The twin passions of his native Genoa were religion and business, and it was much the same in his adopted Spain. In both fields, politics also played a considerable part. Columbus's religious fervor is not in doubt, nor is his business acumen seriously questioned. His real misfortune would seem to be that he was no politician, and so—in his lifetime—he failed. He could lead to the promised land, but he could not govern when he got there.

From the practical seaman's point of view, Columbus's first voyage, far from being really difficult—given his immunity from hurricanes—was just about the easiest voyage ever made by any of the great discoverers, even with the ships he had. It was a simple fair-wind run, made in good weather. It was the way that all the sailing ships sailed outward, for centuries afterward, if they had no heart or need to fight the west winds farther north. It is the way small yachts go, the way that Dr. Bombard took his rubber raft.

I have sailed that way myself in a small sailing ship not much larger than the *Santa María*—from Madeira to landfall on Watling Island. My ship was an iron full-rigger, staunch, able, and sound, and not for a moment could the two passages be compared except in these matters of wind and weather. My run to landfall was a perfect sail, which took a month. I could set the studding sails for days on end, so steady were the winds, and I ran 700 miles once in three perfect days. Flying fish flew into the scuppers, and swift albacore swam with us. By night the watch could rest, heads down on a disused sail, for only the officer of the watch, the helmsman, and lookout had duties. Not a sail had to be trimmed nor a tackle touched (except for a swing or two to tauten it, night and morning) for days on end. I thought often of Columbus as I made that run. We had a little thunder and lightning, and sometimes it blew up fresh for a while, or fell calm for half a day or so, for the Atlantic trades are not so constant that there are no variations. I thought of Columbus's fearful crew, gazing at the lightning in horror, prepared to be alarmed at anything. But the passage was wholly delightful, and it was much the same time of the year.

Almost every sort of vessel, craft, or object which will float has been sailed that way, except a bathtub with an outboard motor. Why then had no one gone that way, before Columbus? The short answer to that question, surely, is that it took a fanatic like Columbus, with his unalterable belief in his personal divine right to make that voyage, to point the way. No court noble wished to make such a voyage, for none believed in it; no practical seaman would have set out to reach Asia by sailing west, for he would be too much aware of the difficulties and unable in any case to find backing. The learned critics were right, as the event proved, to cast doubts upon

Columbus's proposition that Asia was not far from Spain and Japan was to be found where in fact there is now the state of Florida. What they could have no idea of was that there would ever be a state of Florida, or the other forty-eight states, or Mexico, or Central America, or the continent of South America.

His critics could entertain all the doubts they cared to; Columbus went steadfastly on, holding to his strange beliefs, determined to put them to the practical test, and somehow assured that the divine will would see that he did so. What God had ordered man could not upset. In those days there was a readier acceptance of the wonderful workings of Providence than there is generally now. Columbus lived in an age that, whatever its shortcomings, could accept the idea of a God-given mission, which had to be fulfilled.

From an impartial examination of the arguments which he put to them, it appears to a seaman that Ferdinand and Isabella must have been swayed by the divine will, too, for otherwise they would assuredly never have compelled their protesting subjects in Palos to help Columbus on his way at all.

THE SPANISH MAIN

6

OF ALL the ironies and indignities which surround the story and the achievements of the great Columbus, surely the worst is the name by which the world came to know the new continent he gave to it. The name America is from Amerigo Vespucci, whom no man called sailor, and who discovered—very probably—nothing, except perhaps the ease with which some sort of a reputation can come to him who writes the first book.

Whatever academic conflict there may be over aspects of Columbus's life, the historians from Bishop Las Casas onward have, with few exceptions, regarded Amerigo Vespucci as an unmitigated liar. According to the biographers, he was born at Florence on the ninth of March, 1451. His father was a lawyer and the family was well connected. His uncle, a Dominican friar, saw that he was properly educated, and in due course Amerigo was taken in as a junior member of the great mercantile house of Medici. For them he went to Spain, arriving there the year Columbus sailed on his first voyage. He continued to act as an agent of the Medicis, also going into the ship-broking and ship-chandler businesses apparently in his own right, on the side. This was his first active connection with ships and the sea.

Three years after his first arrival in Spain, he contracted in this capacity to supply at least one of the later Columbus expeditions, and so must have come to know the discoverer. According to his own story, he decided to retire from business and go to sea professionally in 1499, when he was about fifty years old. After this—according to himself—he made no less than four remarkable voyages to the New World. According to the historians, if he made any voyages at all it was most likely with a marauding upstart named Hojeda, whose despicable behavior in the West Indies and along part of the South American coast appalled Columbus.

If Vespucci was with Hojeda, says Bishop Las Casas, it was in a subordinate capacity, and he had gone along as a merchant who had helped to finance the voyage. The Bishop was in a position to know the facts. Hojeda himself says that he took several pilots, including Juan de la Cosa and one "Merigo Vespuche." The Hojeda voyage was scarcely one of discovery, except of the main chance. Back from that—or after that—Vespucci claimed not one but three more long voyages in which, he alleged, he sailed almost the entire length of the Americas.

It is significant that he recorded nothing in Spanish of these great voyages of his, but wrote of them in Italian only, which a man might do if his accounts were meant for the consumption of those who were in no position to check his statements. These were often contradictory, frequently wild, and sometimes downright falsehoods. It was he, he said, who came first upon the mainland of America, and he modestly claimed also to have sailed to within thirteen degrees of the Antarctic Pole—where, of course, there was no land save Antarctica. Elsewhere he had "sailed," by his own account, to somewhere in what is now British Columbia, but overland—not in a prairie schooner, in a ship. The Portuguese had also sent him on a Guinea voyage, and on a further mysterious errand to the New Land.

Amerigo told a good yarn. Among those he convinced was a professor named Waldseemuller, professor of cosmography at the University of St. Dié, who, accepting all his statements at face value, put forward the ingenious suggestion that the new continent should be called America in his honor. This must have pleased Vespucci very much, although he could not know that the foolish suggestion would be acted upon so thoroughly. It is an odd quirk of history that caused the name to be taken up. No one seems to have given a thought to calling the great new land Columbia, and in the whole length and breadth of the enormous continent today Columbus's name is honored chiefly by a city in Ohio, a Federal district, a river in the Northwest, and a South American republic.

The oddest thing is that Columbus regarded Vespucci as a friend, and once entrusted him to carry some important letters to the court. "The bearer of this letter," wrote Columbus, "is going to court on matters relating to navigation. He always showed a desire to please me, and he is a very respectable man. Fortune has been adverse to him, as to others. His labors have not been as profitable to him as might have been expected. He leaves me with the desire to do me service..." Strange words! It is an odd service that Vespucci has done his fellow countryman. The pity is that where so many fine navigators, cartographers, cosmographers, and seamen served Italy and the world so well, this lone Munchausen among them should have been so outstandingly honored.

As for the New World, the principal object of the early Spanish voyages was soon to find a way past it, or through it, once it dawned on them that it could be no part of Asia. Neither Spain nor Portugal, nor any other kingdom in Europe then, had surplus capital and population to found new colonies overseas. Though it might be desirable and indeed wonderful to convert the heathen, the material rewards had to be sufficient to finance the necessary voyages, and material rewards were to be found in trade. The Caribbean offered little trade, at first, and it was obvious that a considerable amount of capital and human endeavor would have to be poured into the area before it was really worth much to Spain. As the Spanish navigators and their backers became the more aware of the immensity and complete originality of Columbus's discovery, they were the more depressed.

The idea of a continent being in their way was, to say the least, a serious disappointment. How were they now going to sail to the rich markets of the East, where the Portuguese were already establishing themselves? They continued their quest for a useful exit, for some sort of straits through: but there were none. Caribbean gold was not all that abundant, and the Caribs persisted in dying off, rather than permit themselves to be properly organized for the working of it. It took the best part of a quarter of a century before the discoverers heard of the Aztec empire: after that, the West Indies (which was a general name for any part of the new discoveries then, south of Newfoundland and north of Brazil) took on a more inviting expression.

There followed the wonderful conquest of Mexico by Cortes, Balboa's crossing of the Isthmus of Panama and first sighting (from its western shores) of the mighty Pacific Ocean, Pizarro's conquest of the civilization and vast riches of Peru. The exploitation of this sort of New World was well worthwhile, and it proceeded. All the western part of South America, all Central America and Mexico as far as California in the west and Florida in the east, became a Spanish empire. Before long, slow mule trains were plodding across the Isthmus of Panama, carrying Spanish gold, and Spanish galleons were being built, not only in large numbers at home, but also in the Pacific to carry on the rich trade there. There was talk of cutting a canal at Panama, but the project was beyond the capacity of the time. There was still no useful way out of the Atlantics save by Good Hope, in spite of the courageous Magellan's successful passage of the straits which bear his name. Those straits were not for galleons, nor for steel four-masters of later days either. The galleons could not dare to fight it out off the Horn for a westbound rounding, as a regular means of making a voyage. The odd ship might get through, but the grim and storm-infested land reached too far down into the savage Antarctic for that turbulent and bitter passage ever to be much use to old wooden sailing ships, with hempen rig and too-high hulls.

The Spanish conquest turned inland, and stayed there, for there was land enough. The Atlantic became a highway merely for the laden ships, sailing outward and homeward from and to Panama and the Carribbean ports. Across the Atlantic, on the Portuguese side, a flourishing trade continued, and after da Gama and Affonso d'Albuquerque the long-voyage Indian trade was profitably established. A great and growing fleet of larger ships took part in this trade. The weatherly but small and low-capacity caravel would do no longer, and *Niñas* and *Pintas* were relegated to the coastal trades.

Through the broad waters of the North Atlantic now came the great lumbering galleons of Spain, and the heavily built navs of Portugal, running up from Good Hope with the southeast trades, working through the Doldrums, standing up the northeast trades upon a bowline, their great balloonlike sails distended, hempen cordage tugging at every clew and weather leach, taut tackles humming, spritsails trimmed to the wind. Navs and galleons, how marvelous a fleet were these! The clippers and the bigger ships of later days had grace and beauty too, and in abundance, but the Atlantic sea had never known before and would not know again ships such as these richly laden, tremendous wooden hulls with their high masts of swelling sails, growing higher and higher. Topsails became deeper and deeper, and topgallant masts were stepped above the high topmasts. Lofty wooden sides bristled with the business ends of heavy guns. Great tops were full of boys like crows and could be filled with fighting men, when need arose.

Discipline was strict in ships like these, as it had always been at sea: keelhauling, ducking from the yardarm, tricing up with a knife stuck through the hand, or by the thumbs lashed to the lower rigging, with the victim's feet just off the deck—these were the punishments for the insubordinate, the slipshod, the careless, those who by their misdeeds threatened the good discipline of the ship and imperiled their shipmates' lives. It was the rule of the sea. Ducking from the yardarm meant hoisting a delinquent aloft with a bowline beneath the arms and letting him come down into the sea with a run three times, each drop being marked by firing a heavy gun above his head as he was below the water, as close to his head as possible. This was a "lesson" only. Keelhauling was a punishment which none but the most hardy might survive.

For persistent troublemakers, and any who were caught asleep on the lookout for the second time, there was a punishment which none survived. This was to be lashed in a basket slung from the bowsprit-end, before the spritsail, to swing above the blue sea there with nothing but a little water and one piece of bread, and the criminal's own knife, well sharpened. Here he could stay until he starved to death or, in the last moment of desperation, took the knife and cut himself down, to take his chance in the sea. There the ship would run over him, and he would drown. No one dared turn a hand to save him. There were big crews in these ships: discipline must be maintained, and the seaman had only such rights as his own community and his officers suffered him to have. The price was competence. Who endangered the ship, through any reason, was a poor shipmate, and deserved what was coming to him. This was the way of the sea.

Abaft the mast, in the spacious great cabin—decks of great cabins, as they soon became—life could be pleasant and, indeed, luxurious. As wealth created wealth and prosperity grew, not only noblemen could go clean and perfumed, and dine and wine well on nothing but the best. From Brazil, from Equatorial South America, from Panama, from Central America, and from the Caribbean, the great ships came sailing and the voyage of each was like a royal progress. There was no hurry: it was nothing to occupy a year on the one round voyage—outward to America with the trade wind and back with the antitrades and the Gulf Stream Drift, as Columbus had gone, or down to the Cape in a wide swing through both Atlantics, the way square-rigged ships went to the end of their days.

Farther to the north, another kind of commerce grew even more quickly, and steadily prospered. This was the Grand Banks fishery, off Newfoundland. Here the cod were so abundant that they could be taken with baskets, sometimes, and a ship might fish her fill from her own decks, in a month or two, and go back to Europe with a rich cargo. All was not necessarily metal that could be turned to gold; the dried codfish were gold, too. In those days of little meat and no refrigeration, dried fish were a staple food much sought after, and many a Western European fortune was founded there on the cold, stormy, and fog-ridden Banks. A very different type of ship pursued that trade—not gracious galleons but tough little ships, staunch, low in the sea, and above all, strong, and sailed and fished by tough, hard-bitten crews, greatly enduring.

They came first from Portugal and northern Spain and, soon afterward, from Biscayan France, from St. Malo and all the coast of Finisterre, from Bristol, from the Channel Islands, from Ireland, and from Wales. Previously, the Iceland and the Norwegian fisheries were the greatest sources of fish available to Europe, but the cod fisheries on the Banks off Newfoundland and along the New England coast were infinitely richer and not so much farther to sail. The little ships could come across and base themselves ashore, if they wished, for Spain attempted no dominion here, nor did Portugal. The New Found Land was in that half of the world which the Pope had allotted Spain, but what did it matter? Spain had enough, and so had Portugal, once Good Hope was safely rounded. Spanish mariners had never sought to use the Atlantic exit round the north of Canada: that way, pioneered by the Vikings and then the Portuguese, was later left to tough Englishmen. It defied them all until the powered age. European fishermen based themselves on Newfoundland, Nova Scotia, and the New England coast very early: being rough men and illiterate, they kept no written records. Their job was fishing, not discovery. They took a good fill of fish where they could find it, and made merry on the proceeds when they returned to port.

In these waters, too, the story is obscure; and shadowy, ill-chronicled pioneers abound. Well before the date of Columbus's first voyage, for example, there are brief references to Bristol seafarers, from the west of England, who apparently made a habit of roaming far to the westward in the North Atlantic in quest of the fabulous islands of "Brazil" and of the "Seven Cities." Bristol, on the river Avon near the point where it joins the Severn to flow into the Bristol Channel, was a bad port for sailing ships to make, but an ideal point for handling commodities, both for shipping out English wool and the other products of its rich and pleasant hinterland, and for distributing salt cod brought from Iceland. Early in the fifteenth century, if not before, there was a considerable trade with Iceland, and also to Madeira and the Azores. Portuguese merchants were established there.

Because the port itself was a bad one, with a swift-running river where ships were alternately dried out (which strained their hulls) or afloat in a turbulence, the port developed exceptionally able seamen. "Shipshape and Bristol fashion" is still a watchword of the sea, meaning that a ship is in first-class order, and fit for anything. Bristol ships had to be kept in the best order, both to accept the strain of handling cargoes in such a place, and the stress of beating out of it to gain an offing at sea. What one cannot understand is that any Bristol ships wasted either their mariners' time or their owners' substance beating about an ocean as foul as the Atlantic in their latitudes, searching for an island or islands that were not there. The inference is—at any rate a sailor's inference—that they knew what they were doing.

What they were most likely doing was voyaging to the Grand Banks for a fat and handsome cargo of well-paying cod, and they deliberately obscured the source with the yarn about "Brazil," and the like, to keep away both jealousy and competition. A market flooded with fat cod would cease to pay: and if the Bristolians knew the place at all, they were aware that their market could easily be spoiled if too many ships came dipping into the rich Banks off Newfoundland. They did not have to cross the whole Atlantic to find those cod, for the Banks stretch far to the east. They could, if they wished, fill their little ships for years without ever approaching the coasts of Newfoundland or Nova Scotia. The outermost Banks yielded as good cod as any, and it is reasonable to think that those Portuguese merchants from Angra, Viana, and from Lisbon, knew that very well, and passed the information to their close-lipped Bristol friends. The yarn about "Brazil" comes from the Spanish ambassador who was in London, anyway: it was a good yarn for him.

It was not until 1497 that an *official* voyage was made from Bristol, toward those Banks. This was led not by an Englishman but by another Italian, named John Cabot (or Giovanni Caboto), a Genoese like Columbus who—also like Columbus—chose to live away from his native land. John Cabot of Italy sailed west from Bristol in a little ship called *Matthew,* sailing in May, 1497 (when he would have a good chance of getting an offing with the east winds of spring) and fetching up we don't know where. Controversy rages over his American landfall, which may have been in Newfoundland, Nova Scotia, Cape Breton Island, or even somewhere on the coast of Labrador. It is generally considered today that his landfall was most likely in Newfoundland, and there is a statue there at St. John's to commemorate the "fact."

If Newfoundland was all he saw, it was an intense disappointment to Cabot, for he seems to have held the same theory which Columbus put to more profitable test farther south, and, indeed, he might have forestalled Columbus, for his quest of backers was well under way before 1492. It took the Spanish success to find him the necessary funds even to equip so small a ship as the little *Matthew*, in hard-headed Bristol, and when, after two attempts, he failed to find any Asian markets, or strait or usable passage anywhere through North America, his sponsors (who included the King in London) seem to have dropped him fast.

Both John Cabot and his son Sebastian tried hard, and one of them very possibly sailed down with the Labrador Current, inside the Gulf Stream, past much of the eastern seaboard of the United States. If he did sail that way (and there is evidence that he probably did), it did him no good, nor the merchants who financed his voyage and filled his ships with trade goods. There was no place there to trade. The great nation we now know as the United States was then a mere place which treasure-laden Spanish galleons left out of sight on their larboard hand as the Gulf Stream bore them northward toward home. The Cabots got a few pounds out of the English royal treasury—very few—and then the merchants forgot them, though the son Sebastian, when he settled permanently in England, was a prominent figure later in the Company of Merchant Adventurers.

Wherever he may have gone in his first voyage, John Cabot certainly was on the coast of Newfoundland on his second run, for he saw the Straits of Belle Isle and mistook them for a bay. He sailed both toward the south and north, searching for a passage through, but it is odd that he seems to have missed altogether the great

St. Lawrence River. If the Gulf of St. Lawrence was no pathway to China, it was surely the most obvious lead in that direction. It was left to the St. Maloman Jacques Cartier to sail the St. Lawrence in 1534—or rather, it seems, Cartier was the first to make that great waterway known. His fellow citizens, tough, fearless, and competent fishermen from St. Malo and its environs, had then been fishing in the area for at least thirty years if not longer, and they were accustomed to run into various bays to take their bait fish, to catch squid to eat and for bait, to repair their ships, and dry their cod.

Cartier sailed by the regular Grand Bankers route to Newfoundland, setting out on April 20 (probably with those good east winds of spring, which the westbound fishermen waited for as long as sailing ships from the Channel went to the Banks), and was on the coast by May 10. He looked at Labrador, then called generally just New Land, and sensibly remarked that the place should not have been given that name since there was little land there, but sterile rocks. He was home in France from his first voyage by September 5. The following year, Cartier was back again, and this time he sailed into the St. Lawrence as far as the first rapids, through which he could not pass with the ship's longboat. This time he wintered before returning to St. Malo; again, in 1541, he sailed into the St. Lawrence. But he found no way through, though the result of his efforts was the establishment later of the French dominion of Canada.

All this voyaging by the Cabots, Cartier, the Italian Verrazano (who sailed in French employ), the Englishman John Rut (who sailed from the Thames in 1527 "to seek strange places" but does not seem to have found much), and others was, in a strict sense, unauthorized and illegal, for the Pope had already divided the world between Spain and Portugal, and Papal Bulls were international law. This left little but a share in the home trades to anyone else. Such an idea was unacceptable to the French, Dutch, and English, where merchants and seamen were already hampered by other restrictive practices. All three nations were sending illegal expeditions toward the Guinea coast, quite early in the sixteenth century. English businessmen were soon on the coast of Brazil and in the Caribbean ports, engaged in trade: they could trade, using Spanish ships, but not discover, nor sail their own ships to those waters.

Spain and England then were allies, but, as early as 1527, an English merchant named Robert Thorne (a Bristol merchant with interests in the West Indies and Brazil) put forward the idea that the English might concentrate on finding a passage toward the East through one of the other and as yet unused exits of the North Atlantic. The only two useful exits which in fact there were—down to Cape Horn in the southwest and Good Hope in the southeast—were already then discovered and were the monopolies of the Spanish and Portuguese. It was not just a route which the other countries needed, but a *new* exit with usable bases along the way. They had to have bases to be ports of call for the merchant ships and naval bases for their protecting ships-of-war. The Portuguese held all the good wayside stops both in Africa, toward Good Hope, and in Brazil, toward the Straits of Magellan, and the Straits route was in fact fit only for tough pirates and determined discoverers. But what about a route round the north of Asia, or the other way, round all North America?

It was an obvious idea, and the English—those late starters but great stayers, with a flair for being good losers and winning in the end—got on with voyaging in both directions, almost forthwith. Even the harsh realities of the appalling difficulties against ships which tried to sail in either direction, northwest or northeast, did not deter them, and for many years, grim little ships manned by Englishmen and financed and led by incurable optimists set out on one or another of these hopeless quests. John Davis, with the 50-ton *Sunshine* and 35-ton *Moonshine*, sailed into the Straits which bear his name, and suffered fearful hardships. Martin Frobisher and Richard Chancellor were others who pioneered the Polar routes, though neither got very far—the one toward the northwest, the other to the northeast. They added vastly to the sum of bravery but little to geographical knowledge and nothing whatever to the realm of useful voyaging (beyond the founding of a Russian trade).

That great Elizabethan, Sir Humphrey Gilbert, thought Columbus and his compatriots had really found nothing but the long-lost Atlantis. He considered that there must be a usable way around the place, in all directions. Atlantis, after all, had always been represented as an island.

"I am of the opinion," wrote Sir Humphrey, "that America by the north-west will be found favourable to this our enterprise, and am the rather imboldened to beleeve the same, for that I finde it not onely confirmed by Plato, Aristotle, and other ancient phylosophers: but also by all the best modern Geographers." But both the philosophers and the geographers were wrong, as far as any practical usefulness in a route round Canada was concerned, and it took the Soviet Russians, with their fleets of icebreakers and other highly specialized vessels, to make anything of the northeast passage. To date, no one has made any real use of the northwest passage at all. It has been passed but rarely, and not at all until the twentieth century. It was conquered, in the end, by a highly experienced Norwegian ice pilot named Roald Amundsen, who found a way for the pack ice to drift his little auxiliary sloop—the famous *Gjoa* —around.

If the ice wastes were best left alone, it was not long before the English and the French were sailing in their own ships into both the Spanish and Portuguese zones of the Atlantic. By 1530, a Plymouth shipmaster-adventurer named William Hawkins was sailing cheerfully to Brazil, in his 250-ton ship, and trading there, not once but at least three times. Since he was a good trader, he was well received. He also made Guinea voyages. His son John, born in Devon in 1532, improved upon the father's enterprise by beginning the slave trade to the West Indies, collecting Negroes in the Portuguese area of Guinea and selling them, at an enormous profit, to the settlers in Spain's West Indies. A ghastly and wholly illegal trade thus begun flourished for centuries, and its consequences are still with us.

The Spaniards in the West Indies did their best to throw John Hawkins out, though there were many who were grateful for his trade. English businessmen who settled in Seville helped English Atlantic interests too, and after Hawkins other English seafarers sailed the Atlantic. There was an English fort put up by a company of Southampton men in Brazil by 1542. At the same time, other Englishmen were sailing in their small ships and making piratical attacks on Portuguese vessels bound up-Channel toward Antwerp. They soon extended these profitable activities to more distant waters. A French settlement was established in the Spanish land of Florida, and in due course the Spaniards threw them out again: but they came back.

The younger Hawkins, tossed out of what he regarded as lawful trade in the West Indies (where at least he had been doing his best to give value) sailed back there with more Devonians, his kinsman Drake among them, as pirates and freebooters. What Spain would not trade they would take. In the meantime England had become non-Catholic, and it was considered fair enough to conduct well-organized raids to the West Indies and to prey on Spanish ships—and even, before long, to make warlike raids on ports both in Spain and Portugal. While Mary of England was married to Philip II of Spain, her own Lord Admiral was conniving at the charter of her naval ships to make clandestine but highly profitable voyages to the Gold Coast—a trade which Elizabeth I made legal when she got the chance. It was she who put forward the doctrine that to hold a colony there must be "effective occupation" of it, knowing very well that both Spain and Portugal held far more than they could ever occupy. In England, the Pope's edicts were regarded as having no validity. The merchants and seamen of northwest Europe could never placidly accept a world which the head of a foreign church had partitioned for the sole benefit of their rivals in the Iberian Peninsula. When Portugal was joined to Spain by Philip's inheritance to its vacant throne (or perhaps by the fact that of the three possible successors, he alone was in a position to force his claims), the situation was worse.

After Hawkins came Drake, and from the Spanish viewpoint, Drake was worse, for his depredations were worldwide and their effects were permanent. Neither Hawkins nor Drake was the first corsair in the Caribbean, by any means, for the French had been raiding there more or less successfully for years. Both Hawkins and Drake were at San Juan de Ulua, a port in Mexico, when the Spanish

Viceroy's ships attacked them under a flag of truce and brought their project to ruin. This was a wrong which the English captains could not forgive. In those days, seeking personal redress for injuries done at sea was regarded as fair enough, and the farther waters of the Atlantic soon became a sort of great grab bag for the English, French, and Flemish pirates to try their luck in. Drake—and Cavendish after him—made a grab bag out of the whole of the watery world, for a while.

In the meantime the Dutch were fighting against Spain for their independence, and the English supported them, despite England's old alliance with Spain. In 1583, Sir Humphrey Gilbert was annexing Newfoundland for Elizabeth, and went on to try to establish a colony in Nova Scotia, which failed when the colonists were lost in shipwreck. Not long afterward, the redoubtable and farsighted Sir Humphrey was drowned himself, but not before he had turned English eyes across the Atlantic for purposes other than piracy and war. It was he who put forward the idea of colonizing Virginia, which Sir Walter Raleigh later acted on.

This Sir Humphrey Gilbert was an interesting character. Forthright, outspoken, educated at Eton and Oxford and trained for the law, he was more soldier than seaman. Indeed, like many of the pioneers, he was not a professional seaman at all, and a good part of his military career was spent fighting in Ireland, where he wanted to "plant colonists." He became a leader of voyages, not a seaman. The first voyage he led was from Dartmouth in Devon in 1578, sailing on September 23, the day of the autumnal equinox. He had eleven small ships and 500 men ("choyse souldiers and saylers," he calls them) when he first set out, but, at that time of year, the lot of them were bounced about in hard westerlies in the Channel for weeks, and many sickened of the enterprise before it had even properly begun. Some of the ships quit: others turned pirate. The others kept the seas for eight months or so but achieved very little. It was five years before Gilbert could sail again.

On June 11, 1583, he sailed from Plymouth, with five ships and his Queen's blessing. Within less than two months he was at St. John's, Newfoundland, where he began to set up the first English colony in North America. His ambition was to become there (or at any rate, somewhere in North America) the great landed proprietor which he was not in England and had failed to become in Ireland. But he had chosen the wrong place, despite Newfoundland's beauty and its rich resources in fisheries, forests, and (though he did not know it then) iron ore. So he sailed south with three ships, lost the largest of them off Cape Breton Island, and, giving up the voyage, tried to reach England again with the surviving ships. In a wild blow off the Azores, his ship went down, and the last picture we have of the redoubtable Sir Humphrey is of the bearded old gentleman, seated on his high poop clinging to a piece of the mizzen rigging with one hand and, with the other, reading a book, shouting across to his fellow adventurers in the other ship, "We are as near to Heaven by sea as by land!" The seas were breaking over his little bark then, and the gale howling.

Not long afterward, the waters of the North Atlantic, which drowned so many who sought to conquer them, knew an enterprise as colorful, as vast, and as fraught with tragedy and meaning as any it had ever known, or was to know for centuries afterward. Disgusted at last with the warlike behavior, the piracies, and the continual pinpricking tactics of the Pope-defying English, Philip of Spain collected a mighty fleet and sailed against them, and this was a very foolish thing for him to do. His Invincible Armada ("armada" is both a Spanish and a Portuguese word meaning simply "fleet": it can be seen on the cap bands of Portuguese sailors to this day) was more frightening than effective, and not invincible at all. Badly led by a seasick nobleman whose selection for that responsible and difficult task is reminiscent of Spain's earlier choice of Amerigo Vespucci as the chief royal pilot; lumbering along with incredible slowness, hindered by the vast heterogenity of its extraordinary collection of well over a hundred ships, delayed at Lisbon for months until the ships had to beat north against the summer north wind, and then delayed again off Finisterre, scattered by the slightest squall, the marvelous fleet (carrying 22,000 soldiers in ships manned by more than 8,000 sailors) failed absolutely in its mission. It sailed north to be decimated both by the action of the smaller, better fought, and more mobile English ships, and the assault of an even worse enemy—onshore storms in narrow waters which the Spaniards were unaccustomed to navigate.

The soldiers never landed at all, except from wrecks; the half-hearted nobleman in command proved useless—as the poor man had himself foreseen and for that reason tried to resign not once but many times—and the English captains arrayed against him included experienced, enterprising, and highly competent hell-raisers such as John Hawkins and Francis Drake. They were in their home waters, handling good ships, home-based, manned by mariners who knew both their seamanship and their gunnery. They sailed among the vessels of the lumbering great Armada now like wolves, clinging to their flanks and demolishing them one by one, now together like a squadron of fire-belching dragons dealing destruction in the mass. Far from base, harassed by wind and tide, unable ever to come to close enough grips to pour their superior numbers of well-armed men onto the decks of the little ships which stung them like a horde of wasps, the ships of Spain blew on up-Channel to anchor in an ill-defended mess off Calais. Here the English sent fire ships among them, which created panic. Great ships-of-war, fearfully watching the burning hulks drift down on them with the relentless tide, slipped their cables and ran. One beached and was boarded by the English, who had to hand her over to the local authorities, much to their chagrin.

Never again were the remnants of the mighty Armada properly assembled, and the threatened invasion of England did not take place. The Armada's chief operational purpose was to join forces with a Spanish army in the Netherlands, which it was to transport for an assault landing in southeast England. But the Armada never kept the rendezvous, nor did the Spanish army either. In the face of continued westerly winds, the big ships lumbered on northward through the North Sea and home again by way of the north of Scotland. The English ships continued to harass them until off the Firth of Forth: from there onward, the storms took over, and the storms were worse.

The summer of 1588 was remarkable even in British annals for its long-continued sequence of violent storms—Caribbean hurricanes blowing themselves out across the Norwegian Sea—and the poor Armada fought against an impossible combination of misfortunes. How many of the great ships went down in those waters will never be known, but eighteen of them were cast up and wrecked on the coasts of Scotland and Ireland. Others simply foundered. Less than half the ships which set out ever returned to Spain.

It was an utter rout not only of the Invincible Armada. England's defeat of the might of Spain marked the true opening of the North Atlantic. Henceforth transatlantic colonies could flourish as they willed and where they willed, more or less. The no man's land between Florida and the Banks fisheries was on the threshold of its tremendous career. The "Spanish" Main was now become the Main Ocean.

THE ROANOKE MYSTERY

7

THE REAL BEGINNING of the United States of America was in the Jamestown story, but before that came the Roanoke adventures. Before success came failure. Before the founding of Jamestown came the unsuccessful voyages from England to establish a colony—"plant" was the contemporary word—on Roanoke Island, on the coast of the present state of North Carolina. What was wanted, at first, was a useful base for attacking Spanish shipping and prosecuting the sea war against Spain, and it was hoped that the colony might quickly become self-supporting. It should also produce profitable surpluses, and establish a trade in timber, dyestuffs, furs, pelts, and anything else that might offer. It might provide gold and silver, and it would also be a base to find a way westward to the Great South Sea.

All these were good ideas: but unfortunately, when so many better harbors were waiting to be found, it was a pity to select a place so close to Cape Hatteras. There were four headlands dreaded above all others in the sailing-ship world, and one of these was Hatteras. (The others were Cape Horn, Good Hope, and Cape Flattery.) As a notorious storm breeder with more than its share of maritime dangers, Hatteras was—and still is—preeminent. It was a place to sail by quickly, preferably out of sight of land. Its selection as a base for Elizabethan ships was made by soldiers, not sailors, and one of their chief considerations was to find a base which was not too far from the Caribbean while at the same time not obvious, and capable of being defended against both the Spaniards coming from the sea and the American Indians coming from the land. These soldiers, who sailed the Atlantic sea in curious vessels, were interesting and often fascinating characters. The pioneer was Gilbert; after him came that strange, ruthless, far-sighted, but in the end, so completely unsuccessful character, Sir Walter Raleigh, who took over Gilbert's patent for the establishment of Virginia.

In my mind's eye, I see the courtly figure of this extraordinary Elizabethan every time I go to the National Maritime Museum at Greenwich, near London. The museum, standing in a wide green park athwart the low hill on which the famous Greenwich Observatory is built, faces across a busy road the magnificent buildings of the Royal Naval College, with an occasional view of the shipping passing in the Thames beyond. The central building of the museum itself is the Queen's House, begun by Inigo Jones in 1635 for Anne of Denmark, James I's queen. It is a beautiful building of perfect proportions, fascinating in itself, and its contents are even more so. To me, one of the main attractions is the old original roadway which, dipping between the two flanking colonnades which span the lawns from the museum's other buildings, goes through and under the old palace. There was a royal palace near here before the Queen's House was built, and the tradition is that here, or very near here, was the place where Sir Walter Raleigh flung his cloak down in the mud that Elizabeth I might pass dry-shod across a puddle. Raleigh was a tall, handsome man of polished manner, and a good gambler. When he threw his cloak at Elizabeth's feet, it was a big risk he was taking, for most of his little capital was tied up in his gay and costly court attire. This was no boat cloak or soiled old mackintosh! It was a gloriously embroidered and colorful triumph of the tailor's art, created for the perfect figure: and there was not another to replace it. But the gamble came off.

And so, as I pass along that way over the rough cobbled stones, looking in vain there for a puddle now, or a gay cloak, I think of that gay adventurer of another age, and admire his nerve. His gamble came off, then: but so did his head, in due course. Playing the game of being royal favorite was a dangerous pastime. This Raleigh was stepbrother to Sir Humphrey Gilbert, and like his stepbrother, Raleigh was an impecunious and ambitious younger son. He was briefly a student at Oriel College, in Oxford, but Oxford was not the place for him. He went to London, to become first a minor, then a leading, finally (and temporarily) the principal courtier at Elizabeth's court. For some time he was the Queen's prime favorite, and he used his temporary power in that position unscrupulously in his own and his relatives' interests. He picked up so many useful and valuable perquisites that his name became notorious, and his enemies bided their time. He put money in his stepbrother's North American schemes, and lost it there. To make up for that, perhaps, he took over the schemes themselves, and when Sir Humphrey Gilbert was dead, Raleigh was granted the rights which he had held, to plant a colony in North America in the area loosely called Virginia.

This Virginia was an enormous tract of territory stretching from Florida (which also was ill-defined) northward to beyond the Hudson River, which was then unknown (that wonderful harbor had to wait for Henry Hudson, an Englishman in Dutch employ, to sail into it or at any rate to add it to the map, which he did while on a voyage for the Dutch in 1609) and westward to the Great South Sea. This was a good area to stake a fat claim in, nor was Raleigh unaware of the advantages of a base on that coast to use for privateering raids against Spanish ships, homeward-bound in the Gulf Stream. Raleigh then had money, influence, and ideas, and he set about the interesting business of founding a colony in Virginia straightaway. But he did not go himself. He took over his stepbrother's rights in 1584; the same year, he sent out two mariners named Amidas and Barlowe, who made their passage west from somewhere off the Canaries and fetched up, in due course, off Pamlico Sound, by Cape Hatteras, and sailed inside.

They were back again before very long with a glowing account of the land, and a cheerful unawareness of the dangers of Cape Hatteras.

The following year, Raleigh sent out his colonists, under another of the great Elizabethan adventurers. This was a cousin of his named Sir Richard Grenville, a Cornishman, who had sat in the House of Commons as member for his native county, and had once been Commissioner of Works at Dover Harbor. Grenville, too, had been a soldier, distinguishing himself by his fearless leadership: like the other soldiers, he was also capable enough to lead an expedition by sea. The French had the same idea twenty years before, and a party of French Huguenots had tried to set up a colony in Florida in 1565. The Spaniards found them there and killed them to a man, themselves establishing a post at St. Augustine. Another French group then came, and killed the Spaniards. Fear of being forestalled by further Frenchmen, or Hollanders, was a spur to Raleigh's colonial plan.

The number of Grenville's colonists was something in excess of a hundred. Neither arithmetic nor spelling was a strong point in Elizabethan records, and names and numbers vary in each account. So do spellings of the Grenville name, which is given variously as Greenfield, Grenfell, Greenville, Granville, and (by his own signature) Greynvile. Raleigh sailed with Grenville, but seems to have put about and run back to England at the first blow. Sir Richard's instructions were that, upon arrival in a safe and secluded harbor, he was either to "tarrie himself, or to leave some gentleman of good worth with a competent number of souldiers in the countrie of Virginia, to begin an English colonie there."

With a stop on the way at Puerto Rico, where the Spaniards did their best to throw him out, Grenville sailed on to Virginia. As he entered the sound, his ship the *Tiger* took the ground. A nasty sea was running, and she pounded so violently that she opened up, and a great deal of the provisions which she was carrying for the colony was spoiled. The *Tiger* came off again, and in due course the colony was established. It consisted of 107 persons under one Rafe Lane, another soldier, described as a "gentleman of good account," who was appointed "generall." Then Grenville set off to sail back to England, having the good luck to take a valuable Spanish prize on the way, not far from Roanoke Island. His *Tiger* was a royal ship, loaned by the Queen, to further her favorite's schemes and her own profit. The ship was well suited for taking prizes. The Spaniard was carrying bullion, pearls, sugar, ginger, and hides. Raleigh welcomed his kinsman back to Plymouth, and it was resolved to send out a supply ship to keep the colony going.

The supply ship sailed, in due course, but the colonists did not wait to be relieved. When Sir Francis Drake passed that way in 1586, he took them off at their request. This was an extraordinary incident. The "colonists" were an ill-assorted group, and it did not take long before life at Roanoke palled. It was all very well for the theorists at home to write that Virginia was "a fruitfull pleasant countrey, replenished with all good things necessary for the life of men, if they be industrious who inhabit it." Fruitful and pleasant it was, certainly, but the colonists—many of them, at any rate —saw no future in being particularly industrious. The low sand bars and windy islands in Pamlico and Albemarle sounds were neither the most "fruitfull" nor pleasant places for the pioneers to start on.

"Beyond Roanoak are many Iles full of fruits and other Naturall increases," Amidas and Barlowe had reported. "Those Iles lye 200 myles in length, and between them and the mayne is a great long sea, in some places 20, 40 or 50 myles broad, in other more: somewhere lesse. And in this sea are 100 Iles of divers bignesses, but to get into it you have but 3 passages, and they are very dangerous..." There were cedar and oak, fish, pumpkins, venison, hare, cucumbers, and birds. The Indians readily exchanged furs and skins for trinkets. Captains Amidas and Barlowe had made the round voyage from England in five months, but it was a different thing to stay. Roots and oysters soon became the colonists' chief fare. The provisions brought from England were quickly used up. The Indians, noting the quarrelsome dispositions of some of these paleface newcomers and having soon no high opinion of any of them, turned nasty. There was some bloodshed, and after that the Indians would not barter anything.

The principal industry of the colonists quickly became looking for a ship to take them off, and parties of lookouts were stationed near Cape Hatteras. One sunny day, they were astonished to see not the longed-for one or two sails, but a dozen of them, then a score or more! At first delighted, then alarmed lest this be a Spanish force sent to wipe them out (as had happened to the Huguenots), they kept an anxious watch, out of sight. The astonishing fleet of ships big and small stood on, as if aware of the settlement. What spy had told them? But—these were English ships!

Indeed they were, for this was Drake, homeward-bound from depredations in the Caribbean, and he had been asked by Queen Elizabeth to look in on Raleigh's colonists, and bring them sustenance. This he could well do, for his cruise had been successful. But, soon after the ships had been identified and the delighted watchers allowed themselves to give a cheer, old Hatteras blew up a sudden gale which nearly forced Drake's ships ashore. Like the good seaman he was, Drake clawed off the land, and stood to the open sea again. He did not like the look of Hatteras, nor of those sandy islands and their shallow sound. However, here were the colonists; when the weather allowed, he beat back again. This time he got in, and there was much "drinkinge and ryott" in delirious welcome. The "generall" and his lookouts had had enough. Grenville was supposed to send a ship to their relief and had failed to do so. The whole colony voted to be taken off, "so with prayses to God we set sayle in June, 1586, and arrived in Ye Portsmouth the 27 of July the same yeare."

And that was that—but those soldier-seamen leaders of the Elizabethan age were determined men. Raleigh had in fact been doing his best to get a relief ship to Roanoke, but had been delayed. He must have been astonished to see his settlers all back in England, when he had put up so much capital to get them out of it and safely across the North Atlantic. But he began at once to try again. His relief ship had in fact arrived off Roanoke soon after Drake had gone, to find the colony deserted, and feared a massacre.

To add to the curious sequence of events, Grenville himself arrived off the coast very soon after the supply ship had gone, and he, too, was astonished to see the colony so completely deserted. His soldier's eye could quickly see that there had been no fighting, and no massacre, nor was there any letter left to show where the quitters had gone. No quitter himself, Sir Richard did something about it. He hustled some more colonists out of his ship, quickly, and left them there.

Again the problem of supply was to prove the chief stumbling block. The Spaniards in the Caribbean had more than they could do to try to protect what they already had, and they had no men, time, or ships to come ferreting out the English. The chief difficulty at Roanoke was continuity of supplies, and maintaining the contact with England. Grenville left his second lot two years' supplies and strict orders that there was to be no quitting. Then he, too, sailed off: and again, the months passed, and there came no other vessel —month after month after month. In the meantime, Raleigh also organized another band of colonists, and these sailed across from England, under one John White, who was yet another military man. White took twelve assistants and some hundred-odd new colonists, of which the most interesting was perhaps his daughter. She was married to one of the assistants, and made the westward passage in a state of advanced pregnancy. Her daughter, Virginia Dare, was the first English child born in North America.

White sailed in 1587, with three ships, but one of these (as Raleigh had done previously from Grenville) deserted in the Bay of Biscay. It took seventy days to cross the North Atlantic by the southern route. When they arrived at last, they found none of the men that Grenville had left—nothing but some bones, ruined houses, and a gutted fort. Nor was anything of this party ever found. Undeterred by this tragedy, White's people landed, and got on with establishing themselves at Roanoke, despite the fact that they had been instructed to give up that place and go to a better harbor farther north. Perhaps it was easier to start things again where at least some of the pioneering had been done. White sailed back to England to report, before the year's end, and to see to the sending out of more ships; but that proved much more difficult than he could possibly foresee. Even when supply vessels were sent, sometimes they failed to arrive. Navigation was still in the rough. English mariners had not long given up the habit of measuring distance at sea by what they called "kennings," a kenning being the distance that a man with good sight could see from a headland on a reasonably clear day. A pilot who had been successfully across the Atlantic twice was a rare and much sought prize: each ship had to find the way for herself. White fetched up in Ireland on his way home, not England. Even experienced pilots made such mistakes as thinking Cape Fear was Hatteras, and that Hispaniola was Puerto Rico. An English Route Book, or Rutter as it was called, which was printed for mariners about the middle of the sixteenth century by a man named Robert Copland, offered some extraordinary advice, as follows: "Gentle marriners, on a bonne voyage, hoyce up the saile and let God steer."

White and Raleigh between them did get a supply ship off, but she did not reach America. One reason for the failure of these alleged supply vessels to do their job was the masters' intense interest in the more profitable pastime of taking wayside prizes, and they preferred to go privateering for anything they could find, rather than set about the job in hand. And why not? The Atlantic was a glorious grab bag in which the English did not stand to lose much, at that time, except the small ships they ventured in, and there was little profit in relieving a struggling colony. It was not at all unusual for a vessel, sent out ostensibly for a voyage to Virginia, to begin by running down toward the coasts of Spain and Portugal to pick up a prize or two, cruise awhile in the waters near Madeira or the Canaries with the same intent, slip up to the Grand Banks to steal provisions from some poor fishermen there, and then, in the end, perhaps to put in a token appearance off America somewhere. More likely, she would go back with such plunder as she had been able to secure, and report that bad weather had kept her from her proper destination.

There is, for instance, a record of a certain Captain Facy, a pirate if ever there were one. In the general shortage of better shipping caused by Queen Elizabeth's standstill order (to keep English ships at home in order to be ready to fight the Armada) Raleigh had to send two very small "barks"—the *Brave*, of 30 tons, Arthur Facy master, and the *Roe*, 25 tons. With a small group of additional colonists aboard for Roanoke (including a number of women) and supplies of food, Captain Facy took his cockleshells to sea from Bideford in Devon on April 22, 1587. Within a few days of leaving port, Facy was boarding any ship which he could find that was smaller and less well armed than his own. A Scot ship and a Breton ship were boarded and robbed, though they had very little. From April 26 to 29, Facy chased a Flushing ship which he could not catch, and so they continued toward Madeira. Near here, he was chased himself by a larger vessel, which took the *Brave*, but the tiny *Brave* lived up to her name and fought hard.

> The same day about 2 of the clocke in the afternoone they were come with us [reads Facy's account]. We hayled them, but they would not answere. Then we waved them to leewardes of us, and they waved us with a sword amayne, fitting their sails to clappe us aboord, which we perceiving gave them one whole side: with one whole shotte their master Gonner's sholder was stroken away, and our master Gonner with a small bullet was shot in the head. Being by this time grappled and aboord each of other, the fight continued without ceasing one houre and halfe. In which fight were hurt & slaine on both sides 23 of the chiefest men, having most of them 6 or 8 woundes, and some 10 or 12 woundes. Being thus hurt and spoiled they robbed us...

The little *Brave* had to struggle off back to Bideford the best way she could. Even at that, though she was fighting against big odds, the chronicler adds that she would have done a great deal better if they had not been "pestred with cabbens and unserviceable folkes" who got in their way during the fighting.

And so the Roanoke colonists were not relieved by the *Brave*, or the *Roe* (which disappeared), and that year there were no other ships which could sail to their aid. Relief had to wait until the Armada was defeated, but by that time it was too late. Once again, the surviving Roanoke colonists had disappeared, and where they went or how remain mysteries.

It was 1590 before the final relief expedition sailed from Plymouth (which had seen so many of these adventurers set out). They went in March, which was a good time to use the northern route, but they sailed by the usual route of the Canaries and the West Indies. The northern route then was left to the Grand Banks fishermen, and the colonist barks believed in the sunny way, with its magnificent departure point of the Canaries (whose high land could be used to check the westward course eighty, ninety, and even a hundred miles on their way) and similar bold and high, clear landfall on the mountains of Dominica. The warm waters there might fill the under sides of their wooden ships with the borer worm, sour their beer, foul their water, and discontent their too large crews by providing them with too much sunny sea time and too little work to do. But they knew that route and they stuck to it, though it was not until the following August that the ships were again off Hatteras. Here they anchored and fired their guns. There was no answer. They sent in boats. There were no colonists.

At first, this caused no great surprise, as it had been intended that the colonists should forage well inland. But it had been arranged with them that whenever they went off anywhere, they should leave word of their intentions, in a code message carved into a tree; nor should all go at once. If there was serious trouble, the first thing in the message was to be a cross. White searched diligently. At length he found what seemed like a message. "CRO" it read; but there was no cross. He searched again. The houses had been knocked down, and the place fortified by the erection of a high fence. On one of the posts of this fence was a single word. "Croatan," it said; and again there was no cross. Looking about closely for further clues, the sailors found some sea chests which had obviously been hidden, and then dug up. One of these White recognized as his. While he was looking quickly through the chest, it began to blow and the sea rose. One of the boats had been turned over in the surf, coming in, and drowned some men. Not wanting any more of that, White got back to the ship as quickly as possible. They were anchored in the open sea, off Hatteras: it blew a hard onshore gale that night, which almost forced the ship ashore. In the morning, with the weather eased a bit, White tried to weigh and sail to a better anchorage. But the wind got up again. He lost most of his anchors and cables, and the last anchor would not hold. (August is a hurricane month, and some hurricanes pass to the north off Hatteras.) The sailors would not have any more buffeting off this most dangerous coast, whether there were colonists to be saved at Croatan or not. So they sailed away with the mystery unsolved. They went off toward the Azores to raid shipping, intending to come back to Roanoke later. But they did not come back, and other passing ships, hearing of the story, visited the area later and learned nothing to solve the mystery.

The missing party included ninety-one men, nine boys, and seventeen women. What happened to them? How could they so completely disappear? "Croatan" was the name they had given to the island on which stood Cape Hatteras (which they knew as Cape St. John). White's ships were anchored close enough to see smoke signals at Croatan, had there been any to see. There were none.

There was plenty of room for 117 people to disappear into Virginia, the Lord knows. But it was odd. There almost seemed to be a curse on the place—Gilbert drowned, Grenville fought to the death, two parties of colonists mysteriously disappeared. There were persistent yarns that at least some of the missing colonists survived when Indians massacred the rest on an inland trek, and there was said to be a queer tribe, half-Indian, half-white, speaking a curious Elizabethan English, somewhere in the area, as late as the mid-nineteenth century. Maybe. Maybe they went off and became the first wild hillmen in the Kentucky mountains, where a good deal of Elizabethan English (of a sort) is still spoken. Even such an authority as Sir Clements Markham, the president of the Hakluyt Society, accepted the story that the surviving colonists had mixed with the Indians. Whatever they did or however they died, their disappearance was the end of the Roanoke adventure.

Sudden death, savage fights against tremendous odds, unbridled piratical instincts relieved at least in part by sublime courage, a careless and uncalculating inability to know when the odds against them were impossible, and fearlessness in the face of death were shipmates in any English vessel which set out to sail the Atlantic seas in those stirring, eventful, and bloody days. Grenville himself went down in circumstances of the greatest bravery when fighting, alone, against a fleet of fifteen large Spanish vessels off the island of Flores in the Azores. For this he achieved the greater immortality from the poet Tennyson's pen.

At Flores in the Azores
Sir Richard Grenville lay—

and all the rest of it. I learned that at school, in Melbourne, before I had any idea where Flores in the Azores was, or why Sir Richard should have chosen so sticky and certain an end, and not sailed smartly off with his compatriots who had left the scene. It was Grenville's ship *Revenge* against a Spanish fleet, 150 men against 5,000, and those West Countrymen fought it out in a savage, bloody, and obviously hopeless mess for fifteen hours. Sir Richard slipped at last below the surface of those same Azorian waters which had already closed over the head of Sir Humphrey Gilbert: but the nobility and the inspiration of his last fight have echoed down the centuries.

This was in 1591. Glorious the action off the Azores might have been, but it did the colony at Roanoke no good, nor the Virginia project, except perhaps to remind the Dons that the English fighting man was worthy of respect. They knew that.

In the meantime Raleigh had dropped from favor at court. He had brought the potato to Ireland and introduced the habit of smoking tobacco into Europe, but he could not get his colony going. It is to Rafe Lane, really, that the credit (if it is credit) for introducing tobacco smoking to England should go, and not to Raleigh. Raleigh never saw Virginia. Lane brought him the tobacco and the pipes and Raleigh simply started the fashion. If he had been able to foresee then how great an industry he was starting, he would have been a wise man to keep his holdings in Virginia. For not gold or silver, or sugar or spices, or an easy way through to the Great South Sea, made Virginia's fortune. It was the golden leaf of the Indians' "physick"—plain, unadulterated tobacco. The new smoking habit swept through Europe. A lovely silver pipe, a bit of a walnut shell and a piece of straw, a hollowed piece of hardwood, or a stem and a bowl of clay—all served equally well. Tobacco smoke was a delight to rich man and poor man (and woman) alike, and there was a fortune in it. Virginia rode on the habit's back, for here was something which could be grown fairly easily and dried in the sun, calling for no big investment. Tobacco soon became the principal eastbound cargo, and duties clapped on it kept many a monarch happy. When it was discovered, with pleasure, that the stuff would grow quite well in southwest England, the King clapped a total prohibition on its production forthwith. English fields were for growing England's food, he said: where would Virginia be if the Virginians could not sell their tobacco? He needed the duties, too, and it would have been difficult to tax the home product effectively. So the prohibition stayed, and it took World War II, almost three and a half centuries later, to get it lifted. Not knowing of the fortune in tobacco, Raleigh cut his losses (which he put at a modest £40,000) and sold his Virginian rights to a group of merchants, retaining the ground rent and one-fifth the value of any gold that might be found there. There were other favorites at Elizabeth's court, and soon he was in serious trouble for having got one of the Queen's maids of honor with child. Elizabeth was much concerned with her maids of honor, who among other things could not marry without her consent. Sir Walter was thrown into the Tower of London to reflect upon his misdeeds, but his imprisonment was hardly rigorous. He was able to marry the girl, and to put up some money for a piratical expedition which captured the treasure galleon *Madre de Dios*. This ship had bullion and goods aboard worth a million in our money, but the all-seeing Queen took the lion's share for herself, leaving Raleigh (released from the Tower for the time being) sufficient to finance a futile voyage to the coast of Guiana, to look for El Dorado. On his return, he wrote a good travel book which sold well. In this he was supported by his friend, the Reverend Richard Hakluyt, of Oxford.

This Richard Hakluyt was yet another of those amazing Elizabethans whose work has continued down the centuries. He was a don of Christ Church, later an archdeacon of Westminster, who never led an expedition anywhere or voyaged anywhere either, except across the English Channel. Hakluyt—a Welshman by origin and not a Dutchman, despite the name—was the first ardent student of English voyages, and collector and editor of accounts of them. He was a warm supporter of the American colonization idea and promoted the project, by his writings and his influence, as much as he could. He did his work so well that it is carried on in England to this day, by the well-known Hakluyt Society, in London, which still publishes accounts of the old voyages. His collections of travels are classics, and his propaganda for "planting the English race in North America" has borne great fruit. Hakluyt died in 1616 and, alone of the characters mentioned in this chapter, is buried in Westminster Abbey. Many of his papers may still be seen at Oxford, and I never look at the Christ Church meadow, or the college, without giving the industrious, farsighted, and able cleric a warm and grateful thought.

With the support of Oxford dons and sundry dignitaries in high places, Raleigh continued his propaganda, but his day was done. He sold his Irish estates to the Boyles, who became the Earls of Cork and pretty good seamen in their own right. When Elizabeth died and James I came to the throne, Raleigh was tried for treason, found guilty, and clapped once again in the Tower. This was in 1603. The unfortunate Raleigh was to remain a prisoner there until 1616. Again, his imprisonment was not rigorous. He was able to write, to invent a wonderful elixir, and above all, to keep on hoping for reprieve. Always inclined to be credulous, always ready to listen to ideas for grand schemes, however impractical, and to lend them a hand if he could, Raleigh at last promised the King that he would find him a gold mine in Guiana, if only he were allowed to sail in search of it. This was an impossible idea, and the Spanish ambassador in London at once protested. He would not, said Raleigh, infringe Spanish rights. Then, asked the ambassador, how could he go looking for a gold mine in Guiana, which was Spanish? The King answered that if Raleigh were guilty of any piratical acts, he would lose his head when he came back, gold mine or no gold mine.

With this pleasant thought to reflect upon, Raleigh sailed on the seventeenth of March, 1617, on this last desperate, hopeless, and tragic venture. It was a day of ill omen for him. It was impossible to recruit good men for such a harebrained expedition, and his ships were ill equipped and worse manned. It took the best part of a year to reach the mouth of the Orinoco, which they should have sailed to in a couple of months. By that time Raleigh was left behind sick of the fever, in Trinidad. His son sailed on with five small boats into the Orinoco, in quest of the mine which was not there. On the way, there was the inevitable quarrel at a Spanish settlement. Some Spaniards were killed, as the ambassador had foreseen they would be. This was piracy. Raleigh's son was also killed in the fracas, and the leader of the river expedition committed suicide as soon as he had given Raleigh his report. Raleigh sailed back to England, broken and ruined. Promptly thrown into the Tower again, this time he did not get out. He was executed there on the twenty-ninth of October, 1618, smoking a pipe of Virginia tobacco as his last act and going nobly to his death in the end. His name survives in English, American, and Spanish history, and is perpetuated in the state capital of Raleigh, North Carolina.

Almost the only immediate results of Gilbert's and Raleigh's efforts were some dead colonists, and a name. The sixteenth century ended before any lasting settlement was made in their Virginia. The real and continuous colonization of North America began at Jamestown, and the real leader of the enterprise was yet another of these astonishing soldier-seamen. This time he was no court dandy, Queen's favorite, or landless gentleman in search of fortune. His name was the plain one of Smith—John Smith, Captain John Smith, from Willoughby in Lincolnshire. He was a forceful and competent character who was not only soldier and sailor, but colonist, administrator, and statesman besides; and Virginia needed him. So did England.

THE JAMESTOWN STORY

8

I ADMIRE Captain John Smith. His is a story which shines on an otherwise somewhat dark page of transatlantic history. When the English first tried to establish their American colonies, the only colonies they had tried before were the settlements in Ireland. After Raleigh came his company, and one of the principal attractions to those who put their money into the Virginia idea then was the hope of getting quick returns from gold and silver, and pearls and precious stones, as the Spaniards had done farther to the south. They were out of luck, and this discovery understandably annoyed them. The hopes of easy reward which the investors deluded themselves with spread through the majority of the colonists they sent. Too many of these were soft-handed gentlemen who had been not too successful at home, or strong-minded old soldiers with a sharp eye on the main chance but not always the ability to detect it when in sight, with a mixture of riffraff from the London streets.

There were too many gentlemen, too few hard workers, too few experienced leaders. There was too much quarreling, too much discontent, and group after group, after the hard voyage, landed to make the abrupt and awful discovery that not only was there no quick road to fortune here but they must immediately turn to with a great will and strong backs to carve out from the wilderness even a bare sufficiency to support life. They lacked both the organizing ability and the competence to get on with the job. Misled before they left, misgoverned on their arrival, hungry, dispirited and soon, all too often, hopeless as well, the pioneers with whom the illustrious John Smith landed at Jamestown in Virginia would certainly have quit the place, alive or dead, were it not for him. Yet he was not at first their leader, and his fellow colonists tried to murder him not once but several times. It was his fellow Englishmen who were his greatest enemies from first to last, not the Indians, whom he understood and could get along with, male or female.

This John Smith had a considerable experience of getting along with people and escaping from impossible situations, long before he went aboard the good ship *Susan Constant* for Virginia, in London in 1606. His adventures read today like those of some imagined hero of a radio serial, yet there is no doubt that they were real and they went on for twenty years and more, at much the same tempo. Smith was born a yeoman, which was not much help to him in those days. His father was a prosperous tenant farmer on the Lincolnshire estates of Lord Willoughby d'Eresby, where the son was born in 1579. Not much inclined toward farming, when he was about sixteen he set off on what may be regarded as the adventurer's "grand tour" of Europe in those days—the bloody, rioting, battle-filled wandering across the face of the land, fighting for whoever would hire him, for the English, for the French, for the Dutch. Now assisting at sea in the capture of a galley from Venice, now fighting lustily ashore against the Turks in Transylvania, warrior Smith gave himself his idea of a splendid tour, career, and road to fortune rolled into a glorious and eventful one.

That sort of thing generally leads to a bad end and, before long, the redoubtable Lincoln fighting man was taken prisoner by the Turks. Found badly wounded on the battlefield, his rich dress saved him from the usual fate of instant slaughter, and the hope of ransom saved his life. Marched overland to Constantinople, he became a slave, for none would or could ransom him. He was a remarkably

Construction of *Mayflower II* at Upham's Shipyard, Brixham, England

The *Mayflower* model at Pilgrim Hall, Plymouth

Launching of the new *Mayflower*, Brixham, England, September 22, 1956

Ship close-hauled on the starboard tack, 1565

New England, from Mercator's *Historia Mundi,* 1635

Virginia, from De

The *Susan Constar*
God Speed,
and *Discovery*

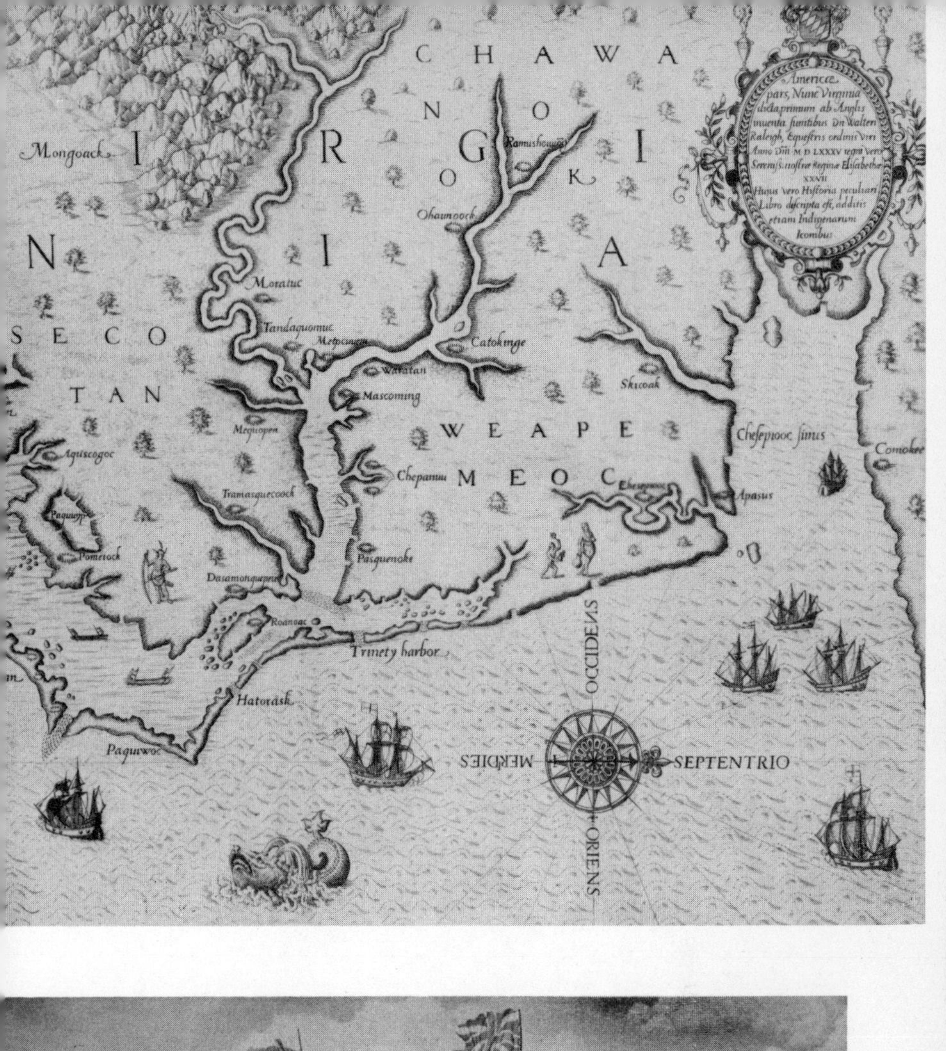

Americæ
pars, Nunc Virginia
dicta, primum ab Anglis
inuenta sumtibus Dn Walteri
Raleigh, Equestris ordinis Viri
Anno Dñi M D LXXXV regni vero
Sereniss. nostræ Reginæ Elisabethæ
XXVII
Hujus vero Historia peculiari
Libro descripta est, additis
etiam Indigenarum
Iconibus
CHAWANOOK
VIRGINIA
SECOTAN
WEAPEMEOC
Mongoack
Ramushouuog
Ohaunoock
Moratuc
Tandaquomuc
Metpeuuem
Catokinge
Waratan
Mascoming
Skicoak
Chesepiooc sinus
Comokee
Mequopen
Aquascogoc
Chepanuu
Tramasquecoock
Apasus
Paquipp
Pometock
Pasquenoke
Dasamonquepeuc
Roanoac
Trinety harbor
Hatorask
Paquiwoc
OCCIDENS
MERIDIES
SEPTENTRIO
ORIENS

The battle of Trafalgar, 1805

The *Serapis* and *Bonhomme Richard*, September 23, 1779

handsome fellow and had the luck to be acquired by a household mainly of women. Here, it seems, the most beautiful daughter fell in love with him. She sent him to a brother for safekeeping, until she could perhaps marry him, but the brother did not approve this idea and gave Smith a dog's life. Goaded by the cruelties of his master, Smith killed him and escaped in his clothes, though he still had the slave's steel collar round his neck. He rode for nineteen days and reached a Russian township on the Don. After many further fighting adventures, he turned up in the Mediterranean again, and shipped off with an English vessel which he thought was homeward-bound. But she sailed toward the Canary Islands where she gave battle to a couple of Spanish ships, which she took, Smith leading the boarders.

From this adventure he came home with a small fortune and a great liking for even more stirring deeds, and arrived in London in good time to learn of the new Virginia adventure. It must have been just the sort of thing he was waiting for—a new land to conquer, a land of challenge, of mystery and of gold, with the Spaniards to the south of it and the Great South Sea beyond. Captain Smith put down his stake to sail in the *Susan Constant*, with alacrity. He became one of the patentees in the London Virginia Company and thought, for a while, of founding a settlement of his own. One of the Company's shipmasters named Bartholomew Gosnold had already made a profitable voyage or two across the Western Ocean on his own, fetching up off Cape Cod, which he named for the abundance of good fish which he found there.

Gosnold not only took fish but landed at Martha's Vineyard, which he also named, and traded with the Indians. If fishing were good business, why go to the trouble always of bringing ships across from England to do the fishing, and then waste time sailing back again? It would be better sense, surely, to set up bases in good harbors on the far side and dry the fish ashore. Here was a basis for real settlement, and Gosnold and Smith tried to sell their idea. It was vain: the Virginia company (or companies: there was also one in Plymouth by that time) was more interested in the glittering prospect of a return from gold, though the Plymouth company did make an early and abortive attempt to settle colonists in Maine.

Captain Gosnold was an important member of the pioneer group which included the *Susan Constant*, a cockleshell of a three-master of only 100 tons, as its best ship. With this vessel (small even in those days) went two much smaller craft, the *God Speed*, of 40 tons, and the *Discovery*, a pinnace of 20 tons. Gosnold was master of the *God Speed*, and the three ships were under the command, at sea, of the master of the *Susan Constant*. This was Capt. Christopher Newport, who also had previous experience of American voyages. The three little ships, carrying 105 colonists, among whom there were not enough John Smiths, dropped down the river Thames from Blackwall on the twentieth of December, 1606, and the Virginia Settlers' Memorial just upstream of the present entrance to the East India Dock today marks the spot where the colonists boarded their ships. There was a ceremony there on the twentieth of December, 1956, to mark the 350th anniversary of the historic sailing.

It was a bad time of the year to sail, and Blackwall—or anywhere else in the Thames—was about as difficult a departure point as could have been chosen. From there the little ships, crowded with stores, utensils, armament, and people, had to work their way right down the London River and round the wreck-strewn, tempestuous waters off the coast of Kent, down the whole length of the English Channel in the face of whatever southwesterly gales might choose to blow at a time of year which could be confidently expected to provide them in profusion and at maximum strength, then somehow make and keep an offing out of Biscay and then—and only then—begin the long ocean voyage. The *Susan Constant* had seventy-one colonists aboard, as well as a full crew, and even the minute *Discovery* was carrying twenty-one.

The smallness of these three ships for the voyage they were making is today almost incredible. The whole three could fit on the flight deck of any large aircraft carrier, and scarcely impede the flying. The smaller pair could sail in the swimming pool of one of the larger Atlantic liners, and neither would be acceptable to serve as lifeboat in such a vessel. The *Susan Constant* herself was nothing like the size of an oceangoing tug. Replicas of these three ships, built at Norfolk, Virginia, in 1956, for the 350th anniversary of the founding of Virginia, showed how amazing such vessels appear to us today. They looked fit to sail up the James River, and that was all, and how the original cargoes and passengers had ever been carried across the Atlantic aboard them was very difficult to understand. But in 1606 they were tolerable ships, though not the best, and it must be remembered that the acceptance of necessary hardship was a plain man's virtue then.

So the little trio sailed, but at first they did not get very far. The gales shrieked at them, the short dark days of the North Sea and Channel winter gave them scarcely time to work out of port, the cold sprays drove over them, and the spars, sails, hempen rigging, and the hulls themselves were soon facing impossible strains. They did the only thing that they could do. They sheltered, and waited. The amount of time that a ship could stay at anchor in those days, sheltering, is exceeded only by the months she can spend waiting for military orders today, should she suffer the misfortune of being subject to them. The *Susan Constant* and her consorts anchored in the Downs for a couple of weeks, then passed on with difficulty to anchor again in the face of another gale.

"Sheltering" is hardly the word to use for the rough, exposed anchorages where the ships had to wait. The ships themselves were safe enough, under the lee of England, so long as the wind blew from southwest or anywhere west, but the sea ran constantly, and the little ships jumped and rolled at their anchors, plucking at their hempen cables, flinging themselves about with a wildness and continual and extremely uncomfortable motion which was enough to make any but the hardiest mariner thoroughly seasick. These colonists were landsmen. There were gentlemen, soldiers, a drummer, a carpenter, a blacksmith, several bricklayers and laborers, a barber, a tailor, a stonemason, a surgeon. Before they had been sheltering a week, many of them had had enough of it and wished themselves back home again; but they had contracted to make the voyage and to stay in Virginia. None was to be allowed to return to England except with a special passport signed by the president and council of the colony. None was even to write a discouraging letter. And so the little ships continued to bounce about in the gray, wretched waters of the January Channel, and the "colonists," shivering and suffering together, cursed their fate.

But those were patient days. In due course the gales eased, and there was an easterly slant in the wind. With that to help them, the ships passed down-Channel and out to sea, to bounce around again in a hard southwesterly in the Bay. Gosnold had made the passage directly across to the New England coast in 1602, but it was not the season of the year for that. The little ships had to go the long way round, down by the Canaries and then westward the Columbus way. In time, as they sailed southwest, the weather became fine for them, and they bowled along before the northeast trade winds.

But the leisure and the long warm days served only to bring home to the colonists and the crews how woefully overcrowded they all were, and they took to fighting amongst each other. The discipline was harsh, but difficult to enforce in such crowded little ships. The sea captains were instructed to take prayers every day, and were charged with the religious and moral welfare of their crews. It was laid down that there should be "no blaspheming of God, or detestable swearing, nor communication of ribaldrie, filthy tales, or ungodly talke; neither dicing, carding, tabling, nor other devilish games, whereby ensueth not only povertie to the players but also strife, variance, fighting, brawling, and oftentimes murther." This was taken more as a list of the mariners' diversions than a solemn warning of what they were not to do, and strife, fighting, brawling, etc., were all in the daily routine, not only among the mariners. At least they had a job to do, which they understood: and they would be homeward-bound again from Virginia.

As for the passengers, they were herded together like migrant Bedouin in an Arab dhow, with the added discomfort that they were not in the habit of changing their clothes and wore far too many of them. Garments were regarded as permanent by the poorer folk of those days, and changing underwear—or even owning any—was regarded as a luxury. The official of the ship charged with feeding the supernumeraries was known as the "undertaker," a name which was far too appropriate. Pease, gruel, biscuit, a bit of salt meat—these were their chief diet, regardless of the weather. The gentlemen in the cabins could have their luxuries, but these were not for the common folk.

"Conserves of Roses, Clove-gilliflowers, Green-ginger, Burnt-wine, English Spirits, prunes to stew, Raisins of the sun, Currence, Sugar, Nutmeg, Mace, Cinnamon, Pepper and Ginger, White bisket, Spanish rusk, Eggs, Rice, juice of Lemmons well put up to cure or prevent Scurvy"—these were all recommended to be taken, and also "Conserve of Wormwood" to prevent seasickness. The settlers were supposed to have a year's provision on their own account, but many of them seem to have had very little. While the adventure appealed to the adventurous, unfortunately it struck also the shallow responsive chords of too many no-goods, quarrelsome and useless fellows who would have made trouble anywhere and found it expedient to leave their native land for that reason. Relieved of the perpetual misery of the winter gales, these pitched into one another, or collectively complained about the voyage, or their food, or the discipline, or the heat.

There were too many people aboard for it to be possible to sleep on deck in hot weather, even if they were so inclined. There they would be under the sailors' feet, and sailors tending the ship's gear had scant regard for the comfort of passengers. So they huddled down below, and sweated, stank, quarreled, and moaned. They stank, the ship stank, and the accumulation of old bilgewater and new drainage in the bottom steamed with odors which could almost be seen. Nothing can smell with quite the same degree of foul loathsomeness as the bilgewater of an old ship. Going the southern way meant that the voyage, already protracted by the long delay in the Channel, dragged on for months. It was all very well to go the Columbus way, but in the winter ships had to get well down to the southward to find a true trade wind. Shipmasters were reluctant to sail too far south because they knew that by so doing they would increase the number of miles they had to sail. So some dawdled and doodled at the trade wind's edge, and their unfortunate ships wallowed there, dribbling a few miles a day when they should have been running along at an average 120. In the deep-sea sailing ship, it was never the miles she had to sail that mattered but the miles where the wind was, and those she had to find. If she did not, the voyage became both tedious and trying. The adventurers might be patient in real adversity, and they knew how to die: but they were fierce individualists, too.

John Smith, being used to disciplined troops, found these persons hard to suffer, and said so. He found some of his fellow gentlemen-adventurers hard to take, and said that too. His experience, and his talks with men like Gosnold, showed him that the challenge of the new continent would be ill met by a crowd of bickering loud-mouths, most of whom had no intention of doing an honest day's work if they could avoid it, some of whom could not if they tried, and all of whom had bolstered their spirits with the thought of easy gold. Smith became understandably unpopular with the gentlemen, who resented his air of superior knowledge and suspected that he wanted to seize leadership by force. He found it hard to accept fools gladly, and he must have been a headstrong fellow. On March 24, 1607, over three months after leaving Blackwall, the ships were off Dominica. They called at several islands in the West Indies. At the island of Nevis, Smith was made prisoner, because it was feared that he was plotting to overthrow the leaders and take the expedition over for himself. He was tried for "conspiracy," condemned to death, and a gallows was put up to hang him. But he got out of that, turned the tables on his captors, and soon had them in his power. He did not execute them: bodies were too valuable to leave strewn to wayside gallows, even some of theirs.

After a week to refresh the ship-weary, the ships sailed on, with stops at various points, including the Virgin Islands. It was April 10 before they got away from the West Indies, and almost the end of the month before they came sailing into Chesapeake Bay—still largely mutinous, still rife with discord and conspiracy, still hoping for quick fortunes from gold, or maybe privateering and piracy, or precious stones—anything so long as it was quick and reasonably certain. It was by good fortune and not good navigation that they sighted Cape Henry, for a Gulf Stream gale had forced the ships to wallow under bare poles for some days, until they had little idea where they were. Cape Henry loomed up obligingly from a rain squall, and they slipped quickly into Chesapeake Bay, or Chesepiuc, as they called it.

Sailing in between two headlands which they called Capes Henry and Charles for members of the English royal family, they passed Old Point Comfort, entered Hampton Roads, swung round the point where now is the busy port of Newport News, and sailed into a wide river which they named the James, for their King. Sailing on up the James River, going carefully with a longboat sounding ahead, they came to a spot which they thought would do for a settlement. The banks of the river there were steep-to, so the ships could lie alongside: the place would be difficult for the Spaniards to find, but simple to sail into for those who knew about it. The headlands of Chesapeake Bay were easy to make and identify from seaward, the entrance of the bay was clear of dangers and good for ships, and inside there was sheltered anchorage for a fleet. They landed, thanked God, called the place Jamestown, opened a box they had brought from London in which was the constitution of the new colony, read it through, and promptly disregarded its instructions. The company laid down that Captain Smith was to be a member of the ruling council of seven, but the other six refused to have him. The seven were to be the three sea captains, and four others, who were to elect their own president forthwith. They elected a man named Wingfield, but it was not long before they regretted their choice and there were serious troubles.

It was on May 14, 1607, that the landing was made at Jamestown, since a little time was spent on preliminary exploration. They put up tents at first, and did not try to fortify their position. But within less than six weeks the Indians were attacking them and President Wingfield had an arrow through his whiskers. That shook him. Smith was forthwith elected to the council, and the defense of the little settlement was organized.

It seems odd, looking back today, that these pioneers should deliberately decide to sit down on the banks of the James River when they had all America to choose from. It is even odder that, where there was so great abundance of natural resources, they should quickly find themselves almost starving, and continue in that way for the following three years. Here they were, landing from their three cockleshells in Virginia in springtime, with a great nation smiling before them.

"Heaven and earth never agreed better to frame a place for man's habitation," wrote Captain Smith, adding that all they needed was industry. "Here are mountaines, hills, plaines, valleys, rivers and brookes all running most pleasantly into a faire Baye encompassed but for its mouth with fruitfull and delightsome land." Oysters and fish were to be had in abundance from the waters of Chesapeake Bay. Wildfowl of many sorts, including ducks, swans, and geese, were there for the taking. The "fruitfull" soil provided the Indians who tilled it with all the rich corn they needed. As the Honorable George Percy (brother to the Earl of Northumberland and a member of the pioneer expedition) remarked, beautiful strawberries "foure times bigger and better than oures in England" were growing wild. But there was neither farmer nor fisherman among them and, instead of the wholesome spirit of energetic industry, there was bickering and quarreling. There were good men besides Captain Smith, but the whole spirit of the enterprise was poor.

The pinnace *Discovery* was left at the settlement for exploring and store-carrying, and so forth, and the bits of a longboat called a shallop, which had been brought from England, were assembled on the beach. This shallop could carry twenty-five people and had a couple of masts. Smith was in a party under Captain Newport which went off in the shallop to look at the surrounding territory, with the idea of discovering a passage through to the South Sea. They reached as far as the site of Richmond, the present capital of Virginia, but there was no passage through to the Pacific, or anything else, except rapids which prevented them from going any farther. Captain Newport staked his King's claim to the land, erected a cross marked *Jacobus Rex, 1607*, called on the Indian chief Little Powhatan, established friendly relations (they hoped), and sailed back to Jamestown just in time to find the local Indians attacking the place.

The *Susan Constant* sailed for London with a freight of wood and sassafras, instead of the hoped-for precious metals and pearls. It was midsummer when she sailed, and the colonists were soon in trouble from drinking bad water, from sickness and fever, and from shortness of nourishing food. Many died from the bloody flux and from fever. A few were picked off by Indians. Even Smith became ill, but that tough citizen quickly recovered. Already, within a few months of landing, George Percy was recording "there never were Englishmen left in a forreigne countrey in such miserie as wee were in this new discovered Virginia." Smith and a few more might reflect that if this were so it was their own fault, but the reflection made no difference. Smith took the shallop and got provisions from Indians. Fish, oysters, deer, turkey, fowls, and some thirty bushels of golden corn were brought back.

On one of these foraging-exploring trips of his, Smith was captured by the Indians and two of his companions were killed. He was too wily and experienced a bird to allow himself to be killed in that manner. Diverting his captors by means of an ivory compass and some other trinkets, he presented the compass to the chief and entered into a long discussion with him on magnetism, astronomy, etc., to the Indians' considerable diversion and his own immediate safety. Though the Indians were very interested and pleased with him personally, his safety was only temporarily assured. The Indians already had a natural feeling of anxiety at the encroachment on their lands which was inevitable with the coming of the colonists. The only useful colonist to them was a dead colonist. So Smith was hailed before the mighty chief Powhatan. Powhatan had not seen any of the English before this. Smith was paraded before him as he sat in state before his royal wigwam, surrounded by his braves and—very fortunately—by some of his women. He received Smith kindly at first but then, since what was to be done was obvious, he called for his braves to bring some large stones and bash the Englishman's brains out.

Smith had his head on the stone "block" when, suddenly and without reason, Powhatan's little daughter, called Pocahontas (the "playful one"), ran forward and laid her small head on the stone beside him, saying to her father at the same time to put an end to her, too. This was her way of interceding for Smith's life, which it was her prerogative to do if she felt inclined, and Smith was immediately reprieved. It might all have been arranged beforehand; but it worked, to the intense relief of Captain Smith and the incalculable benefit of the colony of Virginia.

Pocahontas did more than save Smith's life, for she did all she could afterward to see that the colony received urgently needed supplies of corn and other things and, on at least one occasion, she brought warning of an impending Indian attack. At the time she saved his life, Pocahontas was a mature thirteen years old and Smith was a bearded soldier of about twenty-eight. He was a bachelor, and it is to be regretted that he did not marry the girl. But he remained a bachelor to the end of his days, and Pocahontas married another Englishman and came to live in England. In the cold damp climate of southeast England she sickened and died, and her remains are interred in a churchyard at Gravesend, on the banks of the Thames.

This story about Pocahontas and John Smith has been discredited by some moderns. There is no reason not to accept it. Smith reported the incident to his Queen, which he would never dare to do were it not true. Pocahontas was respected in England as his savior, while she was alive: why throw useless doubts upon her, three hundred years after her death? "At the minute of my execution she hazarded the beating out of her own braines to save mine," wrote Smith, who was in a position to know, and his contemporaries (who were not given to praising him) accepted the account, and Pocahontas.

When he returned to Jamestown, Smith was once more in grave danger of his life. Though he was then acting virtually as president (Wingfield having been deposed and being in disgrace, because—among other things—he had tried to steal the pinnace and sail off in her to England, and he had no Bible with him) he was seized, tried for the deaths of his two companions, and condemned to be hanged. All this despite the fact that he had made a friendly and most useful alliance with Powhatan, for which he had risked his life; that he and he alone could get corn out of the Indians in any useful quantities; and that he now had the Indian princess Pocahontas on the side of the English. His incompetent and shiftless contemporaries, who included far too many lazy, quarrelsome, and insanely vindictive nincompoops, demanded that his life be forfeit. Once again they hastily erected a gallows and were actually leading the pinioned Smith to be strung up on it when—yet again—occurred one of those miraculous interventions which so often had saved that man's life.

A sail! A sail! The shout was raised. All turned to see, forgetting the prisoner. Right into their own James River a big ship came sailing. For a moment they stared at her. She might be a Spaniard, informed of their presence by spies. A quick, anxious look showed this to be no Don from Spain! This was an English ship, her big foresail and spritsail bellying in the sunshine, her main topsail being gathered into the commodious top by a group of merry boys, her lateen mizzen sheeted into the wind by lusty, singing sailors whose English accent was unmistakable.

Captain Smith quietly slipped his pinions and stared, though he still stood near the gallows. Now they could read the name of this strange ship. *John and Francis,* they read—not the *Susan Constant* come back to them, then. But what was that? Here came a familiar voice, booming across the river.

"Ahoy there, President Wingfield! Ahoy, Captain Smith!"

It was the voice of Captain Newport, who had sailed the *Susan* away, coming back with a new supply ship.

President Wingfield was lying prisoner in midstream aboard the pinnace he had tried to steal, with her rudder and sails stored ashore lest others try the same thing (as many had a mind to do), and Smith was even then standing in the shadow of the gallows.

Captain Newport was as forthright and competent a sea dog as Smith was a fighting man. He landed, and put things to rights at once. He could put things right, unfortunately, only for the handful of survivors of the Jamestown colony. Of the 105 who had landed, not 40 remained. Disease, starvation, and the Indians had taken the rest. The *John and Francis* brought more to join them, but the new colonists were horrified to observe, instead of the wonderful settlement they had been led to expect, a poor place of a few wooden dwellings and a palisade set in what looked horribly like a swamp. Instead of brave and prosperous young fortune hunters swaggering about, they were met by two-score bickering skeletons. Instead of an orderly and harmonious, properly organized colony, they found a disorganized, near-starving, poverty-stricken group of quarrelsome pessimists who, even then, had not properly mastered the first lesson—that they must pull together for the common good.

Instead of farmers, fishermen, and carpenters, the *John and Francis* had brought an odd group which included some gold refiners, for the London company was still determined to find gold. Where Spain had found so much, might not England also be given a little? The real gold was in the soil, in the Indians' pipes of peace (which they had smoked too seldom) but it took years to realize that fact. In the meantime the new colonists landed, and Captains Newport and Smith got them at work improving the settlement. They put up a new storehouse and a church, and started clearing several acres of ground for crops. There seemed to be a curse on poor Jamestown. No sooner were these very necessary jobs done than the township took fire. Being built of wood and thatched with reeds, the houses burned with a furious speed and the fires could not be quenched. Within an hour or two, the colonists were reduced to putting up tents again.

Almost everything went—"armes, bedding, apparrell, and much private provision. Good Maister Hunt our preacher lost all his library and all that he had but the cloathes on his back, yet none ever see him repine at his losse." Preacher Hunt had the right spirit, too. A young man fresh from Cambridge when he sailed with the first ships, he put up his first reading desk by the simple means of nailing a piece of wood between two convenient trees, and got on there with his preaching. Indians and other alarms frequently interrupted the devotions, but Preacher Hunt carried on. The Jamestown fire was too much for him, coming on top of all the other hardships and after he had so greatly used up his stores of energy in trying to keep the peace among the unruly council, mutinous leaders, and hungry colonists. Worn out by it all, Preacher Hunt died not long after the fire.

When the *John and Francis* sailed back for London, Captain Newport took the worst of the surviving mutineers. Not long after he had gone, another supply ship (which had sailed with him but had dawdled shamefully on the way) came into the river, with yet more supplies and more colonists. These included twenty-nine gentlemen and twenty-one laborers, six tailors, a jeweler, a perfumer, two more refiners, and two goldsmiths. These promptly caught the local fever and the perfumer, goldsmiths, and the gold refiners obligingly died. Indeed, the London company was slow to learn! But it did learn in the end—though not before the colony came within an ace of being abandoned. Even with the supplies brought by the two new ships (and it cost $10,000 a trip, in real golden money, to send those ships, without reckoning the cost of the supplies they carried: the return freight was mostly cedar) and with the corn bartered from the Indians through the good offices of temporary President Smith, before long the colony was in serious want again. The poor tailors, the jeweler, too high a proportion of the gentlemen, and a good many of the laborers too, proved useless against the challenge which man and nature flung at them.

For that, they were not to be blamed. This was very much a new venture for Englishmen. There they were, thousands of miles from their homeland, flung almost entirely upon their own inadequate resources with no proper facilities, or even with any awareness of what properly adequate facilities might be. Ill selected, untrained, used to city life, they landed on the banks of the James River and got on with the job as best they could. A great many of them quickly died. They bought their knowledge with the high price of their lives; but they gained knowledge. They learned by their mistakes, in time, and the London company learned after them.

Smith spent a good deal of his time in the shallop on voyages of exploration and discovery (which after all was one of the chief purposes for setting up the colony). He made a map of Virginia, wrote a short book about America, explored some 3,000 miles of coastal and inland waterways. Never flagging (except temporarily when under sentence of death) in industry or enterprise, Smith carried on. While Smith was getting energetically on with the job, back came Captain Newport again with yet another vessel, for a round trip to England could be done in four or five months. This time she was the supply ship *Mary Margaret*, and she brought more colonists, more orders, more impossible plans, for the company had not yet learned its lesson. Newport brought firm orders to find gold, to discover the South Sea, to set up Chief Powhatan with a crown, to find Raleigh's lost colonists and profit from their knowledge of the country, and to get on with the manufacture of at least pitch, soap, tar, and glass, and to produce large quantities of sawn timber.

It is difficult to decide which order was the most preposterous: it was a waste of time to obey any of them. Powhatan was given his crown (to which he raised understandable objections, having gotten along very well for years with his own ideas of such trimmings), and an attempt was made to set up a factory. But the gold, the South Sea, and Raleigh's colonists were all three as remote as California, where in fact both the gold and the South Sea were waiting to be found. Newport and others sailed up the James River as far as the site of Richmond, found nothing, and returned. Then Newport sailed away with yet another cargo of timber, soap ashes, and such, almost sailing into Henry Hudson who was off Chesapeake Bay at the time, in the little *Half Moon*. Hudson did not sail into the Bay, which he knew was already an English colony. He was chartered by the Dutch, at the time, and stood farther north, to sail into the Hudson River and do the groundwork that led to the founding of New Amsterdam.

With Newport gone again, Smith was for a time the undisputed president. Never the diplomat, he took no pains to hide the true state of affairs from the overoptimistic company. "When you send again," he wrote to London by the *Mary Margaret*, "I intreat you rather send but thirty carpenters, husbandmen, gardiners, fishermen, blacksmiths, masons, and diggers up of trees, rootes: than a thousand of such as we have." He added that he had no confidence in the discovery either of gold or of a way through to the Great South Sea. Henry Hudson was more likely to find that, he said, by sailing far to the north. "As yet," said Smith, "you must not look for any profitable returnes."

All this was very truthful and very necessary for the London promoters to know, but they were far from grateful to such informants. This was the kind of thing they hated to be told; they already had a lot of money in Virginia, and bad news made it difficult to raise the further capital which they needed. So bad news was suppressed, and its reporters frowned on. It is all very reprehensible and it was most unfair to the farsighted Smith. But the same thing would happen in similar circumstances today. The very next ship to arrive brought news of a great fleet of nine large vessels which was coming out under the command of Lord de la Warr. The noble lord, in due course, was to be Captain-General of Virginia, and he would get the place on its profitable feet once and for all. As for Captain Smith, no one was very grateful to him; but he continued his work of trying to create efficiency and organized harmony, until the Captain-General should arrive. He continued to treat warily with the Indians and to gain their cooperation, to organize at least some defense against them, and to get to know more of the wonderful country.

On the fifteenth of May, 1609, seven of the promised nine ships sailed from London. Picking up two smaller vessels at Plymouth, they continued the voyage before the end of the month. They were carrying 500 new colonists, headed by Lord de la Warr with Sir Thomas Gates as his Lieutenant-General, Sir George Somers as Admiral, and several other knights in positions of authority. Just how 500 worthwhile citizens could be recruited to sail over the Western Ocean to a remote, struggling and poverty-stricken colony which had so far not been able even to supply itself with the barest necessities of life, we are not told; but the inference is that they had no idea what they had really let themselves in for, or, possibly, some had been misled and others forced to go. That prohibition against discouraging letters still stood, and what John Smith told the company the directors kept to themselves.

A ship called the *Sea Venture* headed this peaceful armada. With her were ships called the *Blessing*, *Unity*, *Diamond*, *Falcon*, *Lion*,

Swallow, and *Virginia* (which had been built in Maine). They sailed in midsummer, went the southern route (but without the usual time-wasting stops at islands), and promptly sailed into a first-class West Indies hurricane. They were off the tail of the Bahamas when the storm struck them and, fortunately for them, it was only its outer perimeter that overtook the fleet. Even that was more than enough. The wind screamed and the sea rose in frightful violence. The buoyant wooden ships rode "a-hull," meaning that they made fast all their sails and ran under bare poles, rolling and pitching horribly but always yielding to the sea, not fighting back. In this way most had the luck to be blown out of the storm, after two whole days of it. But the fleet was scattered and only four of the ships arrived together at the James River. Two young women in the *Unity*, scared out of their wits by the storm, had chosen the height of the hurricane to give birth to boys, but both births were premature and the infants died. The *Swallow* was dismasted. All the ships suffered deaths among their passengers. "Out of two shippes was throwne overboarde thirtie-two persons," reads one report, and this casualty rate was general.

At length six of the ships arrived, with less than 300 of the colonists. The ships carrying the leaders did not come in. While waiting for them, Smith was accidentally shot and so severely wounded that at last that redoubtable and hitherto indestructible warrior was laid low. It was a foul blow. His enemies promptly suggested murdering him, now they had so good a chance, but the general view was that he would die very shortly anyway and, until he did, he was best left alone. So the badly wounded man was packed off back to England in the first ship which turned round. If he lived, he would have to stand trial from the company for his "misdemeanours," consisting, according to them, in his headstrong and roughshod disregard of his fellow councilors, but in truth, mainly in his failure to find gold or to produce profitable manufactures or other products. If he died he would be flung overboard, and that was that.

It was the fourth of October, 1609, when the ship carrying Smith back to England slipped down the river. In spite of everything, the colony then had every chance of succeeding. By sending so great a fleet, the company at least made it clear that it was going to stand by its undertakings and not leave the settlers to suffer the fate of Raleigh's colonists. There were 450 people ashore, of whom at least a nucleus was now experienced and competent. They had stores, arms and ammunition, livestock, tools, at least sixty houses protected by a strong high wall of good timbers, and a fortress in which were twenty-four guns. They had ships and—when Lord de la Warr arrived (if he ever did) they had the assurance of continuity of good government. The place at last was on its feet, and Captain Smith, more than anyone else, had put it there.

He went back to England, and did not die then; and, while he was gone (in the continued absence of Lord de la Warr) all that he had built up so painfully came again to nothing. Within a few months less than a hundred of the colonists new and old survived, and this remnant, ill-led, half-starved, and misgoverned, was grubbing along on such shellfish and herbs as they could find, like castaways, not colonists. The whole lot of them, utterly depressed at last, decided to throw in their hand, and there was now no leader strong enough to stop them. The Indians were openly against them. They were reduced to such starvation that there was some cannibalism. One Virginian put his dead wife in pickle to have something to eat, but he was discovered at the gruesome barrel, and executed. The rest of the colonists, face to face with the fate of Raleigh's pioneers, despaired. They had no ship fit or large enough to take them anywhere.

And then occurred yet another of those almost miraculous happenings with which the story of Jamestown so strangely abounds. The best part of a year overdue and long given up for lost, two ships came sailing in, with the long-missing Sir George Somers and Sir Thomas Gates aboard. These were strange little ships, for the two knights had been driven to the strange island of Bermuda in that hurricane. The *Sea Venture* was stranded on a reef there and could not be refloated, so the survivors built a couple of small ships out of the local cedar and pieces from the hull of the wreck. These sloops were aptly named the *Patience* and *Deliverance*, and it was these which came sailing up the James River.

Once ashore, seeing the state of things, Somers and Gates came to the conclusion very quickly that there was no hope for Jamestown. The best thing they could do was to write off Virginia, get the survivors together, and go. Having made their decision they acted on it, and were sailing off with all hands when, even before they were out of the river, they saw three ships come sailing in from the sea! It was Lord de la Warr, arriving at last. The date was the tenth of June, 1610.

It was the last miracle. John Smith had gone, and came back no more to the shores of Virginia, but the wonderful story of miracles which he had begun went marching on. Lord de la Warr put the colonists ashore again (fortunately they had not burned down the town as they had intended to do) and, with the fresh people he had brought from England and Sir George Somers' party, refreshed from the Bermudas, got things going properly.

At long last the faltering rhythm of the new colony's life steadied to an even beat, and faltered no more. There were further difficulties and once a massacre, as Smith had foreseen, but Virginia's future was assured, and North America's with her—not only North America's. The successful settlement of Virginia at Jamestown, achieved with such difficulty, was to change the course of history.

(Mindful of its importance, the 350th anniversary of the founding of Virginia is being celebrated on a large scale in 1957, and work toward this has been going on over the past two years. At Jamestown, archaeologists have unearthed the sites of some 135 buildings which show the site and character of the old town. The foundation lines of more than a score of the earliest buildings are being marked by means of low brick walls. Excavation has brought to light many interesting objects, including pottery, sword hilts, and old tools and old Indian arrowheads. A full-size restoration of the original fort is also being built at Jamestown, and the ships *Susan Constant*, *Discovery*, and *God Speed* will be moored off the town. A replica of the old glassworks and the sawmill will be running, and the lodge of Powhatan will be built just as it was—as far as is known—when Pocahontas saved Captain Smith's life. The research for the reconstruction of the ships was carried out, very largely, by the late Comdr. Griffith Baily Coale, with the cooperation of the Mariners' Museum of Newport News.

The anniversary celebrations are centered on the old Travis House at Williamsburg, Virginia, the wonderful old town which has been restored to its appearance in colonial days by Mr. John D. Rockefeller, Jr. Settled as the "Middle Plantation" of 1633, Williamsburg was first an outpost against Indian invasion before becoming the capital of Virginia in 1699. For the following eighty years it was the political, cultural, religious, and economic center of what was then the largest and most populous of the English colonies in America.)

GOD WORKS A "MIRAKLE"

9

IN THE STORY of the North Atlantic, the voyage of an obscure and commonplace little ship called, presumably, the *Mayflower* stands preeminent. Neither picture nor any sort of plan of the vessel survives, and even her name was not mentioned by those who sailed in her; yet there are good reasons for her immortality. The ship known as the *Mayflower* carried the heroic band known later as the Pilgrim Fathers, who in the year 1620 landed at Provincetown and later at Plymouth, Massachusetts, and founded New England. More than that, they laid there, in great part, the foundations of the United States of America.

There had been settlers in plenty who sailed westbound across the North Atlantic before, but the Pilgrim Fathers may be regarded as the first of the true pioneers. They set out from Europe not with an eye over their shoulders at the land which they had left and intending to return at the first opportunity, nor misled by promoters seeking to make a quick profit out of them, careless of what then might be their fate. They were the first cohesive and united body of men, women, and children who sailed for the new land seeking neither a way around it to a richer East nor quick wealth from the easy exploitation of its precious metals. They sailed for the new land to make a new life in and of that new land, to bring up their children and their children's children there, with a new freedom, a freedom of body, of spirit, and of mind.

These were great ideals; but not one of their contemporaries would have looked twice at the Pilgrim Fathers, nor—if they could help it—once at their famous *Mayflower*. The thing they did grew after them. The fame of the ship came long after her undistinguished timbers had dissolved to dust or had been transferred ashore to a multitude of allegedly historic barns. The Pilgrims did not call themselves the "Pilgrim Fathers"; that title came afterward too. They thought so little of the ship which carried them upon their now most famous voyage that, as far as the records have come down to us, not a single one of them ever mentioned her by name, and the only contemporary account of the voyage makes no mention of her name at all.

The English exiles who were later to achieve so much undying fame did not regard themselves as heroic. What they sought was peace, not immortality. The *Mayflower* voyage, grim and profoundly uncomfortable as it must have been, was just another incident in the long story of trials and persecution and hardship which had formed their lives. The immense moral courage and infinite fortitude with which they took that voyage in their stride, and then proceeded in the harshest months of winter to carve out a colony upon the hard shores of New England, were already well established in their lives long before they sailed for America.

The *Mayflower* story is one that has been often told, and yet, as for the actual ship and her crossing, it is one that we still know very little about. The fact that no one who came over in her thought enough of her to mention her name may well indicate that the winter's crossing she gave them, fifteen weeks of painful, cold, and unrelieved misery on the heaving sea, was so grim that they preferred to forget it if they could. In addition, the names of ships did not mean as much then as they do now. There were many *Mayflowers* at that time in the British registry. It was a common name to give a cargo ship. Just as the Arab dhows of today are known not by their names but by their captains, so also were European ships known in the sixteenth and early seventeenth centuries. Bradford's *History of Plimoth Plantation* does mention the captain's name. He calls him Jonas, though the name apparently was Jones—

Capt. Christopher Jones, of Rotherhithe, by London. There was a Capt. Christopher Jones who owned a fourth part of a bark called the *Mayflower*, of about 180 tons, in London in 1620. It is regarded as reasonably sure that it was he who made the voyage.

All that we can say for certain about the *Mayflower* is that she was about 180 tons, had been in the wine trade with French ports, had at least a main topsail (because the main topsail halyards trailed overboard and John Howland was able to save himself by grabbing them when he slipped overboard while the ship was hove to in a gale), and was exceedingly decrepit and ripe, because one of her principal beams cracked while she was working in the sea, and had to be jacked up with a large printing press that fortunately was aboard. A ship whose main beams break in a seaway is a poor thing, and the *Mayflower* must indeed have been an old ship. She seems to have staggered safely across the North Atlantic the one time—possibly she had made previous passages toward the Grand Banks, maybe to the Greenland whaling ground—and then sailed back to London, to be laid up. The hulk of Captain Jones's *Mayflower* was certainly sold off for a scrap price—little over £100—by 1622, when Jones himself was dead.

The Pilgrims were poor folk, who neither had nor sought money. It is reasonable to expect that the ship which took them to America was the cheapest that could be found. There were no passenger ships for long voyages in those days. Any ship had to do. In a sense (in that she carried whole families, and many of them) the *Mayflower* may be regarded as the first transatlantic passenger vessel, but she had no amenities for passengers. She was just any old ship which was unemployed at the time and available for cheap charter. Not that the Pilgrims themselves chartered the *Mayflower:* that was done for them. They were a group of plain English folk from a diversity of places as far apart as Scrooby in Nottinghamshire, Chelmsford and Billericay in Essex, Cambridge, Colchester, and Duxbury, and their common bond was exile—exile for their religious principles. Refusing to conform to the strict dogmas of the established Church of England, they were Separatists who had been forced to leave England and live at Leyden, in Holland. Here they made a hard living among the Protestant Dutch, but they feared that their children would grow up neither good religionists nor good Englishmen, for the Hollanders took life as they found it and made merry while they could. So the Pilgrims looked abroad for a new homeland, where they could go their own ways in peace and worship God as they wished.

At first thinking of going to Guiana, in South America, they abandoned that idea because there was gold there and strife with the Spaniards. They wanted no part of either. They thought also of Virginia, but feared that large as Virginia was, there would be no true religious freedom for them in a colony under the control of the Church of England. But there was a lot of room in North Virginia and there was also room in New England, and along the Hudson River in what is now New York State. It was decided to make for North Virginia, and an agreement was made by the Pilgrim community at Leyden to sail in such ship or ships as might be provided, toward this land.

At that time, the right to form colonies in Virginia was restricted to two companies, the one in London and the other at Plymouth, and the Pilgrims made their agreement with the London company. The agreement was that the company would finance their voyage and some outfit, and they would "plant" a colony in North Virginia. The products of that colony would recoup the merchant adventurers for their outlay. The agreement was naturally loaded on the adventurers' side, but that could not be helped. If they were to go at all, the Pilgrims had to take—more or less—what was offered them. The negotiations took some time, for many reasons. In the first place, there was opposition among the Pilgrims themselves to the idea of going to America, where there had already been several abortive attempts at setting up colonies. The savagery of the Indians, the harshness of the winter climate, the difficulty of supply were all well known. In the second place, the Pilgrims were not in good favor with the English authorities, either political or religious. It cost a lot of money to set up a colony, and most ventures of that sort had yet to yield a profit. The long and hard sea voyage was no pleasurable anticipation, and might well prove more than some could endure, for the loss of life on the earlier Virginia voyages had been heavy.

However, all difficulties were overcome. The *Mayflower*, lying in the London docks after putting out a cargo of wine in casks from France (Bradford says she was a sweet-smelling ship, and as she is also said—on what evidence I do not know—to have been a Greenland whaler, it would take a cargo of sweet wine or attar of roses to get the reek out of her) was chartered on a one-voyage basis. Another, much smaller vessel, a fore-and-aft named apparently the *Speedwell* (her name is never mentioned in the Bradford chronicle either) was bought outright. This *Speedwell* was about 60 tons—smaller than a Thames barge or an ordinary Chesapeake Bay schooner—and it was intended to keep her in American waters for local fishing and trading.

The *Speedwell* went to Holland to embark the party, some of whom were to stay with her for the Atlantic voyage, and the others were to transfer to the London ship at Southampton. Everything was as well arranged as it could be, and—so far, at any rate—the pattern of the voyage followed that set by the dozen or so which had preceded it. The *Mayflower's* cargo included the hull, masts, and rigging of a small vessel known as a shallop, about thirty-five feet long and rigged with either two masts or one, and this vessel was carried in parts for assembly on arrival in America. The purpose of the shallop was to assist in landing the people and the cargo, and to make exploratory voyages. In those days, ships did not carry lifeboats. Boats were for use in ferrying goods ashore and generally tending on the ship's needs, for there were neither docks nor harbors, and ships and their people were much dependent on their boats. There was also a longboat, carried on the main deck, and this was usually as large a boat as could be stowed there and swung outboard and in again with the ship's tackle. This, too, was no lifeboat as such, but a general-purpose boat for the ship's use. When a small ship like the *Mayflower* had her main deck cluttered with a longboat and the parts of a rigged-down shallop in the 'tween-decks below, she was already fairly crowded.

As far as the longboat is concerned, the same thing can be seen today. Such boats are still in use aboard Arab, Pakistani, Indian, and Maldivian dhows, and they still take up a great deal of room. They are not launched at sea, though they might float off a sinking vessel. They are strictly for use in port and, in quiet waters, are usually towed. There are no quiet waters in the open North Atlantic, and both the *Mayflower's* and the *Speedwell's* longboats were carried aboard the ships.

It was in 1617 that the Pilgrims began their negotiations to sail to America, but it was already the middle of July three years later when at last the *Speedwell* set out from Delft Haven, near Leyden, with as many of the party as could be accommodated aboard. There was not money enough to take them all, and the bigger ship was bringing some other persons engaged by the merchant adventurers in London to help the enterprise. The idea was that the balance of the Leyden party should follow later, as supply ships sailed across to keep the settlement going and to carry back its cargoes for sale. The departure of the *Speedwell* presented a scene so moving that the Dutch bystanders, who had never seen the poor Pilgrims before, stood and wept in the rain as the little ship spread her sails. The wind was favorable and she ran quickly across the North Sea and down-Channel to the rendezvous at Southampton.

Here the *Mayflower* had arrived; but all was not settled, by any means. There was some bickering with the speculators, the outfitters, the ship chandlers. There was an iniquitous contract thrust under the Pilgrims' noses, designed yet further to enslave them to their London backers. This they refused to sign, and, in consequence, they found themselves so short of funds that they had to sell some of the already inadequate stock of provisions laid in for the settlement in order to clear their immediate debts. This was a serious matter, but even then there appeared to be no real misgivings.

Putting their trust in God, of Whom they were asking a great deal, the Pilgrims sailed at last in their two ships, intending to make the westward crossing directly from Southampton to somewhere in North Virginia—the farther north the better, in order to be well away from the English, who were already in the Jamestown area and whose clerics could be expected to be as bigoted as their fellows in England. The wind was favorable, coming from the north, when the ships went quietly down Southampton Water, two little wanderers of incredible smallness carrying a load of the stoutest hearts that ever put to sea. Trials awaited them almost at once, trials beyond the ordinary and difficult bouts of seasickness and the attendant misery of life in crowded cargo ships, in which passengers were allowed only on sufferance and the lowest knave among the crew could add to their discomfort, almost at will.

It was soon obvious that the captain of the *Speedwell* had no stomach for the voyage. Among so many of great courage, he was a gutless wretch whose mind was already made up not to proceed with the voyage. After a few days at sea and a bit of a minor blow, he said his ship was leaking. He hailed Jones in the *Mayflower*, reporting his alleged plight and demanding that they put back. Jones may have looked at him dubiously (or he may have been in the plot, as he appears to have been in that not to deliver the Pilgrims to their agreed destination); but they put back. They ran back to Dartmouth, where no serious fault could be found with the *Speedwell*. Again, after an exasperating delay, the two ships put to sea. Again they sailed down-Channel with a fine fair wind, foaming along at their maximum speeds of perhaps 7½ knots, making good progress.

Again they got to windward of Land's End, clear of all the Channel, with the worst of the passage already behind them (for it was still summer, and they might then have made a reasonable run over the rest of the Western Ocean). But again the *Speedwell's* captain complained that his ship was sinking, though she stayed afloat. Once more he demanded that the fleet put back. Again Jones listened to him (and the Pilgrims had to listen with their sea captain, for none among them was a sailor and they had declined the assistance of Captain Smith, from Virginia). Once more the two ships, having beaten so far and having also consumed considerable stores and water, put up their helms and ran back for the English Channel.

This time it was the port of Plymouth they made for and so,

fortuitously and at the last moment, the great Devon port was associated with yet another of the heroic maritime enterprises which have so distinguished its long history. The *Mayflower* and the *Speedwell* anchored off Plymouth, and now the master of the smaller ship disclosed his hand. He would not go on, he said, for his ship was not fit for the voyage. No serious fault could be found in the wooden hull, though it was true that she had been making water: but her master got his way and was allowed to abandon the voyage. All the people and stores which could possibly be crowded into the *Mayflower* were thereupon transferred to the bark. She had been crowded enough before, and must now have been packed intolerably.

In the meantime, the summer had gone and it was early autumn, a windy, stormy time upon the sea lanes of the North Atlantic. The advantage of the earlier sailing had been the fact that the days were longer and warmer then, which would have softened the hardships of the Pilgrim passengers. Now that was gone. Some lost heart, and left. Some with large families of small children, for whom space could not be found in the *Mayflower*, had to leave whether they wished or not (all had realized the whole of their assets before leaving Leyden and had nothing to return to, there or anywhere else). One wrote despairingly to a friend ashore, "Freind, if ever we make a plantation, God works a mirakle. . . ."

Though some left and others could not be taken, in due course the *Mayflower* departed again. This time it was final. The date was already well on in September, toward the autumnal equinox, and all hope of a reasonable passage was now gone. Few ships, except those in Bartholomew Gosnold's small expedition, had until then made the passage direct by the northern route between the English Channel and New England, although there had been at least a century of sea experience in sailing westward to the fisheries on the Grand Banks of Newfoundland. The way to sail there was well known, but it was not customary to make such a passage in the fall. The time for sailing west was spring: autumn was the time to come home again.

What experience Captain Jones had of sailing in the Atlantic we do not know, but at any rate he has proved abundantly that he was a prudent, careful, and courageous mariner by making the voyage successfully at all, in such a ship with such a cargo and at such a boisterous time of the year. It is reasonable to assume that he was availing himself of whatever knowledge was commonly available. He might have known Captain Gosnold, or others who had sailed to New England for the fur trade or the fisheries or to the Banks. Small shipowners of Bristol and Plymouth, as well as other ports, had been sending their ships westward then for many years. It is known now that the best way to make the autumnal westward crossing in a sailing ship is to stand first well toward the north, as if making for Cape Farewell in Greenland, and then to make for destination from a point about 30 degrees west and 55 degrees north, with the Arctic Current to assist. In this way the Gulf Stream's effect is avoided, but there is an increased expectation of meeting heavy weather, in a sea and at a time of year when gale-force winds are more or less normal.

What way Captain Jones tried to go we have no idea, except that it was not the southern route—the trade-wind way which would have given sunny days but a much longer voyage. In his time, it was neither customary nor possible for master mariners to know, with any degree of precision, where their ships were, when making ocean voyages in bad weather. It was sufficient for him to make a good offing and head west, for he must come upon America somewhere. He had no means for fixing the position of his ship precisely anyway, for he could not establish her longitude and his means of working out latitude were primitive, to say the least. But he must have known the Western Ocean, especially if he had been in the Greenland trade. He would know how to punch and fight his ship toward the west, and that he did.

But he took sixty-seven days in getting to the westward, which is a very long time even for a small square-rigger, and the adverse weather was so continuous and alarming that he almost gave up the attempt at least once. We know that much from Bradford's journal. (We have no *Mayflower* log, or anything whatever from Captain Jones, his mates, his "bootson, quartermaisters, cooke," or any others of his numerous crew.)

> After they had injoyed faire winds and weather for a season they were incountred many times with crosse winds, and mette with many feirce stormes with which ye ship was shroudly shaken [says Bradford, remembering the unhappy events some years afterward], and her upper works made very leakie; and one of ye maine beames in ye midd ships was bowed and craked, which put them in some feare that ye shipe would not be able to performe ye vioage. So some of ye cheefe of ye company, perceiveing ye mariners to feare ye sufficiencie of ye shipe, as appeared by their mutterings, they entred into serious consulltation with ye master and other officers of ye ship, to consider in time of ye danger; and rather to returne then [than] to cast themselves into a desperate and inevitable perill. And truly ther was great distraction and differance of opinion amongst ye mariners them selves; faine would they doe what could be done for their wages sake (being now halfe the seas over) and on ye other hand they were loath to hazard their lives too desperatly.

But Captain Jones said they would stand on. The ship had opened up in her upper works, and the 'tween-decks where the passengers lived were awash; but she was sound enough down below, he said, and provided that he did not try to carry too much sail, she should come through. So the vital decision was made. It was a sailor's decision, and it was indeed a brave one. Captain Jones has not been given his due share of credit for the success of the Pilgrims' voyage. To fight on westward in a seriously weakened ship, with the weather steadily worsening and a New England winter to expect at the end (if they survived at all), was a most courageous thing to do. Captain Jones, plain man as he was and no Pilgrim, was cast in as great a mold as they. As for the water in the 'tween-decks and the acute discomfort, that much was unavoidable. The high, crank little ships of those days carried their enormous superstructure only because these upper works were additional to the ship's main hull, a sort of lighter-built house erected afterward and strapped on with vertical timbers along the ship's sides. No wonder they worked, and let the water in! The wonder rather is that they were not washed over the side, the whole of the aftercastle and the forecastle as well, to expose the passengers completely to the elements.

One reason the *Mayflower* kept in one piece, decrepit as she was,

was that she did not try to fight the sea. No matter how the storm raged, she was *with* it, *in* it—never against it. She could not stand against it. "In sundrie of these stormes," wrote Bradford, "the winds were so feirce, and ye seas so high, as they could not beare a knot of saile, but were forced to hull for diverce days together." What he is saying is that in very bad weather the ship just lay in the sea with no sail set at all, which was the best and the safest thing that she could do. But it got her nowhere toward her destination. Those little ships, with their low prows and high poops, would practically heave to of their own accord, provided they were not pressed, for the aftercastle acted as a lying-to sail which would keep them shoulder to the sea, yielding, drifting, rising and falling with an abominable and frightening motion, but not fighting back, not in danger. So it was in Cape Horn ships to the end of their days. I have been hove to several times in winds of near-hurricane strength in such vessels, though some were of more than 3,000 tons and were built of steel. As we had no longer high aftercastles to keep us to the wind (for the modern sailers were long and low, and very wet in the sea) we kept a rag of sail set there, perhaps a weather cloth lashed in the jigger rigging, or a rag of close-reefed storm trysail. The principle was the same. We drifted, yielding, and suffered nothing, as the *Mayflower* did, and our motion was probably every bit as violent. But our ships were dry down below.

So the *Mayflower* struggled on, fighting when she could, stopping when she must. John Howland went overboard once when she was hove to, and because he went to leeward and the ship was drifting slowly that way, without forward speed through the water, he was able to grasp the end of the trailing topsail halyards and be hauled back aboard again as, indeed, were many seamen in similar circumstances in the days of sail. Washed overboard by one sea, washed inboard by the next, was not an uncommon fate. John Howland was a lucky young man. A little boy was born and christened Oceanus; one of the seamen—a "proud and very profane young man, of a lustie, able bodie," as Bradford calls him—and one of the passengers died. "After longe beating at sea," at last, more than two months after sailing from Plymouth, the *Mayflower* made the land off Cape Cod.

This may have been where she was going according to Captain Jones, but it was not where the Pilgrims thought they were bound, for this was no North Virginia. They had Jones stand toward the southward to make a better landfall at least somewhere near the Hudson River, but the ship was soon in shoals and among breakers. This would never do; they allowed Captain Jones to put about, and run in for the shelter of the encircling, sandy arms of Cape Cod. Sixty-seven days out from England, on the eleventh of November, 1620, the bark *Mayflower* anchored off Provincetown, in what is now the Commonwealth of Massachusetts and, to all intents and purposes, the great crossing was made. The anchorage was sheltered and there was sea food and firing in abundance, but there was precious little else, not even a sufficiency of fresh water.

The Pilgrims did not appreciate a diet of clams and Cape Cod oysters, though both are sea delicacies supreme; as a main food supply they palled, and were otherwise inadequate. The *Mayflower* dallied a month while the shallop—its planks and thwarts much strained by the people who had been forced to sleep on them for so many weeks—was put together and used for discovery. Poor Mrs. Bradford fell or jumped into the sea, so discouraged did she become at last with the appalling cold and the bleak prospect of the sand dunes about Cape Cod. (She must have drowned herself, though no chronicle says so. A woman who had survived that crossing would hardly fall into the quiet waters of Cape Cod Bay, unless she wanted to do so.)

The cold was savage, ceaseless, and beyond all bearing, even after a decade and more of winter's east winds in Holland. Some of the poor people, deluding themselves that New England was in the same latitudes as Spain, had thought the climate might be as warm. It was not. They had to build their homes, to plant their crops, to do all things for themselves. They were weak from the long crossing in such crowded conditions and from the great turbulence of the ocean. If they had not had the hearts of lions they might all have jumped into the bay, as Mrs. Bradford did. Instead they signed their famous compact, by which they bound themselves to each and all for the furtherance of their great project, and having found at length the better site of Plymouth, shifted the ship to an anchorage near there, and went ashore. Half of them died the first winter, but when the time came in the spring for the *Mayflower* to return to England, not a single survivor sailed with her, nor wanted to. That is the measure of their spirit.

God had indeed worked a "mirakle"—and at that a greater even than the Pilgrims knew. For harsh as was the combination of natural circumstances against them, they were spared the worst. This was the armed and determined hostility of the aborigines, the unfortunate Indians whose land, after all, they had invaded and appropriated. It so chanced that all that area had been denuded of Indians by an epidemic which was most probably some minor ailment introduced by previous Europeans (as the common cold almost wiped out the Tahitians who, never having suffered it, had no immunity). The few Indians who had returned, and met them, were friendly. One of these was a brave named Squanto who spoke passable English, having been carried off as a captured slave some years before and taught English in England and Newfoundland. Squanto and the friendliness of the Indians were worth a battalion of armed soldiery to the decimated Pilgrims, which was just as well, for they had no such battalion. Their resources in arms were small, and their soldiery but a fraction of a company under the hotheaded Miles Standish. If there had been serious fighting to be done, the chances are that they would have been lost.

Yet this factor was entirely fortuitous and could not have been known to any of them. Rather should they have expected implacable hostility and treacherous murder. They were prepared for such things. Night after night, as their decimated menfolk died, the survivors carried them silently and without lights to a secret graveyard, where they buried them and leveled off the new graves in order that the Indians would not know how dreadfully their numbers were reduced. They need not have worried. With Squanto's help and the friendliness of the chief Massasoit (whose statue stands nobly over the Plymouth of today), the Pilgrims were suffered to establish themselves, and before long their own nobility and steadfastness of purpose, their indefatigable determination, abiding and inexhaustible courage, and strong faith in God had "planted" the firm foundations of such a settlement that flourished and grew, prospered, spread, and in due course, became a nation.

THE NEW *MAYFLOWER*

10

WHAT WAS IT really like aboard the famous *Mayflower?* Bouncing about for fifteen weeks in that so dreadfully small and inadequate ship, with neither warmth nor dryness anywhere nor even adequate food, with 150 persons (counting the 102 or 104 passengers who finally sailed from Plymouth, and the very large crew) crowded into the low, unlit, ill-ventilated cargo 'tween-decks of a pitching, decrepit, and noisome little bark which if she existed today would not be allowed to take twelve holiday-makers on a weekend vacation run across Chesapeake Bay! What *did* those hundred-odd passengers, cooped up like that for fifteen weeks, find to do with themselves? How did they pass the time?

Well, the answers to those two last questions are simple enough. I have learned them the hard way for myself. What they did, and their principal occupation, was just plain surviving. That's what I did when I was for months in an Arab dhow, and it is an absorbing and full-time occupation from which most of us are freed in these days, when a transatlantic voyage is made either in some wondrous aircraft or a superliner where every possible need is both foreseen and pampered almost *ad nauseam*, and even the cheapest of dormitory accommodation in the oldest and slowest liner is princely by comparison with conditions of only thirty years ago. In the dhow, I was crowded with something like 200 other passengers. The ship was about 180 tons, with a high poop rather like the *Mayflower's*, with a longboat cluttering up the deck, with little spare fresh water, a small smokebox for the only galley, and a couple of boxes slung outboard over the sea as the only bathroom and lavatory accommodation. She smelled. She rolled. She pitched. The passengers all lived on deck (except the women, who were crowded into a loathsome great cabin below the poop), and the smoke from their little fires and the clutter of their living and their cooking drifted over the whole vessel. They filled every nook and cranny, sleeping wherever they could stretch out and—many of them—where neither man nor child had room even for that elementary comfort, for there were so many that there was not deck space enough to allow 6 feet by 2 to all.

In the *Mayflower* it must have been much the same, except for two further disabilities which were both appalling. In my dhow the weather was good and the wind was generally favorable (or she would not have gone to sea, nor have survived when she got there) and, since all hands slept on deck, the problem of ventilation —light and air—did not arise. Moreover, the voyage was in the tropics and the weather was warm. The *Mayflower* Pilgrims had to sleep below, in a space more confined than the main deck of my Arab, and far less satisfactory. The Arabs, many of whom were migrating to East Africa either in small tribal groups or families, each made a part of the deck their own, where they put their few belongings and set up house for the voyage. Some camped below the longboat, many inside it; others by the break of the poop, or in the lee of the little smokebox galley, or by the wooden water tanks (which were carried on deck). The higher type, merchants known to the captains and lesser seyids, minor sheikhs, and such, were allowed to inhabit the poop. Except for these exalted ones, all prepared their own food and looked after themselves in all ways. The ship carried them, and that was the end of her obligation toward them. She had neither to feed them nor provide them with quarters, nor heat nor light, nor save their lives if they went overboard. The matter of preparing three meals a day (though none was truly nourishing and food was always scarce), looking after the children to see that they did not go overboard or get too much in the sailors' way, washing out their few clothes, and so forth and so on, occupied all the passengers' days.

The sailors also lived in the same way, except for the fact that the ship fed them. All their work was in the open, on the main deck, round which they were wont to rush at headlong speed shifting the huge mainsail, or stretching the mizzen, or some such job, and woe betide any stupid passenger who then got in the way! The 200-odd passengers led full and eventful lives, punctuated by the five daily prayers of good Muslims and exalted by an awareness of God; and I reclined on a patch of carpet on the captain's bench high on the poop and watched it all, and took such scant exercise as I was able to, and warded off the malaria and the dysentery, and blindness, and all the rest as well as I could.

And so I learned there how the *Mayflower* passengers lived, for they were in small groups, with women and children too: and, unlike the Arabs, the families were allowed to be together. Each made its own "pitch" in such portion of the dark 'tween-decks as they might (when the main hatch was covered with a grating only, as it was usually in anything but very bad weather, there was both a little light and a sufficiency of fresh air) and settled in as cheerfully as they could. They had no cabins. There was room for no such things, and the *Mayflower* must have been hard put to it even to allow Captain Jones room to spread a chart, or work out his cumbrous noontide sights and dead reckoning. Those aftercastles were very high but they were also narrow, and even the great cabin in that ship must have been comparatively small, paintings of the signing of the compact off Provincetown, etc., notwithstanding. The mates, of whom there seem to have been four, and the senior petty officers such as the boatswain, master gunner, carpenter, and cook, must have had some sort of better accommodation. The ship was their permanent home, and it merely offered transportation to the passengers. Therefore the crewmen would keep their cabins, if they had any, though for private gain one or two might have parted with such hutches as the ship allowed them. The seamen huddled together the best way they could, probably somewhere in the for'ard 'tween-decks, dossing down in their clothes and a rag of blanket, or an old cloak.

The ship's galley turned out meals, normally, only for the ship's company, not for the passengers, and the cook must have been hard-pressed as it was. Forty lusty men is a big gang to cook for, ashore or at sea. The Pilgrim families had their own charcoal braziers, and cooking, eating, and cleaning took a deal of their time. In the dhow, food was very poor and always insufficient for the passengers, for they economized too greatly on that, nor were they able (like the Pilgrims) to forecast accurately the length of time they would be aboard. A few pieces of dried fish, a small sack of rice, a bit of a tin containing curry stuffs and condiments and another with some low-grade coffee beans—these were their provisions. Yet they survived for a month or more. Coffee flavored with cardamons or cloves stilled the rumblings in their empty bellies, and, also like the Pilgrims, they had good spiritual control of their bodily needs. What was there they ate, in silence and with dignity, nor did they pine for what they had not. Sometimes a fish caught in the sea was large enough to provide a mess for a hundred of them, and then they were grateful. Order was kept aboard the dhow by the lesser sheikhs, and the seyids, and a minor chief among the Beduin. In the *Mayflower* the Pilgrims appointed their leading men to be governors and assistants, to keep order.

And so the little *Mayflower* rolled and lurched and stumbled along, wallowing her low wooden waist in the sea, with the green water licking up the fat tumble-home of her sides and the high aftercastle creaking, and the wind howling in the cordage rigging —now with a screaming note like a hundred demons, now quietly upon a quieter day and, when the sun shone, the Pilgrims could air their poor bedding. Some, woefully seasick, would stretch out upon such spot as they could find where their inert and all but helpless bodies would not roll or slip too greatly with the motion of the ship. In a sailing ship this was more easily contrived than it could have been in a powered vessel, for the wind when on the side held the ship steadier, at least so that human heads could be kept up to windward. With the wind on one side the ship would list and roll always toward the other, and a body kept fore-and-aft—in the line of the keel—would always roll, and not slip endways. The Pilgrims would quickly learn these things, and make themselves as comfortable as they could.

As for fresh water, that was most strictly rationed, for the ship could not carry much of it and what she had was in wooden barrels, which could leak. For sanitation there may have been wooden buckets for the children and the womenfolk, but for all others it was necessary to go to the heads—an expression still in use at sea, especially in navies, but then all too real. The "heads" were the beaklike, exposed, and windy areas in the front of the ship, and it was here that the mariners and male passengers eased themselves, perched out in a windy row to leeward, breeches down and one hand hanging for dear life to some piece of rigging.

It was a grim life indeed, but it must be remembered that life was grim ashore too, in those days, and the Pilgrims were of good yeoman and plebeian stock which knew how to endure. If they slept in water (as they must often surely have done), it is amazing what the human frame can stand, when it has a mind to—in other words, when it must. As I write this I recall that I also have slept in sea water, too, in an undermanned full-rigged ship 57 days off Cape Horn, where the crew's living quarters consisted of a steel house on the wet and sea-swept foredeck, the doors of which could not be properly shut. The sea seeped in and the deckhead leaked, nor was there any form of warmth, nor any relief from suffering. We slept wet, in our wet clothes, with no chance of drying them. The sea water and the hard cordage brought up great sea sores on our hands and wrists, which would not heal. We were crewmen, not passengers. The ship's motion was horrible and endless, nor had we any hope of improvement until we were long past Cape Horn. It was midwinter. The year was 1929. I slept in the water then and I caught no cold.

Today, as I write this in the warmth and comfort of my home, I look now upon my softened hands and well-clad dry and nurtured frame with some mild astonishment. Is it really true? *Have* I slept and lived in some semblance of the conditions which those Pilgrims knew? Yes, it is true enough; yet I recall the hardships now with wonder, though I know that they bothered neither myself nor my shipmates unduly at the time. The crew of that ship were tough citizens, good yeoman stock, used to hardship.

So also it was on the *Mayflower's* famous voyage, for 67 days of what Governor Bradford briefly refers to as "longe beating at sea" and then, thanking God, hurriedly forgets. If a group of moderns was suddenly to be flung into such conditions as the Pilgrims then suffered, at first they would find things wholly intolerable. But after a while, as their awareness grew of the real problem—just simply that of their own and the ship's survival—I don't doubt that they would face up to it too, and soon cease to be astonished at how vast an amount of punishment and hardship their bodies could absorb. Such tests come often enough in wars.

In order—in part—to gain experience of what sailing a square-rigged ship like the *Mayflower* might be like (as opposed to the experience of reenacting the voyage, which in these days would not be possible), I offered myself for command of the replica of that vessel being built in England, in 1956–1957. Replica, did I say? How could there be a replica of a vessel of which, for all her fame, there exist no precise records at all? The answer to that is, of course, that there cannot be; but our new *Mayflower* is authentic, for all that. It so happens that there do exist sufficient data on a vessel of the *Mayflower's* date, size, and rig, and it is upon this that the new *Mayflower*—called the *Mayflower II*—is based. The data have been worked upon by experts, of whom the first was Dr. R. C. Anderson, president of the British Society for Nautical Research and a trustee of the National Maritime Museum. Using the data available, Dr. Anderson built an excellent model of a bark of the *Mayflower's* size and period, and it is this model which stands today in the Pilgrims' Hall at Plymouth, Massachusetts. It was the first really accurate model of such a ship, though alleged models of the *Mayflower* are legion and—all too often—about as wrong as they could be. In rigging, in fittings, in gear and all other details of that kind, this model is wholly accurate; but of course no one can say that it is of the *Mayflower* herself. It *could* be. It very probably is. It certainly is near enough to give a very good idea of what that ship was like and how she was handled, and therefore it is reasonable to base the replica on her.

The actual building plans for the new *Mayflower* are not the same as those which Dr. Anderson worked out for his model, though similar. A model, after all, is a model, and a ship is a ship. The building plans were prepared by a well-known American naval architect, Mr. William A. Baker, of Hingham, Massachusetts (who worked also on the restoration in San Francisco of Roald Amundsen's famous ship, the *Gjoa*). Mr. Baker's plans are of a ship a foot more in height and a foot less in beam than Dr. Anderson's—the greater height because she has a little better headroom than the original, the less beam because it is hoped she will sail that much the better. (For myself, I wish she had all the beam that Dr. Anderson gave her: but there was nothing arbitrary about his dimensions—given the formula, the actual dimensions could follow a somewhat wide possible range.)

It so happened that Mr. Baker had prepared his building plans quite independently (and of course an actual ship is a very different proposition from a model, for people must live in and work a ship) when an Englishman named Warwick Charlton, after thinking over the idea for some years, decided to go ahead with building a *Mayflower* replica as a tangible and—he hoped—more or less permanent expression of British good will to the people of the United States of America, as well as a lasting and very real expression of gratitude and esteem and a reminder, too, of the common heritage, and largely common interests, of these two leading nations of the English-speaking world. Mr. Charlton's idea grew to fruition, Mr. Baker's plans were ready, and in Plymouth itself a great project was afoot to provide a fitting berth and background for the ship, all at the same time. All that remained was to build the ship and sail her over.

But how could you build such an awkward little ship today, of good British oak and without a straight line in her? How could you rig her, with hard hemp cordage for the standing rigging, and cumbersome and awkward leads, and not a splice in all the fourteen tons of rope that she must carry? Who could lay up such rope, or use it when it was laid up? And where could one find a crew to sail the ship, supposing she ever was built and rigged and finished? As to that, the building of such "replicas" was not wholly a new idea. There have been others. There was for example, a whole fleet of Columbus's ships which was built for the Chicago Exhibition of 1893.

Again, the problem was much the same. No detailed plans survived of any of these ships. What was built were accurate examples of ships of the same size, period, type, and rig, and painstaking research turned out good vessels. The *Santa María* was sailed across. The others were shipped. The *Santa María* was built in 1892–1893 at Caraca, by Spanish shipwrights, under the general direction of Señor Leopold Wilke. The result was not unlike the *Mayflower* in many ways, and much the same tonnage. The new *Santa María* displaced 233 tons and was almost 61 feet on the keel. The new *Mayflower* should displace about the same, and her keel is 58 feet long. The *Santa María's* rig was slightly more simple than the *Mayflower's*, for she set only a main topsail above her big main course. The foresail was the only sail on the foremast. The *Mayflower* has topsails on both fore and main.

When the new *Santa María* was sailed, she proved to do quite well, though her best recorded speed is given as 6½ knots, and she took 36 days to make the trade-wind run from the Canaries to Watling Island. I hope the new *Mayflower* will do a little better than that! It was also said at the time that the Columbus replica "pitched horribly," though I do not understand that. She was a short, fat little ship: she was bound to pitch in a short steep sea. But I should guess that a 45-foot fishing boat could pitch much better, or even a 75-footer. Whoever reported the excessive pitching of the *Santa María* has little experience, possibly, of small ships at sea.

The *Santa María* stayed in Chicago, with her freighted sisters *Niña* and *Pinta*, and eventually all three went to pieces there. There was also a replica of Henry Hudson's famous ship, the *Half Moon*, built and presented by the Dutch government for the Hudson-

Fulton celebrations in New York in 1909. Like the *Santa María*, this *Half Moon* was an excellent job, but she, too, suffered the same fate in due course. There was no site, and there was no organization, to give the necessary (and expensive) after-care to these vessels, and so the *Half Moon* went to pieces. Her purpose was pure pageantry and she served that very well; but now all those ships are gone.

The new *Mayflower* serves a deeper purpose. She is to be maintained at Plymouth Plantation in perpetuity, funds for this purpose being raised, and the site already donated by the Hornblower family. From my point of view, the new ship is very much worthwhile to sail across, not only because the sailing of her will be most interesting. I am accustomed to square-rigged ships, but no one has sailed a vessel quite like that (except for the single run in the reconstruction of the *Santa María*) for the best part of two centuries. Spritsails, lateen mizzens, cumbersome brails, and awkward rope rigging went out many years before I went to sea, the spritsails and lateens for upward of a century. The placing of the masts, the windage of the high aftercastle, the more or less cheerful acceptance and use of what to our minds are the unnecessary inefficiencies of the too awkward rig, and the method of steering (which is by means of a staff called a "whipstaff" attached to the head of the long tiller), will present many problems. But essentially the new *Mayflower* is still a small bark. She is a little square-rigger with a couple of square sails on the fore and main, and her only other canvas the lateen mizzen (set on the aftermost mast) and a spritsail, which is a sort of square spinnaker set on a yard on the bowsprit. The foremast is right for'ard, like a Chinese junk's, and I don't doubt there were reasons for putting it there, as there are good reasons in a junk. I have watched many a junk beat to her anchorage off Singapore and elsewhere and marveled at the ease with which they handled, for all their awkward appearance. I saw that every piece of apparent awkwardness had its purpose, and all the seeming inefficiency disappeared when the junk was handled by people used to her. So it must also have been in those old galleons of the *Mayflower's* type. At any rate, I hope so.

One illusion should be dismissed at once, and that is that such vessels were excessively tubby, so much so that they could scarcely get out of their own way. Some models are like this, I know, but no ship ever was—no ship that went to sea and survived there. The underwater lines of the new *Mayflower* are good. When she was launched from Mr. Upham's yard at Brixham in Devon in September, 1956, she slipped down the ways like a bird, and the manner in which she kept her way through the sea and sat upon the gray water were a delight to behold. I don't doubt she will sail well. Her awkwardnesses of shape are above the waterline—far above it. The top of the highest house on the aftercastle, for example, is 40 feet above the keel—40 feet in a little ship with a keel 58 feet long! I would have razed that deck, had it been left to me, and built it up on arrival at Plymouth, but then the result would have been no *Mayflower*.

The truly incredible thing is the smallness of the ship—58 feet on the keel, 24 feet odd in beam, some 12 feet deep, and 90 feet from stem to stern. Of course, one realized that the *Mayflower* was a small ship, but to see this little creation of curved wood—not a straight line in her anywhere, until it came to adding the aftercastle—slowly growing on the ways at Brixham was a bit of a shock. One hundred and fifty people, men, women, and children, cooped up in a little thing like that, for a winter's crossing! And not a fine new ship with the best of charts, instruments, weather information, and lifesaving appliances which could be provided. (Ministry regulations insist on these today, and a receiving radio at least.) The original had none of these things, nor dreamed of them. The main beam of the new ship, built of a massive piece of Devon oak personally selected by Stuart Upham, looked as if it would take an outsize in pile drivers, working on the job all day, to crack it, and the little ship's timbers looked fit to break up a coral reef—not break up *on* the reef, but break the reef. (Though I would hate to put them to the test.)

So Stuart Upham and his shipwrights built the ship, of best Devon oak (for which he had to range far and wide): the Gourock Ropework laid up the cordage at Port Glasgow in Scotland, which they did with great thoroughness from the best Italian hemp: and the canvas for the sails was made by the famous firm of Websters in Arbroath, which is also in Scotland (it was these same Websters who made our canvas for the big Cape Horners, where it was put to the test). Nautical instruments of the proper vintage were made by Messrs. Kelvin Hughes, the famous nautical instrument makers, and these are so well done that not a single scrap of material not available for the original navigators has gone into them. The nautical instruments of the period include a cross staff, the seventeenth-century forerunner of the modern sextant, a traverse board for keeping the reckoning by the simple means of shifting a few pegs (designed for the illiterate and the unmathematical, and still of use), a compass in a wooden bowl, an old-style binnacle, and a candle lantern which can be guaranteed to go out whenever it is most needed. A genuine whipstaff has been made to steer by.

As for this last, I could have done without it for I much prefer wheel steering, and I can foresee that the whipstaff will be a gigantic "whip" indeed when the rudder starts to kick in a following wind and sea. Relieving tackles to the tiller head, I hope, will quieten it a little, but it will go hard to steer so inefficiently when one knows how easily a better system could be contrived. The pumps are primitive, but effective. The longboat is genuine (but there must also be rubber life rafts of the type which has shown its worth in recent years).

What about the crew? And what about the practical problems of handling such a ship, and somehow inducing her by means of the wind alone to remove herself from Plymouth in Devon to Plymouth in Massachusetts, by way of Provincetown, and afterward down to New York? As for crew, I have kept in touch with the deep-sea sailing-ship sailors I have sailed with, in vessels such as the full-rigged ship *Joseph Conrad* and the four-masted bark *Parma*. These were good ships, and their crews were lads who came to know their business. The *Conrad* was a former school ship not so very much larger than the new *Mayflower*, though much loftier and more efficient in every way: the *Parma* was a giant of a steel four-master. Sailors who could handle the brutish sails in that big Cape Horner ought to find the *Mayflower's* canvas child's play by comparison, and those who learned their sea ways in the *Conrad* should not be too greatly put out to learn the ropes again in the seventeenth-century vessel. Indeed, she has some great advantages which we were denied, for none of her canvas (except the light topsails) is handled aloft. We had to fight our way aloft in all sorts of weather, day and night, and fight and secure the wind-mad canvas there, taking our chance a hundred feet and more above the reeling, sea-filled decks. The seventeenth-century style was to lower the big yards to the deck, and the topsails were so comparatively small and light that a few ship's boys sufficed to gather them into the commodious "tops." These tops are big working platforms with room for a platoon of men in them, unlike the strictly utilitarian, meager constructions which we knew. Even a first-voyage boy should have no difficulty in climbing to them, or in working in them when he has reached their comparatively low height.

My three mates will be sailing-ship men, from the square-riggers, and so also will a sufficient nucleus of my mariners be—above all the boatswain and the senior able seaman. For the rest, I shall have good fellows from the merchant service, most of them certificated officers (which no one in the original ship was required to be), a group of experienced ocean yachtsmen, mainly from Oxford, and some boys. Boys are always good crew. If they were not sea-minded youngsters they would not be at sea, and there is no dark mystery about the art of sail handling. What their grandfathers and their great-grandfathers did, so can they do also, and well. In the *Parma* we went to sea habitually with boys for crew, and the average age of all hands fore and aft was about seventeen. It was like that in all those last Finnish Cape Horners for the last twenty years of their lives. There were a few older lads who knew their business, and there were the officers and the cook, steward, carpenter (sometimes), and sailmaker. The rest were first-voyage boys. This system of manning worked splendidly: we always had good crews.

I don't doubt that it will work equally well in the new *May-*

flower. If her antique inefficiency in some ways may appall us, she has the great advantage of her exceptional interest. All my life I have been interested in such ships, and on many a dawdle in the Sargasso Sea have kept hopeful lookout as a youth for some old galleon held there in the Gulf Stream's weed. There were no such ships, of course; well, now there is one, and it will be great to sail her. After all, we have only to bring her across the North Atlantic once, to make the one delivery voyage.

The ship is to sail in the spring of 1957, I hope with a nice northerly or northeasterly air stream set in over the United Kingdom that will last a week or two to send her well along her way. The spring is the traditional time to sail for the Grand Banks. I have been in a Portuguese codfishing schooner which sailed from Lisbon to the Banks in eleven days with the east winds of spring (though others have taken thirty-five days, and even forty). Just how well the *Mayflower II* may sail on a wind remains to be seen. But this much is certain—if the decrepit, crowded, overloaded, lonely, and forlorn poor old original could safely make the voyage and battle her way against gales three and a half thousand miles to windward, then in all humility our passage in a well-found, brand-new, and able ship, neither decrepit nor crowded, in the year of grace 1957 ought to be a joyride. Nor may the new ship carry anything like the complement of the old. Present-day regulations forbid it, on both sides of the Atlantic. A passenger ship must be a passenger ship and comply with all manner of strict regulation. For that reason, the new ship is to carry no passengers as such at all, but only guests and friends, and persons necessary to her voyage.

I could have filled her easily with applicants to help sail her over—fill her, and the liners *Queen Mary* and the *United States* besides. There are plenty of adventurous types, men, women, and boys, on both sides of the North Atlantic, only too willing to help to sail her. The pity is that I could not take them all.

THE STRUGGLE FOR POWER

11

FOR THE comparatively brief period that the North Atlantic was an Iberian preserve by right of discovery and divine right as interpreted by the Pope, there were no wars there, for at first no other nation was strong enough to challenge the pioneers. The defeat of the Armada put an end to that. English, French, and Dutch adventurers then began to stake out their claims in the New World, each equally determined to profit from what was readily exploitable and, failing quick riches from gold and the like, to build up colonies which would first supply and then provide markets for their home countries. England in Virginia, Newfoundland, New England; Holland at New Amsterdam and elsewhere; France in Canada, trying for a foothold in Florida, and also in Louisiana, all three competing for a share of the rich West Indies, soon came to quarreling with one another like a group of headstrong children. The English made an outstanding success of their West Indies islands, the French dug in in Canada, the smart Hollanders made a profit everywhere. Each in turn, and sometimes all three simultaneously, felt its security threatened, its hope of profit lessened, by the activities of the others. Those who had gone to pains to plant colonies in Virginia took a poor view of latecomers trying to skim the profit which they regarded as legitimately theirs. The general fear was that there was not trade enough for all. Therefore each sought not a fair share, but the lot. There were no fair shares in international trade, then or now.

The situation was complicated by the very success of the planted colonies, for the colonists soon had a mind to resent their undue exploitation by a group of capitalists far away, and the new Americans, stimulated by the challenge of the great continent whose fringe they inhabited, and fortified and strengthened by their early trials, had no intention of remaining forever a docile source of profit for English overlords 3,500 miles away, whose chief activities as far as they were concerned seemed to be to set up monopolies and to create restrictive practices. Their country was rich—Virginia in tobacco, others in cotton and rice, New England in timber and fish and naval stores—and a fair share of the rewards, they felt, should go to those who did the rough and backbreaking pioneering, on the spot. The New Englanders particularly became thorns in the motherland's side. They turned early to the sea for living. The abundance of good harbors and excellent shipbuilding material, which was theirs to command, stimulated shipbuilding.

By 1631 Governor Winthrop was launching the first all-American ship, the *Blessing of the Bay*, on the pretty Mystic River in what is now the state of Connecticut, and she was the first of a great, growing, and efficient fleet. Soon Boston, developed by the virile, competent, and pigheaded Puritans, was not only a major port in its own right and with its own trade, but was rivaling English ports for the ocean carrying trade generally. New England's sailing ships were being undersold in Europe, to the chagrin and loss both of English shipowners and shipbuilders.

Shipping was good business and New England thrived on it, but this had not been part of the colonial scheme at all. Boston grew rapidly into a great Atlantic seaport, handling a host of well-built and well-run little ships to its own great profit, and the considerably reduced income—as they saw it—of their jealous English forbears. In fact, trade created trade, and the greater prosperity of Boston could be England's too, with a share for all who had the spirit and the sagacity to see their opportunities and to grasp them. But in Europe, too often, the old monopolistic ideas prevailed. Europe, and above all England, clung to the age-old tenets that the strong should by right exploit the weak, that there should be lords and vassals, that colonials might have their place, but it was not and never could be enhanced by successful rivalry with the Old Firm.

It was all very shortsighted, but very human. Restrictive practices applied by England irked the adventurers of the American colonies. In truth, the real spirit of merchant adventure had shifted across the Atlantic. The English, being successful, naturally wanted to keep things that way. The Yankees saw their opportunities and used them. Their ships were in the fish trade, the slave trade, the sugar trade, the rum trade. Round and round the North Atlantic they sailed—taking dried fish from Newfoundland perhaps down to the West Indies for slave food on the sugar plantations, then a load of sugar from Barbados to the States to convert into rum, or perhaps across to Europe, and a cargo of Negroes from the Guinea coast back to the West Indies to be sold for slaves, followed by a run home with more sugar to convert into more rum for further profitable voyages. The English answer to their success too often took the same form—an attempt at more restrictive practices. Wars and rivalries in Europe further enriched the new Americans. Not only Boston became a great port. New York, Philadelphia, Salem, Providence, and Norfolk also became ports of importance.

Within a hundred years of the Pilgrim's landing, the Commonwealth of Massachusetts alone had more than 600 seagoing ships, half of them in foreign trade, most of which was to the West Indies and Europe, and New England fisheries had become so valuable that a quarter of a million quintals of dried fish were exported annually to Spain, Portugal, and the Mediterranean. New England had the finest and the largest masts and spars available in the world. The Carolinas grew the best rice, Virginia the best tobacco, Georgia the best cotton. The states of New York, Pennsylvania, New Jersey, and Delaware, with their rich farming land, produced corn and cattle in great abundance. There was lumber everywhere, and quite an early export was of prefabricated wooden houses framed and ready to set up. The harbor of New York—formerly New Amsterdam, taken from the Dutch in one of the Dutch wars—was one of the finest in the world. In one year alone before the Revolution—the year 1769—the English colonies in what is now the United States built and launched 389 vessels, of which 113 were fair-sized square-riggers, and Massachusetts' share of these was half.

These were English colonies and so these were English ships, and everything was fine so long as British monopolies were not upset, and the Old Firm's profits continued to increase. But British monopolies were upset, and the profits went to new Yankee firms more than to old English ones, and this was not as things were planned to be at all. An act was passed in the British Houses of Parliament, during the reign of King George III, establishing heavy duties on many articles imported into the American colonies, and making it obligatory that all colonial sugar should leave its country of origin in British ships. This kind of thing naturally aroused a good deal of indignation, but the protests of the colonists went unheeded.

Further and even more stringent regulations were applied, the real purpose of which was to force Yankee ships out of the North Atlantic carrying trade. It was illegal for the Yankee ships to trade directly with the West Indies, at their front doorstep, and by British law they were supposed to go to the considerable and stupid inconvenience of using British ports as clearinghouses. This they refused to do, and a good deal of smuggling and clandestine trade was carried on. This did Yankee shipowners no harm, in the long run, for they profited pretty well from it and they also learned to develop and sail splendid fast little ships. When at last the inevitable Revolutionary War broke out, they had the great advantage of having already a fine fleet of swift privateers and experienced men to man them. Lacking a navy to fight with, the privateers did very well, and it was British policy which created and fostered them.

All wars are unnecessary but none was more unnecessary than the war of the American Revolution, nor was any war ever brought on by greater stupidity. Further laws required that the American duties should be paid in hard silver coin, which drained the colonies of their bullion. The harsh Navigation Acts were strictly applied, especially in the West Indies, which formed one of the richest and most important sources of American trade. Direct trade between the colonies and French and Spanish settlements was put down with a rigorous hand, despite the fact that all these restrictive practices also harmed those who initiated them. Restrictions breed restriction, and resentment. The net result of all the English efforts was to create an active anti-English feeling in America, and a resolve on the part of the colonists to manufacture their own goods rather than pay heavy duties on stuff brought across the Atlantic. This they set about doing forthwith, and they have been doing it successfully ever since. They resented, too, the interference with their shipping, and above all else, the silly, galling attitude of those who appeared determined to regard them and their whole existence as created for the profit and benefit of the Old Guard, who stayed in England.

The growing friction between the colonies and the mother country was increased by the Stamp Act of 1765 which, among other things, set out to collect internal taxes in America under the authority of the English Commissioners of Stamps. A consignment of stamps, sent to New York, was seized and burned there. We hear a great deal of the Boston Tea Party, which came later, but this burning of the hated stamps was equally a lighting of the fires of revolution, though they died down for a while. The Stamp Act quickly made business between the two countries almost impossible. Wharves were deserted, American ships were laid up with their colors at half-mast in protest, and idle crews walked the streets of the great seaports. The American merchants made an agreement to import no more goods from Britain, regardless of their own losses, and there was a proposal even to prohibit the profitable tobacco trade from Virginia and Maryland. This sort of thing could not go on. The Stamp Act was repealed, but the act of repeal carried a preamble censuring the Americans and declaring that the American colonies were subservient to the

English crown and parliament, whose authority, it was stated, extended to American subjects "in all cases whatsoever."

Not long afterward came yet more troubles, in the shape (among other things) of a new American Taxation Act, which put high duties on tea, glassware, and other things. The duties in themselves were bad enough, but the real purpose of the act was to assert the homeland's right to tax the colonies, and this was worse. Their successful defiance of the Stamp Act had not unnaturally increased the American desire for self-government. So, when a shipment of tea came across to the port of Boston after the new duties were imposed, the angry citizens got together, marched aboard, and tossed the tea chests into the sea.

At the same time all shipping and trade with England came to a standstill, and an illegal trade was fostered both with France and Holland—the traditional English rivals and, of course, enemies. The British parliament retaliated by declaring that New Englanders were prohibited from fishing on what they regarded practically as their own Grand Banks. After July 20, 1775, any American vessel found fishing on the Newfoundland Banks, or off Nova Scotia or Labrador, was to be seized. The Americans did not wait for this crowning stupidity to come into force. The Old Firm had been too obtuse altogether, completely misreading all signs of the colonists' justified resistance. It was a pity. Even then, it would have been a simple matter for the quarrel to be straightened out.

But the Revolution was on, with the result which we all know very well. The war was fought out mainly ashore. American waters were dominated by the powerful British Navy, though American privateers took a serious toll of British shipping. In 1778, France took the colonists' side, and a French fleet under the Count de Grasse played a considerable part in forcing General Cornwallis's surrender at Yorktown. By 1781 the Dutch, too, were openly on the American side, for the opportunity to harm British trade was too good to miss. But the Revolutionary War was carried on by Britain almost from the start in more or less a half-hearted manner. If British command of the sea, and the full British force of arms, had been used as effectively as they might have been, there is no doubt that the Americans might have been compelled to continue as reluctant colonists for a few years longer.

But there were some English shipowners and others who felt that the colonists' subjugation was not worth the treasure it cost to fight for it. Let the colonies be free and independent, they said, for then, among other things, the young merchant marine of the New England states and New York would be automatically foreign, and so eliminated at a stroke from the profitable North Atlantic carrying trade. This view was extremely shortsighted, too, and when it was put into effect at the end of the war, the enterprising Yankees simply got on with finding new trades of their own, and building even better ships which sailed farther and faster. In due course they passed their own Navigation Acts, restricting their own trade to their country's ships, and since the American coastwise trade included—in time—the long ocean voyage outward to California and back again by way of Cape Horn, the new flag was soon being carried farther and by far more ships than it had been before.

As for the North Atlantic, if it was little of a battleground between the colonists and the English except for more or less private fights, its waters were sailed by some picturesque and important fighting men in those eventful years. Of these, two were outstanding and one was preeminent. These were the American naval officer known as John Paul Jones, and England's Admiral Lord Nelson. There has been so much of romance built up round the character of John Paul Jones that it is difficult to work through to the truth, but, by any standards, he was a remarkable seaman and naval officer. He was a Scot, not an American; he was not trained as a naval officer, becoming such when the necessity arose, after some years in the merchant service; he fought or was prepared to fight equally for the Russians as for the American colonies. Nor was Jones his name, and it is not the least curious fact about the man that a born Scot should deliberately choose to disguise himself with so unmistakably Welsh a surname. He was born in Scotland, sailed in British ships, and died and was first buried in France.

As with the Pilgrim Fathers, later generations made more of the man and of his exploits than ever his contemporaries did. Many among them seem to have actively disliked him, and not a few made it their personal business to thwart him at every possible opportunity—which they did, with no benefit to their countries.

John Paul was born the son of a gardener in Kirkcudbrightshire in Scotland on July 6, 1747, and went into the merchant service early as an apprentice. He must have been a bright and unusually competent seaman, for he was second mate at seventeen and mate at eighteen, and had an interest in a vessel in the slave trade not long afterward, bringing slaves across from the Guinea coast to Jamaica. Before he was twenty he had shown what he could do, by taking command of a ship in which both the master and mate had died from fever. At twenty-one he seems to have been in the American trade. Not long after this, for some curious reason (said by some to have been love, and by others, involvement in a murder) John Paul disappeared ashore in Virginia and emerged some years later as John Paul Jones, a patriot commissioned by the Continental Congress as a first lieutenant in the new American Navy. His commission dated from December 22, 1775; by the following October he had already distinguished himself sufficiently to be promoted to captain. He had taken part in a raid on the West Indies island of New Providence which, though unsuccessful, had served to show his unusual abilities.

After that he cruised in a ship called the *Alfred*, taking prizes of English merchantmen and fishing vessels. This activity, though successful, irked his fighting nature. There was criticism of the fact that the few American naval vessels then in commission deliberately avoided meeting the far superior ships of the British Navy, and their war, when it was carried on at all, was against merchantmen. Such a reflection would not do for Captain Jones. Itching for a fight—a real fight with any adversary—he was given command of a sloop called the *Ranger* and sent off to the friendly ports of France (friendly because they were anti-British, not so much pro-American: any damage done to Britain would help them), with instructions to request the loan of a "swift frigate" with which to harass English shipping where it would hurt most, in their own home waters, and indeed to go further than that and carry the American Revolutionary War right to their own territories.

This was a bold concept and Jones was the man to put it into action, but the French had their own captains in search of fast frigates. Captain Jones was a headstrong seaman who could never bring himself to suffer fools gladly, nor pretend to do so. An able and a forthright man himself, he expected others to recognize the fact, and be likewise. But the world—above all in its services, civil or military—is loaded down with mediocrities, against whom the really able man has always found that he must fight a harder and longer battle than with the national enemies. Jones got no frigate out of France then, though he received many good wishes. Good wishes man no guns, and he sailed off in the inadequate *Ranger*. He showed what he could do by carrying out a personal assault on the English coast at Whitehaven, and then doing battle with a larger British warship named the *Drake*, which he compelled to strike to him.

The attack on Whitehaven, though really a very minor affair in itself, caused consternation, and the shock it gave the complacent countrymen of England far outweighed its very small tactical importance. When Captain Jones returned to Brest in his victorious *Ranger*, with the English ship *Drake* in company as prize, the uproar of welcome was terrific. The French were beginning then their own war with England (not for the first time!) and still they had no good, fast frigate to spare even for the victorious Captain Jones. Instead they gave him a broken-down old East Indiaman called the *Duras*, which he hastily renamed *Bonhomme Richard* (in compliment to Benjamin Franklin's *Poor Richard's Almanac*, which was popular at the time) and hustled off to sea.

With this decrepit vessel he was given the rank of commodore and command of an assortment of privateers and minor men-of-war under individual French and American command. Even then, despite his previous successes, the officers allocated to him proved both inadequate and—what was worse—insubordinate. War is mostly boredom, and in the boring periods his fellow commanders seem to have found Commodore Jones hard to put up with. So, very unwisely, they left. It was an easy thing for them to do. All that was necessary was to lose station some dark night, and thereafter cruise independently.

If this was the French attitude, the English still rankled at the successful depredations of John Paul Jones, the more because they regarded the man as a traitor, despite his naval commission. If natural-born Americans dared not bring their naval ships to British waters, they asked, why should this renegade Scot do the job for them? They prepared a hot reception for him, up and down the Kingdom. At Liverpool, for instance—Liverpool was a port vitally concerned with the American trade—there were many expensive preparations.

"We have the pleasure to inform the public," stated the local news sheet on the first of May, 1778, "that there are two grand batteries here of 27 18-pounders in excellent order, for the reception of any mad invader whose rashness may prompt him to attempt to disturb the tranquility of this town. George's battery is commanded by the Mayor and the Queen's by Captain Hutchinson, both of them accustomed to the thunder of cannon. . . . To these securities will be added the *Hyaena* frigate, a King's ship built here, which in a day or two will be fit for sea and will be moor'd in the river; for our security by land we have two companies of Veterans, and four companies of the Liverpool Blues, commanded by General Calcraft who resides in Liverpool."

They also had half a dozen ships cruising in St. George's Channel. But the Mayor of Liverpool, though accustomed to the thunder of cannon, heard none fired by John Paul Jones, and the Veterans were not called on to repel invaders, either French or American. As for that, the shrewd merchants of Liverpool knew how to profit from the use of their own privateers in the hostilities equally as well as, if not better than, their kinsfolk across the North Atlantic, and Liverpool privateers did very nicely indeed.

Rouse, British tars! Old England's boast:
Drive off her foes on either coast—

Let J. Jones know and feel that we
Can yet avenge his perfidy...

So an "Old Seaman" exhorted his compatriots in a long ode printed in the same Liverpool paper, and Liverpool privateers got on with the job with profit and satisfaction. But "J. Jones" did not exercise their guns. He was elsewhere—in the North Sea, to be precise, and there, despite the greater perfidy of his squadron captains, he was doing battle with the British frigate *Serapis* off Flamborough Head. The date of this action was September 23, 1779. The *Serapis* was the better ship, but Commodore Jones engaged her in a savage, bitter duel, and outfought her.

To know how this battle went depends on whether one reads a British or American account of it, but there is no doubt that Jones's feat was an astonishing one. His ship was by then so decrepit that she had had to be lashed round with cables to keep her old and rotten hull more or less in one piece. She never had been built as a ship-of-war, and would have been inadequate had she been new. Some of her guns were as rotten as her hull was and these exploded when they were used, killing many of her people. The *Serapis* was a 50-gun ship, well manned and properly worked up, with an able commander, good officers, and a full and well-fought armament. The greater part of the action was by night, which may add some confusion to the accounts. At an early stage, seeing the *Bonhomme Richard's* guns exploding and not being much incommoded by her firing, Captain Pearson of the *Serapis* asked Commodore Jones, in a courteous manner, whether it was his intention to surrender, which indeed would then have been the prudent and reasonable thing to do.

"Surrender be damned!" roared Jones back at him. "I haven't yet begun to fight!"

These famous words have rung all down the years of American naval history. With them, and his exploits, Jones became the first great American naval hero, which has served further to obscure the stories about him and his background.

At any rate he meant what he said. With such useful guns as his old wreck could muster, and splendidly supported by a crew who took their spirit from him, he fought the *Serapis* through the night. When the two ships threatened to drift apart (for the night became windless) he lashed them together, and they continued to blaze away at each other, muzzle to muzzle. The *Bonhomme Richard's* sides were so rotten that the British shot often went right through her, and she leaked like a misused old fish basket. Perhaps the bonds that tied her to the *Serapis* helped to keep her up. The action was not aided by the fire of the only French colleague who had remained with Jones, for the fellow aimed more shot into the poor old *Bonhomme Richard* than into the *Serapis*, and when he might have been some use was not there.

The two contestants, locked together as they were, were obscured by the smoke which both were so industriously creating, and as the night drew on the action became even more confused. At its height there was an alarm of fire aboard the Britisher. Fire down below! The alarm was real enough. A Yankee marine, climbing out on his ship's mainyard, which projected above the British ship, was able to drop grenades through the *Serapis'* main hatch, and this early form of aerial bombing had devastating effect. One of the grenades set fire to a pile of cartridges, which promptly blew up and set the ship seriously afire. The small-arms fire from other marines, fighting from the tops of the French-American ship, practically cleared the *Serapis'* decks.

In the confusion, having fought his ship to a standstill and expecting her momentarily to blow up altogether, Captain Pearson surrendered to Commodore Jones, and the greatest single sea battle of the Revolutionary War was over. Their contempt for the Jones victory, and the respect in which his superiors in the Navy and his country held Captain Pearson, was shown by the fact that the Captain was knighted shortly afterward, while a price of 10,000 golden guineas was placed on Jones's head.

"The next English navy captain I meet will get his peerage," was Jones's grim comment when he heard this.

But there were no more gallant duels against the English for him, nor for any other American naval officer of that period. Jones was again received as a great hero in France. King Louis

XVI gave him a gold-hilted sword and the Order of Merit, but no ships. Going back to America, he was at first promised command of a fine new frigate building there, but this ship was given to France and Jones returned to Paris, still shipless, to act as agent for prizes taken by American ships in European waters. He took no further active part in the war at sea, not because he wanted things that way, but because there was no part which he was allowed to play. In 1787, Congress gave him a gold medal in recognition of his services. Gold medals and golden-hilted swords were all very well, but Jones preferred to be a man of action.

A year or two later he took service with Catherine of Russia, but here again the intrigues and jealousies of his less competent brother officers brought his efforts to nothing. By 1790, the redoubtable Scots American with the Welsh nom de plume was back in Paris once more and there, within a year or two, he died. It took much active searching to find the leaden coffin that contained his body, a century later, and in 1905 it was convoyed by a fleet of American warships to Annapolis, with honors, where it was reinterred in the grave of a hero. There, in the adopted land which he served at sea far better than many of its own nationals did, rests the body of John Paul Jones, still a figure of some controversy and endless legend.

John Paul Jones, whatever else he might have been, was certainly a sea fighter of outstanding skill and courage. His fighting spirit, his endless courage against great odds, his immense technical ability made him outstanding in battle, which he loved. But the boredom of war was not for him, nor was the sufferance of those of less ability, whether they were his superiors in naval rank or politics. Like many clever men, he expected others to have an equal ability to see things clearly, and to comprehend at once the clarity and worth of his own solutions of the problems of his times. When they did not, he was apt to be outspoken. He made enemies easily among those upon whose side he fought, and these impeded him in his efforts to come to grips with their real enemies. In appearance he was a comparatively small man of homely countenance, inclined like many small men to be quarrelsome and perhaps a little boastful too, which did not make him an endearing character. Yet he was an able speaker and a clear thinker not only in matters of sea fights, and during his years in Europe he was a welcome courtier at the brilliant courts of France and Russia.

There was another smallish man, of distinctive appearance and no ability to suffer fools gladly, who also sailed ships upon the North Atlantic, a small man with one eye and one arm, and immense courage and ability amounting to genius. He also had some quarrels at times with seniors on his side, but he defeated them and their enemies. Admiral Lord Nelson served as a young officer on the American station and in the West Indies. In 1782, as a very young captain, Nelson was in command of H.M.S. *Albermarle*, a 28-gun frigate which, after convoying merchantmen from Britain to the Gulf of St. Lawrence, cruised for some time against American shipping on the New England coast. Nelson was only twenty-three at the time. What a fight it would have been had Nelson in the *Albermarle* found John Paul Jones coming out of Boston! But it was not to be.

Instead, Nelson had a narrow escape from destruction, one foggy day off Cape Cod, when the fog cleared suddenly to show his frigate almost surrounded by a big French squadron of four line-of-battle ships and a frigate. With characteristic dash and instant decision, Nelson used the breeze that dispersed the fog to be instantly on his way. The big ships could have pounded him to pieces and would have taken huge delight in doing so, but with the freshening wind he sped toward the shoals of the St. George's Bank where the bigger ships dared not follow. The frigate kept up the chase and Nelson led her all day long. When the evening came, he backed the *Albermarle's* main yards, waiting for the Frenchman to come up and join battle. But the Frenchman sheered off.

Round the St. George's Bank are many shoals with depths from 12 to 18 feet, and Nelson, daring and able seaman that he was, would never have hazarded his ship by sailing boldly in such an area if he had not known thoroughly what he was about. He was an expert pilot in his own right, but even an expert pilot in such a place must have either perfect charts or local knowledge—preferably both and above all, the latter. In fact there were no perfect charts, but Nelson did have local knowledge—years and years of it, gained in the best possible school and present aboard the *Albermarle* in the person of one Nat Carver, descendant of the Pilgrim Fathers and fishing skipper on the St. George's Bank, out of Plymouth, Massachusetts. Nat Carver and his fishing schooner *Harmony* had fallen prize to the *Albermarle* a few days earlier. Carver was taken aboard to act as unwilling pilot for the waters of Boston Bay. The youthful Nelson had a way with him, and Captain Carver soon learned to respect his ability and to admire the man. When suddenly those Frenchmen hove up out of the fog, it was Nat Carver who knew the dance to lead them toward the shoals, and it was his local knowledge that made the brilliant piece of sailing possible. Nelson was so pleased with his Plymouth skipper-pilot that he gave him his schooner back again, which was more than an act of grace. The ship's company and his brother officers had a stake in the prize money she represented: they, too, were in agreement with their young captain's generosity, with good cause.

It was that same year that another great British admiral, Rodney, had roundly defeated the French Admiral de Grasse in the Battle of the Saints, off Guadeloupe, in the West Indies: it was the remnants from de Grasse's defeated fleet which Nelson encountered off Cape Cod. If they had sunk the *Albermarle* and disposed of her young captain then, how much might the history books be changed now! Nat Carver did a greater service than he knew.

That same Nelson was destined to know some of his most anxious and trying moments in North Atlantic waters, chasing a French fleet fruitlessly from the Mediterranean to the West Indies and back to the Mediterranean again, to catch up with it at last and bring it to annihilation—not only the fleet, but the dreams of the flamboyant and hitherto all-successful dictator behind it. Nelson's great victory with his wonderful captains—his "band of brothers"—in their line-of-battle ships, off the point where Prince Henry once had brooded, his thorough destruction of the French naval power that windy day off Trafalgar near Sagres, has become the most written-of, analyzed, reconstructed, and publicized sea fight of all history.

But to Nelson, too, much of warfare was but boredom. He used the periods of boredom, seasick and often ill in other ways as his rather frail body was, to good account and, when the moment for great action came, he was always ready—ready and brilliant and, more than that, resoundingly successful. And not in chancy, unimportant ship-to-ship encounters, but fleet to fleet, power to power, with the fate of the modern world depending largely on the outcome.

There were others, of course, and the Atlantic knew them too. If British official stupidity had split the North Atlantic and broken off the most important area of the New World from the Old, now British genius in the person of a frail admiral brought Atlantic peace for a hundred years. There were blemishes—the war of 1812, the Civil War, the Spanish-American War—but these were minor. Sea peace for a hundred years! It was a magnificent achievement.

PRIVATEERS, PIRATES, SLAVERS

12

PRIVATEERS, on the whole, were little better than authorized pirates, and the sea lanes are well rid of them. Though of some popular satisfaction to the new nation whose young navy lacked the power to fight adequately in its struggle for freedom, and often of considerable personal profit to those who engaged in it, privateering did not really pay. It was a crooked, ugly business, for all the "romance" that has been written about it in late years, and the false glamour that was too often associated with its luckier protagonists at the time. In war, technically all subjects of the belligerents were equally at war with all subjects of their nation's enemies, but it was the ships, and the unfortunate shipowners and seamen, who stood most open to attack and suffered the greatest loss. The practice of robbing merchants privately on the high seas was really piracy, no matter what it might be called.

If the new Americans did very well with their privateers in the War of the Revolution, so also did their British seafaring brothers, against whom they fought. Something like 700 privateers were fitted out in Britain, paid for by merchants to operate against other merchants, who had done them no harm nor wished them any. The general effect of the war on Liverpool, for example (which with the port of Bristol sent most of the British privateers to sea), was to bring its commercial progress to a stop, for all the flamboyant successes of some of its privateers and the attendant braggadocio. Liverpool's foreign trade had doubled itself in the fifteen years between 1760 and 1775: from that time onward while the war lasted, it declined seriously. The tonnage of its shipping went down; its population declined (10,000 of them were dependent upon charity for a bite to eat); public improvements were practically suspended (and there was room for many); the business of the port, apart from an occasional auction of "prize" goods, came almost to a standstill, and the manners of the Liverpudlians themselves, we are told on good authority, "made a retrogression towards barbarism."

All this in the most successful English privateering port! Where almost daily, at the height of the war, swaggering little brigs and black brigantines and topsail schooners, bristling with ruffians and with guns, took a run along the waterfront, up and down, to show themselves before sailing (and maybe to recruit more crew). In London, 600 vessels normally engaged in the trade with America were lying idle in the Thames. These were small ships, it is true, or there would not have been so many of them, but each gave employment to a master, his mates, and crew, and each should have helped to keep some shipowner in business, as well as to promote trade.

In the fall of 1775 the Americans were fitting out their privateers, and soon the pesty little vessels were swarming round the West Indies. Not long afterward they had reached the Irish Sea and the waters round the British Isles, and everywhere else that they might pick up a fat merchantman. As the useless war dragged on, French, Spanish, and Dutch merchantmen became equal prey to the English privateers, while marauders of those nationalities attacked British shipping. Each fresh nation in the war meant more legitimate prey for the privateers, less trade for all, and more loot for some. Vessels which could no longer take part in Bristol and Liverpool's slave trade were hastily transformed into privateers. Between the end of August, 1778, and April, 1779, 120 private ships-of-war were fitted out, of a total tonnage of nearly 31,000, carrying among them nearly 2,000 guns and manned by 8,754 men. Most of these were small ships: all were very little vessels by any standards applicable to deepwater shipping today. Many were less than a couple of hundred tons.

A privateer was any vessel which (being properly commissioned for that purpose) carried on her country's war against enemy merchantmen, on her own account. In those days, merchantmen expected such attacks (as well in peace as war, often, for when there were no privateers there were always pirates) and went armed to sea. But a merchantman's primary business was to carry cargo, the more of it the better. Big cargoes could be carried in large ships which were not overmanned: men absorbed profits, and took up space which could earn freight, and so did guns. Fast ships meant lean ships and lean ships could not by their very shape carry as much as fat ships, but fat ships sailed poorly. Privateers were usually fast ships, even if converted from plain merchantmen, for their trim was good when they carried no cargoes, and they could outsail laden ships. Many merchantmen tried to look like ships-of-war, with false gun ports sometimes cut and more often painted on their sides, and false wooden guns bristling from the ports in time of open war. This practice of pretending to look like a sailing warship died hard. I can remember seeing many big sailing ships with these gun ports painted along their sides when I was a boy in Melbourne in the early 1900s. The ships were called "painted-port ships," and they were both French and British. I served in at least one 600-ton iron bark that had had painted gun ports in her day, though built in the 1870s.

The privateers usually took their prey by outfighting them, either with their guns or by boarding. There were some red-blooded hand-to-hand fights and some notable ship-to-ship encounters, but many of the privateers were bullying little ships which hunted in packs, pouncing on the less well-manned merchantmen and using any means at all to bring an action to swift success. Some of the privateers, of course, met more than they could cope with, and were captured in their turn. Sometimes the larger of them took on enemy men-of-war in clean combat, and won, but this was rare. There was sometimes an element of crookedness in the captures of merchantmen. Well-laden ships, especially those in the West Indies trade, would connive at their own "capture" at some convenient rendezvous, and share the prize money with their captors, while their owners at home collected the insurance as well. In this underhand way, legitimate trade took a double beating, by loss of goods and loss of insurance.

Once granted the "right" of private war, there was no end to the iniquities that could be practiced, and were. Even ships in the government service (such as the Falmouth postal packets) soon learned how to work some very questionable though profitable tricks. It was noted, for example, that those packet commanders whose ships were the more frequently captured somehow became quickly rich, and a scandal was exposed which is almost unbelievable. The postal packets carried a lot of freight as the private ventures of the captain, officers, and crew—so much so that these private ventures were generally considered (at any rate by the crews) as of more importance than the mails. A scheme was worked out by which goods taken from England were insured for the passage out and home. Then, these goods having been profitably disposed of at some West Indies port and the money for them transmitted home by bills, the packet sailed again and was "captured" and looted by arrangement with some obliging American privateer. Let go again after the "loot" had been removed, the packet sailed back to Falmouth to collect on the insurance *and* the bills. There was said to be a fixed charge for this small service on the part of certain of the privateers, and everyone was happy —everyone in the packet service, that is.

Only a minority of packet crews lent their ships to such base purposes. There was many a real battle between packet and privateer, and the Falmouth packets had a great name as grand fighters who usually came off best. The trouble was that so common one in government service—the pay was so low that the crews had to make something on the side in order to keep their families alive.

There were other ships, big merchantmen, which sailed by prearrangement to meet some helpful privateer who, by removing their cargoes, was able to dispose of them in some prohibited port at fantastic profits, to the joy of all concerned.

The Liverpool morning newspaper dated September 6, 1776, for example, has an account of this practice, alleging that many of the richer ships taken by American privateers in the vicinity of the West Indies had deliberately arranged to be so taken, in order that their goods could reach the highly profitable market.

> To elucidate this point we must observe that the Saints [West Indies] are in great distress for numberless articles which they cannot procure openly from England [the paper goes on] as all commerce with them is prohibited by parliament and punishable as high treason. Under such circumstances, therefore, directions are privately issued . . . to fit out large ships with the commodities particularly wanted. This is accordingly done, and the vessels sail to a given latitude under the plausible pretext of being bound to some well affected parts. When they arrive at the given latitude, provincial privateers are in readiness to seize them, and they strike without a blow, well knowing that their owners are to be amply indemnified for the utmost loss which they may seemingly sustain in their imaginary capture.

Nonsense, said the shipowners when this charge was repeated to them: the newspaper was seeking merely to keep morale high in the face of so many appalling losses, and their ships were genuinely taken. No doubt the great majority of them were, but there were some curious goings-on, not only in the West Indies.

While only the able Yankee privateers and the swift Baltimore ships ranged the seas, the Liverpool privateers were not so active. Liverpool had no liking for the fratricidal war which worked so grievously to her loss. Nearly 800 British ships were captured within three years, worth upward of £2,000,000, and this was all dead loss. Tobacco jumped from 7½*d.* to 2*s.* 6*d.* a pound, pitch from 8*s.* to 35*s.* a barrel, and all other American goods went up in proportion. When at last it was all over, Liverpool citizens called the war "a most disastrous, disgraceful, unnatural, unnecessary, and expensive war, that might have been averted had a single grain of common sense been admitted to the councils of the obstinate old King."

They went on to complain that many of the Yankee privateers had cruised throughout the campaign without proper commissions —not that that made any difference, except for the well-based apprehension that, when privateering was no longer possible, these would turn pirates. Which some did, indeed, pretending to be privateers again when yet another war broke out between Britain and France. Fast little ships from Baltimore then ranged the seas, flying English colors against French and the French flag when they attacked British ships, ravaging both with equal impartiality and profiting only themselves. Many of these ships could pass as English, as far as their crews were concerned, for there were a good many English naval deserters aboard them. But the hull form and sail plans of the American ships were unmistakable, and the captains at Lloyd's—and the merchants—knew well what was going on.

When France, Spain, and Holland came into the Revolutionary War, one result was that easier and more numerous prizes were to be had off the English coasts, and it was then that the British privateers took their best harvest. Every non-British East Indiaman lumbering home from the Indian Ocean, and every Dutch, French, or Spanish West Indiaman from the Caribbean, was legitimate prey, and the time to go after them was before they heard of the fact that their nations were also in the war. News traveled slowly in those days. When war was declared by France, for example, a considerable fleet of French ships were at sea homeward-bound, but could not possibly be warned and could do very little even if they were warned, except try to hurry home. Such ships were always more or less prepared for attack, but, thinking that a state of peace existed in their own home waters, it was natural that vigilance might be relaxed a little as they came nearer Europe.

One such ship was a French East Indiaman called the *Carnatic*, which was the richest prize ever brought into the port of Liverpool, and the story of her capture is a strange one. When Liverpool owners went in for privateering in a large way, they commissioned every builder they could find to turn them out fast, well-armed ships. One such "builder" was an optimist by the name of Peter Baker—a sound tradesman, and an enterprising character, but unfortunately not much of a shipbuilder. Mr. Baker had been a carpenter, and it was very foolish both of him and the shipowner who employed him to try to turn out a privateer. Mr. Baker built one of the worst abortions of a full-rigged ship that Liverpool had seen in many a day, and the owner, taking one disgusted look at the lopsided, sheerless, ill-fastened monstrosity presented for his use, declined to have anything to do with her. So he threw her back on her builder's hands.

This was the more unfortunate for Carpenter Baker in that he had allowed himself to get heavily into debt on the job. If he could not clear those debts, he would have to go to jail. So he decided that, if the shipowner would not have his vessel, he must take the ugly thing to sea himself. He decided on a privateering venture of his own; if everybody else was doing it, why not he? He had the ship. If he knew little of shipbuilding he knew even less of navigation and seafaring generally, so he took along a son-in-law, named Dawson, to act as master. This son-in-law had been on an African voyage or two and did not know much about ships either, but the idea of privateering appealed to him. The ship —called *Mentor*—was a big vessel for the job, a 400-tonner with 28 guns and a crew of over a hundred men. This was a big ship to man, and a big crew to find for so impecunious an enterprise, and the Baker crew was as lopsided a lot as the ship—loafers from round the waterfront, farmers' boys in search of adventure, unemployables and ne'er-do-wells from the slums of Liverpool and miles around—and, along with these, a few old naval gunners of great age, and a few old sailors.

Manned by this rabble and commanded by the inexperienced Dawson, the *Mentor* waddled down the Mersey and out to sea, foregoing the usual braggart's trial run along the waterfront with colors flying (maybe because another vessel, engaged in that practice a day or two earlier, had got on a bank and broken her back) and, when the tide favored, staggered down the Irish Sea. She would neither stay nor steer, but she was well suited to her curious crew and she managed, most of the time, to sail bows first.

The *Mentor* was hardly out in the open sea before she came upon a large French East Indiaman, almost as unhandy as she was, lumbering homeward in ignorance of the war, with a hold crammed with treasure. The East Indiaman was pierced for 74 guns and made up in all respects to look like a line-of-battle ship. She did not, however, fool the observant Dawson, who, for all his limited experience, knew a gun when he saw one—as did most seamen in those days. A close look through his glass, as he sailed an intercepting course toward the stranger, showed him that those guns were dummies—bits of wood, protruding harmlessly from the side. So he closed the French ship, gave her a broadside, boarded, and took the ship almost in the twinkling of an eye, holding the *Mentor* alongside her in the seaway until the prize was secured.

As soon as he had an idea of the value of his prize, Dawson turned about and made for Liverpool. The town's bells rang for him when he brought the prize in from sea. She was a famous East Indiaman, and her great hold contained, among other things, a box of diamonds which alone were worth £135,000—the best part of a million in today's money. Wedges of pure gold, boxes of silver, precious brocades and silks and jewels of all descriptions were in the ship, which was said to be the richest prize ever brought into the port. Messrs. Baker and Dawson prospered exceedingly on the deal and built themselves a great mansion which the local lads named Carnatic Hall; but the *Mentor* came to a bad end. She foundered in a gale on the Banks of Newfoundland when she was only four years old, and drowned thirty men of her crew. She had amply earned her keep, and Mr. Baker went on from success to success to become the Mayor of Liverpool.

Fantastic stories of this kind abound in the privateer chronicles. Sometimes a ship would change hands twice and even three times on the one voyage, her crew now captured by a privateer, only to rise later and retake the ship from a careless prize crew, and be taken themselves yet again, perhaps, before they reached their destination. It was all in the luck of the game, and a seaman in those days on the North Atlantic, either deep-sea or coastwise, led the adventurous life. There is a story, for instance, of how three ship's boys retook their ship, a little coaster named the *Lively*, from an Irish privateer (which they called pirate) named the *Black Prince*. This *Black Prince* took the *Lively* when she was only a couple of days out of London, and put a prize crew aboard. Then, with a storm coming up, she ordered the *Lively* to follow her. While they were trying to do that, they dropped behind and then had the further misfortune to be captured for the second time on the same passage. This time it was by a French 44-gun frigate, which took all the *Lively's* people off, including the Irishmen, and put another prize crew aboard. They left the three ship's boys. The gale continued and the *Lively*, acting up to her name, bounced about so much that she opened up, and the French prize crew was soon worn out at the pumps trying to keep the ship afloat and their frigate in sight. Weeks passed. The frigate was gone, and the pumping continued. At last only three of the French crew were left fit for duty. The boys, having waited for this, seized them in the dead of night, taking charge of the ship with a couple of cutlasses. Then they sailed the ship to a mile or two off Kinsale.

Here they hoisted a flag of distress, but that was not the end of their adventure. Some half hundred of the local "pirates," coming out by boat, leaped aboard and, finding only the three boys in charge, proceeded forthwith to loot the ship with a greater thoroughness than even the privateersmen had shown. These hoodlums were put to flight if not to shame by the arrival of authority, in the shape of the captain of a letter of marque, and at last the boys were freed.

Capture and recapture on the same voyage became almost commonplace adventures. Early in 1780, for instance, the Guineaman *Hero* was taken by the French, then recaptured by H.M.S. *Champion* when the French prize crew had her within a few miles of Cherbourg, only to be retaken a week or two afterward 30 miles off Cork—again by a French privateer which could not keep her, for she got away yet again. The *Hero* was trying to get through to Guinea to pick up a highly profitable cargo of slaves—then the best of legitimate business—but she did not make it. For the fifth and last time, she was captured—this time by the whole French fleet, which sent her into Cadiz where she was condemned.

Seamen were in prison and out of prison, free men and prisoners of war, with a series of startling changes which must have been difficult to take. They were philosophers almost to a man, and they accepted their fate, if there was nothing to be done about it: but in French prisons a good many died.

> Dear Jenny [wrote a young Scots gunner to his wife from a French prison, after capture from a privateer], this is to let you know I am well in a dungeon at Dunkirk, God be blessed for it, hoping to hear from you. Tell Mrs. Ross I bought her stuffing, but it is gane. Let Jean know that I bought her a gown, and it is gane too.
>
> I bought an anker of brandy and gin to ourselves; but Jenny, they are gane too and a's gane: for the French dogs unrigged me in an instant, and left me nought but a greasy jacket of their ain: but Jenny, I have saxpence a day from the King of England, God bless him, and I have bread and water from the French king, God curse him.... Jenny, keep a good heart, for I'll be out of this yet, and win meikle Siller, and get a bottom of my ain too; and then have at the French dogs....

Whether Jenny ever saw her gunner again is not recorded, but she probably did. As for the French, some of the most successful and courageous privateers belonged to that nation—seamen like Jean Bart, Robert Surcouf, and Duguay Trouin, all of whom served more than a successful apprenticeship at the old game, becoming, in the process, such national heroes that there has seldom been an occasion since when the French Navy had not included at least some sort of ships named after all three. Unlike many of the privateers, these were gallant men and able sea fighters, courageous and skillful in action and gentlemanly and considerate at other times. There were others, fiends who kept up their fire even when their opponents had surrendered, and sometimes butchered whole crews.

On the whole, privateering was an evil business, and the United States was anxious that an end should be put to it, by international agreement. In all its early draft treaties offered abroad, the new country always inserted a clause to outlaw the privateer. The treaty which Benjamin Franklin negotiated between the United States and Prussia as early as 1785 stipulated that, if ever they came to war, neither power would permit the commissioning of privateers to operate against the commerce of the other. But the war of 1812 saw a horde of mercenary, destructive privateers, both British and American, roaming the North Atlantic once again. The pickings were too good, the gamble too stimulating, and international agreement on outlawing privateers (or anything else) too difficult. The war lasted a wholly unnecessary two and a half years. Between eight hundred and a thousand ships of each side were taken by the other, to the loss of both and the real gain of neither.

Over two-thirds of all these ship captures were made by privateers. The Yankee privateers swept the Atlantic for a time, in spite of the British Navy, and cruised sometimes almost off the Mersey Bar, just outside Liverpool. Some of the crew of a privateer called the *Fox* landed at Sligo and at Newport, in their uniforms, and, pretending to be British (perhaps it was not a pretense, for the captain of the *Fox* was known to be an ex-British seaman who had had a command in the trade between Liverpool and Londonderry), bought supplies ashore. Another Yankee privateer called, very appropriately, the *True Blooded Yankee* (though she also seems to have been manned largely by former British seamen) cruised extensively in St. George's Channel, between England and Ireland, and took many valuable prizes there including a Liverpool letter of marque which was well armed, and a Belfast ship called the *Fame* which was bound for London with a cargo of linen. It was customary to allow such ships to ransom themselves, which they did if they could, and one captured privateer had a dozen ransom notes in his black brig worth more than £20,000. The *True Blooded Yankee* was a formidable vessel, formerly a gun brig and owned in her privateering days by an American named Preble, who lived very pleasantly on her earnings in Paris. In one five-week cruise this ship claimed twenty-seven prizes, an island off the coast of Ireland, and—very briefly—a small outport in Scotland. What island, and which port, is not stated.

Another Yankee, called the *Argus*, did all too well in the Irish Sea and the Bristol Channel, but she was a sloop-of-war and not a privateer. Her captain, one W. H. Allen, had been first lieutenant of the frigate *United States* and was a seaman held in respect by both sides. This *Argus* got among the homeward-bound West Indies fleet one day in August, 1813, in a fog off Lundy Island, and captured and sank many of them. A week or two later she was captured herself by H.M. sloop *Pelican*, and Captain Allen was mortally wounded. He was brought ashore at Plymouth, where he died. His body was buried in the Old Church at Plymouth with full military honors, a contingent of 500 British Marines leading the funeral procession, with their band. Two little black boys, one carrying the dead captain's sword and the other his cocked hat, walked immediately in front of the hearse. These were his servants. The armament of the *Argus* included two fine brass cannon which Commodore Decatur had presented to Captain Allen.

Another Rhode Island privateer called the *Yankee* sailed throughout the whole war uncaptured, taking rich prizes, and once made a cruise down the whole length of the West African coast during which she took prizes and property worth more than $300,000. On the whole, the Yankee privateers seem to have had the best of it, despite the Liverpool successes, and when at last yet another unnecessary war was over, all Liverpool—merchants, townspeople, and seafarers alike—rejoiced to see a good Yankee ship come sailing freely up their river, the British colors flying bravely at her mainmasthead and the Stars and Stripes aft, and a much-needed cargo in her hold. It was a fine day, and the town turned out to watch the magnificent and welcome spectacle.

This was the last war during which the British government granted letters of marque. In future wars armed merchantmen had to be truly naval in all respects: in due course, the submarine, sneaking and dreadful, took the place of the marauding little sailing merchantmen, which, with all their kind, had disappeared by then completely from the seas. Such, one supposes, is progress.

If privateers were often rogues and sometimes murderers, on the whole they fought their version of whatever war they were involved in according to the rules. Looking back from this age of mass murder, prospective and real, when every baby in the remotest home ashore stands equal chance of death with the front-line soldier, the old days of the little ships pitching pieces of iron at one another and not, on the whole, doing a great deal of harm, seem almost romantic and adventurous. There was much that was red-blooded about that kind of warfare, which was not destructive to the spirit in the way that international war has now become.

On the other hand, the war carried on by pirates always was wholly despicable. There was never anything in the least romantic about such seagoing psychopaths as Blackbeard Teach, Bartholomew Roberts, Charles Gibbs, and the rest. Piracy flourished where command of the sea was lost, and the West Indies was an especially popular hunting ground for such criminals. Like the privateers, they knew where to seek the richest prizes—in the richest trades, close to ports or at the entrance and exits to channels which ships had to use perforce. There were still thousands of pirates in the Caribbean as late as the 1820s, when the U.S. Navy sent a fleet against them. On the other side of the North Atlantic was an even more ruthless lot on the Barbary coast, but there was some connivance at their existence. Safe conduct could be bought from them at a price considered reasonable by those who wanted to keep rival shipping away: the Moorish corsairs served a useful purpose by discouraging Yankee ships, for instance, to cut too deeply into Mediterranean trade. In due course, the U.S. Navy sent good frigates across to deal with them; but it took time.

The idea that pirates were romantic fellows who spent a deal of their spare time burying treasure dies hard. If they got any treasure, they spent it. They were willful, profligate, good-for-nothing rogues, usually cowardly, drunken, and incompetent. They attacked weak ships which they took by treachery if they could, and butchered the weak and defenseless to remove the evidence against themselves and, sometimes, for the mere wantonness of it. One of the most despicable was Teach who operated along the coasts of the Carolinas, murdering, thieving, and raping. A naval officer finally took care of him, cutting off his head, but the idea that he left sundry assorted boxes or chests of treasure here and there still persists. So, according to the romanticists, did Captain Kidd. Those who can see romance in these reprehensible and thoroughly low-down pirates could invent anything: yet even in very recent years (since the end of World War II) I have seen at least one party of foolish optimists go off in a chartered schooner in quest of some alleged pirate gold.

They had the usual "map," with hieroglyphs and crosses. Any such map of those days which still existed would be a useless piece of paper now, if it ever was anything better. Even if it were the outcome of accurate contemporary survey (which it could not be) the features of the coastwise lands would have changed, frequently out of all recognition (like the Bahama keys and the islets off the Carolinas). The fools I watched did not get very far, for their schooner was wrecked before she was out of the English Channel, but the silly map that one of them had is probably still in existence. There is some treasure to be found in Atlantic waters —or beneath them, rather—in sunken wrecks round the Caribbean and perhaps also round the British Isles. This is the treasure the pirates missed, not their takings. Modern methods, with frogmen and all the rest, have already been able to bring some of this from beneath the sea, but it is a safe assumption that no methods of any kind will ever come upon the Teach or the Kidd treasures. What caches they made were strictly of a temporary nature, and they had good use, themselves, for all the treasure they could find.

Two of the worst pirates there ever were were women. These were a couple of reprehensible and unrelieved butchering bitches known as Anne Bonney and Mary Read, and the less said about them the better. They both came to nasty ends, but not early enough. They both operated in the North Atlantic, and for far too long. They both fooled a lot of men in more ways than one, but in the end they fooled nobody, and swung. Anne Bonney was Irish by birth, raised in Carolina, a big, boisterous female hoodlum of cutthroat disposition and murderous ways, who first came to more than local distinction by knifing a maid in her youth. From this beginning she progressed, in due course, to pirates' mistress and, with Mary Read in her crew, outdid her male consorts in butchery and sometimes also in valor, which was not so difficult. When her pirate ship was attacked by an armed sloop, it was the two women who fought the longest, cursing the men for their cowardice in running below. Mary Read had the excuse at least of having been brought up as a boy, and she had fought as a foot soldier in two armies. The pair of them must have been sexless, shapeless, straight-chested viragos, whose careers at sea were brief, bloody, and unnecessary.

It is almost a relief to consider slavers, after the "girl" pirates, for slavery was a respectable occupation for centuries, and those who took part in it were considered as benefactors. Speaking broadly, there were two systems of slavery, the one the ancient Eastern system which, from long usage, religious regulation, and other factors, was not so bad, and still persists in some countries. The other was the bloody, horrible kind which consisted of seizing poor ignorant natives wherever they could be found, carrying them to wherever a market for their labor might exist, and selling them there like cattle. This was unfortunately the kind the North Atlantic knew, and the very worst of all slave ships and all slavers sailed there, to the eternal pollution of the clean ocean.

New lands could not be opened up without labor, and aboriginal labor too often died off when put to the test of continuous hard work (not being used to that sort of thing, never having seen the need for it) or proved recalcitrant and unemployable. The African Negro was the slave laborer par excellence. Of good physique (proved with savage thoroughness by his mere survival of the dreadful voyages over the Atlantic Ocean) and happy disposition, responsive to the slightest measure of good treatment, his muscles and his broad back carried many a planter in the West Indies, in South America, and the Southern states of the U.S.A. to a fabulous prosperity. On the whole, it was the slave trade that was the more iniquitous, not slavery. The slaves could be brought to market only after a westward crossing of the Atlantic which included, on most passages, the negotiation of the doldrums.

Slaves were loaded under unhealthy conditions, often far up African rivers, sometimes after the poor wretches had been made to walk several hundred miles from the inland villages where their kinsfolk had captured them. They were packed into the stifling and unventilated holds of horrible little vessels where they lay together almost like sardines, except that sardines are already dead, and do not have to be chained. However long the voyage might last, here they lay and here they died, too, on occasion. A dead Negro had no market value, and the traders did their best to keep them alive. They were mortally afraid of mutiny, of the Negroes taking charge, as they did at least once in a Liverpool ship called the *Thomas*, owned by a Mr. Thomas Clarke and commanded by Capt. Peter M'Quie.

In 1797 the *Thomas* was taking a "cargo" of 375 slaves from Loango toward Barbados when her armorer foolishly left his arms chest open one morning while at breakfast. That was the last thing he ever did. Women slaves, who were unfettered, passed the arms to their men who, breaking out their chains with superhuman strength, rushed on deck and massacred the crew. But the slaves had no idea what to do with the ship, which drifted about. After six weeks the slaves took an American brig loaded with rum but, unused to this fiery stuff, they drank so much that they became helpless. Then the brig's people promptly captured them, and took them all off to the West Indies, where they were sold.

All the slaving captains were not brutal. It was not at all unknown for a slaver master to use some of his "cargo" to help fight his ship, although the poor wretches could have had little real interest in the outcome of the battle. They did not pause to consider such things as this, if they were treated fairly. For instance, there was the case of the slaver *Brooks*, a notorious vessel which was commanded by a well-known master named Noble. Captain Noble looked after his slaves. Writing to his owners in Liverpool from Montego Bay, Jamaica, under date of April 26, 1777, he told them that he had roundly beaten an American privateer which attacked him.

"I had fifty of our stoutest slaves armed, and they fought with exceeding great spirit," says the captain, and the privateer was forced to retire partially dismasted. Nor was a single slave hurt in the encounter, the only casualty being reported as the "Doctor, who received a musket ball in his belly, but he has got the better of that already, as it came through the stern before it hit him."

It chances that there is a good deal of information about this *Brooks*, which was one of the ships especially surveyed on one of the many occasions that the British parliament busied itself in rigorous investigation of the whole matter of the slave trade. The *Brooks* registered 297 tons and carried 45 seamen, and her usual "cargo" was at least 350 men, 130 women, 90 boys, and 40 girls–over 600 persons, though she was licensed to carry 450. On one passage investigated, she had lost 13 males and 4 females, the females carrying better because they were unfettered. She had been seven weeks on the passage from the Gold Coast to the West Indies. Her human cargo was stowed on shelves specially built into her holds, and she was in all ways a modern and well-equipped slave-carrier.

At that time, something over 75,000 Negroes were being carried away from West Africa annually, more than half of them in British ships, others in French, Dutch, Portuguese, and a few in Danish vessels. These slave ships were specially built for the job and, as time passed and the trade became illegal, they were given a very fast turn of speed in order to outrun pursuing naval vessels. It was during this period that the most dreadful barbarities were practiced, when sometimes whole complements of slaves were thrown overboard when capture was inevitable, in order that the wretched humans would not remain as evidence. With them, into the sea, went the paraphernalia of the trade—chains, branding irons, thumbscrews, mouth-wrenchers (for forcible feeding), and all the rest of the horrible equipment. In the decade following 1783, 878 slavers belonging to the port of Liverpool alone (and Liverpool was not the only port engaging in the business) carried well over 300,000 African Negroes off to slavery in the West Indies and America, and the total value of these slaves was over £15,000,000. A trade of such dimensions and profit took time to put down, though far-sighted humanists had fought against it for generations.

As for the profit, the figures speak for themselves. Here is the record, for instance, of a ship called the *Lottery*, belonging to a millionaire named Thomas Leyland, who was three times Mayor of Liverpool:

Net proceeds of 453 Negroes sold by Messrs. Bogle and Jopp, as remitted by bills after payment for all charges		*£22,726 1s*
LESS		
Cost of ship's outfit	*£2,307 10*	
Cost of the cargo sent out to Africa	*£8,326 14 11*	*10,634 4 11*
Profit on the voyage		*£12,091—16—1*

This profit was about six times the value of the ship. The cost of a slave on the African coast at that time was £20 to £25, and he was worth £70 in the West Indies. But there was an Anti-Slavery Society already in being and, though at first its activities alarmed the Liverpool merchants, in time they, too, saw that so tainted and inhuman a trade could never be to the lasting benefit of their port, nor to anybody's. By 1808, slavery in British possessions and the slave trade in British ships were abolished, but that was not the end of the matter. So profitable a business could not be suppressed overnight, and the trade continued until well past the middle of the nineteenth century. In the United States it took a bitter Civil War to abolish slavery. Even after that, slave ships continued for a while to sail the North Atlantic. There was a profitable sale for their cargoes in some South American states. It was 1888 before slavery was finally abolished in Brazil: while there was a market, there were ships to carry "cargoes" for its service, and degraded wretches to sail the ships.

When at last the last slave ship had gone forever from the too greatly polluted waters of the North Atlantic, the slavers had gone off to the South Seas where they became "recruiters" whose business was the supply of "indentured labor." Some of these were still at their nefarious work well into the twentieth century. Here and there, some remnants of this system may still survive, though not at sea.

WHALEMEN AND FISHERMEN

13

THE LITTLE privateers and the stately great sailing battleships were alike lovely vessels, seen under a cloud of well-cut sails with a fine breeze or with wind-stiffened canvas swollen in a gale, in war or peace. The brave old *Constitution* (which fortunately is still with us, moored in the Boston Navy Yard), rolling across toward the Mediterranean, with the perfect symmetry of her high rigging and the magnificence of her pure-white cotton sails, must have been a sight for the gods. Nelson's, Hood's, Rodney's fleets of great line-of-battle ships, as beautiful as they could be venomous, sailing in quiet and beautiful procession upon the deep blue waters of the open sea, were indeed glorious sights of unsurpassed maritime loveliness, for all the hideous purpose of much of their being. That kind of loveliness was doomed when two ugly, self-propelled, squablike things, floating forts of incredible ugliness and minimum efficiency, began to throw hot iron at each other off the historic James River on a day in March, 1862, in the Civil War. These were the *Monitor* and the *Merrimac*, the first of the "ironclads," and they spelled the end of the sailing warship.

The sailing merchantman lasted much longer. Nowhere was she at her more adventurous than in the old Yankee whalers, those fantastic, fat little ships which used to sail out of Nantucket and New Bedford, and from Provincetown and New London and a dozen other ports besides, and roam the length and breadth of the sea world in their quest for the sperm whale. From Arctic ice to Antarctic ice, across the whole of the Pacific and Indian oceans they sailed, and the vast area of the North and South Atlantics was to them no more than a sort of sailing back yard. There were plenty of whaleships which were not Yankees—English, Scots, Portuguese, German, French, Danish, Dutch, Tasmanian. But the Yankees had the most, lasted longest, and did best, though some of the greatest names in whaling are British, names such as Scoresby and Enderby.

The port of Bristol was sending out whaleships to the Atlantic grounds in 1594, and the enterprising Captain John Smith, of Jamestown fame, was whaling off the coast of New England some fifteen years later. Whaling is an old, old business; the Red Indians of Massachusetts Bay were old hands at it long before the Pilgrim Fathers landed, and it was indeed the advantages of the Cape Cod area both for fishing and whaling which led the early settlers to prefer that sandy, tide-swept place, despite the comparative poverty of its soil and the harshness of its winters. Whaling there was at first bay whaling, when men watched for the telltale spouts as they tilled their hillside fields and, when a whale was sighted, all the villagers rushed down to the beach and went after it in open boats.

This kind of whaling is still practiced, in 1956, in Madeira and from several islands in the Azores, with boats and equipment practically identical with those the Yankee whalemen used in their sailing whalers a hundred years ago. A sailing whaler merely took bay whaling out to sea, carrying the boats at davits in order that they could be lowered where the whales were. By hunting whales not just spasmodically when they chanced to swim conveniently near a beach, but on their own feeding and breeding grounds wherever these could be found, these ships made a highly profitable industry of the business. This they did with great success, first with right whales and then with sperm, or both.

Right whales gave baleen which provided the bonelike supports for the voluminous and much-rigged-out garments which ladies wore in those times, from the ribbed lace collars high on their necks to the rotund and useless bustle. Few females were sufficiently endowed by nature to fill these monstrosities without artificial aid, and the aid was whalebone. The right whale gave oil, too, and the sperm whale gave a fine-quality oil which was used for lighting, a special quality baled from the head, and sometimes ambergris. Both the right whale and the sperm whale float when they are dead, which the larger whales do not: and so they could be hunted and processed by the primitive means available in the sailing ships. Essentially, these were nothing but the boats, the blubber-cutters, and the beach trying-pots which were fixed up (for safety) in brickwork on the open main deck.

Whaling was a tough life—not so bad while cruises were comparatively short to places like the Greenland grounds (after the right whales: this was one of the mainstays of European whaling but not so much in favor with Nantucket or New Bedford) or the Azores, Madeira, and the Cape Verde Islands in the North Atlantic. Whaleships never went to sea just in the vague hope that, by sailing far and wide enough, they would somehow find themselves alongside a sufficient number of whales to fill their holds with oil. Whaling captains knew where to look for whales. They knew that the schools of sperms wandered by the Azores at certain times of the year, then to Madeira, and, later, round the Cape Verde Islands. Their business was to be in all three places at the proper times but, since before very long far too many brother-hunters also knew the feeding habits of Atlantic whales, more enterprising whalemen beat their little ships around Cape Horn into the Pacific or sailed past Good Hope to the Indian Ocean and northward to the China Seas. Then voyages frequently lasted for years.

On the whole, only owners and masters made anything of a profit out of it. Foremast hands were too profligate and too poorly paid, and the natural result was that, in a great many Yankee whalers, only the afterguard—master, mates, boat steerers, and some of the harpooneers—were American. The crews were foreign, many of them Azorians or Cape Verde Islanders and, before long, it became the practice to run out of New Bedford or Nantucket with minimum crew and to do the real recruiting in these islands, and in

Madeira. The islanders took to the business cheerfully, for they were worse off in their own crowded islands. The Cape Verdes are largely barren, and the lovely Azores have been overcrowded for many years. In this way, the big Portuguese-speaking population of New England was built up, and the Azorians, Madeirenses, and Cape Verde Islanders came ashore by the hundred to make good citizens in the new land. They were brave whalemen, and they were well led. Crews were also recruited round the South Seas islands, mainly from among the beachcombers and runaways who soon became bored with that sort of "idyllic" existence. The Portuguese islanders were all boatmen born and experienced whalemen, before they ever sailed under the Stars and Stripes.

Sperm whales were taken mostly in schools, and that sort of whaling, though precarious and never an easy occupation, was not so dangerous. It was the lone bull sperm, cast out from the herd, who fought back. Some such bad-tempered bulls, quickly acquiring a savage skill from a successful contest or two with puny man in his little boats, really became dangerous. Such a beast was the ill-famed Mocha Dick, who drowned many a whaleman and was the real-life counterpart of Herman Melville's Moby Dick, and another was the sperm whale which sank the Nantucket whaleship *Essex* in the Pacific in 1820. Even with a "docile" whale, the business of dispatching him (or her) from a bit of an open boat on the great broad sea could be exceedingly hazardous, and the brass tablets to the memory of men and boys taken down by whales, or knocked under by flailing flukes, which line the older churches of New Bedford and Nantucket are eloquent. The whaleman took great risks often for little profit, but his was a red-blooded life of real adventure, a free life in which he could feel that he was a man. The exultation of the chase made up for many long days of boredom, and, when on the grounds, there was usually plenty of incident.

Time spent on passage offered the routine work of tending the sails and gear, and there was always in addition the whaling equipment to be looked after. There was no shortage of work and, if the master and officers were reasonable fellows, the life could remain sufficiently harmonious even over a three-year cruise. There were calls at islands to break the monotony. Some masters and officers were anything but reasonable citizens. The very business they engaged in so absorbed their lives that they became almost inhuman. For them, the ships, men, the sea itself existed only to provide their ships with a cargo of whale oil. They had no interest in anything but the business they engaged in, which they followed with single-minded purpose and fierce energy until it killed them and—too often—many of their crews with them.

These small whaleships existed by the hundred and, unlike the great whale factory ships of today (which hunt a different kind of whale which the old-timers had to leave alone because it sank), they could keep going almost until the last whale was killed. A comparatively few whales sufficed to give them a cargo: today's factories must take whales by the thousand, and when whales no longer exist in such tremendous numbers, they will go out of business. In this way, the smaller, wandering sailing whaleships were the greater menace to whale stocks, which seriously declined. But it was the coming of petroleum that put an end to the little ships. In the 1850s the port of New Bedford alone sent over 300 whaleships to sea, and took over from Nantucket as the largest whaling port in the world. In 1860, the United States produced 500,000 barrels of petroleum and, a year later, four times that number. This was the end of the spermaceti candle and the sperm-oil lamp, which could not compete against the cheaper, better kerosene.

The Civil War caused the loss of many whaleships, when Confederate raiders such as the *Shenandoah* and the *Alabama* sank or burned as many whaleships as they could, in orgies of wanton and useless destruction which ranged the waters of the globe. The poor old whaleship was easy prey, for she could not fight back. The whaleships were not armed, except with a few muskets and cutlasses to discourage marauding Melanesians and the like. Well-armed ships like the auxiliaries *Sumter* (Comdr. Raphael Semmes), *Alabama* (same captain), and *Shenandoah* (Captain Waddell) could destroy the unarmed whaleships at will, and the Nantucket and New Bedford men regarded them with unrelieved horror. In the course of the war these three ships wantonly destroyed a great fleet of their fellow Americans' ships, and the whalemen learned to hate them with an intensity which has not yet completely died away.

Both the *Alabama* and *Shenandoah* were comparatively large ships, built in England, and when the *Alabama* was sunk in fair fight by the U.S.S. *Kearsarge* in the English Channel one day in the summer of 1864, all the Cape Cod peninsula was delighted. There was nothing heroic in sinking whaleships. Even a merchantman could fight back a little, but only a few whalers had as much as a bomb gun.

The whaler captains showed what they thought of it in the person of one old-timer, master of the bark *Favorite* of Fairhaven. When the *Shenandoah* tried to board him, the septuagenarian master of the *Favorite*, one Captain Young, offered battle with his bomb gun. He had only the one, and no bombs at the time, but he did not intend his ship to be taken.

"Haul down your flag!" yelled the boarding officer.

"I'll be goddamned if I will!" shouted old Young, leveling his bomb gun.

"Haul down that flag!" repeated the boarder. "If you don't, we will blow you out of the water!"

"Haul it down yourself, if you think you can!" shouted the old man, taking aim with the gun.

"All right then, you asked for it. I will blow you up!"

"Blow away, my buck. May I be damned three times in hell if I haul down that flag for any blasted Confederate pirate!"

But the bomb gun wouldn't work, and the boarding was carried on without further incident, except for a scuffle when they actually hauled down the flag. The poor old *Favorite* was burned. The old captain had to be triced up and lowered into the boat with a block and tackle and, aboard the *Shenandoah*, he was put in irons. The Confederates did not like being called pirates.

This dialogue is one version of an often-told story. According to a midshipman who was with the *Shenandoah's* boarding party, the old hero was drunk. The *Shenandoah* lasted out the war and finally was sailed back to England, where Captain Waddell handed her over to the English authorities, who never would have let her go had they known her real business. She was smuggled out of England and turned raider at Madeira. The *Shenandoah* had sunk forty-six good American whalers. Faced with this sort of loss, and the further loss of fifty-odd ships which the government threw away in a useless attempt to block some southern harbors (they loaded the ships with stone and sank them off Charleston), and another thirty-seven lost in a disaster in the Arctic ice, the whalemen were in poor shape to fight against the inroads of the new petroleum. Though New Bedford continued to send whaleships to sea for another three-quarters of a century, they had had their day. They had founded many a Yankee fortune, and New Bedford businessmen knew how to turn their capital to other things. As for the seamen, they never had had any capital anyway.

It was some years after World War I that the last Yankee whaleship went to sea on a genuine whaling voyage. One of the best known of the New Bedford whaleships, the famous *Charles W. Morgan*, still survives, enshrined for permanent preservation at Mystic Seaport, on the banks of the historic Mystic River, in Connecticut. The *Charles W. Morgan* sailed the seas for eighty years on thirty-seven voyages, during which she earned two million dollars profit for her owners. Today the stout timbers of the old *Morgan* seem fantastically small, for a ship that endured so much and sailed so many hazardous and eventful voyages. Her low 'tween-decks, her minute and crowded forecastle, the cramped quarters for her master, and the primitive arrangements for the cooped-up life she gave her crews—all seem to belong to another age, as indeed they do.

As for the crews, they were paid by shares, but the share system was loaded in such a way that the good Puritans of the New England ports did their best to discourage seafaring profligacy. Things were so arranged (by tying minimum shares to an arbitrarily fixed low price on the oil, by deductions for "leakage" and anything else that could be thought of, and by charges for slop-chest clothing and tobacco at the highest possible rate) that many whalemen returned to port after a years-long voyage in debt to their ships or, at best, with so few dollars coming to them that they were forced to ship out again as soon as possible. The industrious man could prosper, by working his way through harpooneer to mate and master; but the way was hard for those not born into the business.

Except for the land-based whalers of the Azores and of Madeira, whaling now has gone from the North Atlantic Ocean, though in recent years I have seen a few small modern whale chasers at Setubal in Portugal and a laid-up fleet of them in one of the pretty bays of Newfoundland. Modern whaling is a mass industry, carried on almost exclusively in the Antarctic.

Another form of adventurous maritime industry which used to be carried on entirely under sail has almost disappeared, too, and that is deep-sea fishing. Within living memory, the wonderful fleet of Gloucester schooners used to sail to the Banks off Newfoundland, summer and winter, taking their fill of cod which was fished in the time-honored way, by dorymen. There are few dorymen out of Gloucester today, or any other port on either Atlantic seaboard, except in Portugal. St. John's and a dozen other picturesque ports in Newfoundland and Nova Scotia used to abound with them, and many were the stories of endurance, courage, and shipwreck which they could tell.

Dory fishing from small schooners on the Banks off Nova Scotia, New England, and Newfoundland was a dangerous business. It was one of the hardest ways to make a living at sea that could well be devised, old-fashioned whaling included. Whalemen had long spells of passage making, of comparatively easy times when there were no whales to go after: but the poor doryman had to set off in his little box of a boat at dawn *every* morning (unless a gale was blowing and his ship was jumping too much to work fish). Each and every day, sometimes for six months at a stretch, he had to take his chance against squalls, ice, fog, collision with steamers, and the usual hazards of being overturned, swamped, or otherwise drowned. A whale boat was one of the most beautiful sea boats ever built, designed for supreme seaworthiness and strength, and even the largest whaleships could carry only five or six of them and a few spares. A dory is a flat-bottomed open boat, without so much as a keel or even a rudder. It is built up of planks on edge, nailed together on a frame which allows great sheer and flare but is not otherwise distinguished.

By the very nature of the work, dories are frail and unseaworthy in appearance (an appearance they belie), and have to be carried by the score and even by the half-hundred, nested in big stacks on deck, like a child's blocks that fit one inside another. Dorymen work alone or at most in pairs; they are men against the sea, if ever there were any. Today's Banks and most offshore fishing is done by draggers, mechanically propelled ships ranging in size from fifty to a thousand tons, which take their fish by hauling huge nets along the sea bed and hoisting them inboard. The hard work is done on deck, and the vessels are entirely powered. Some of the larger are factory ships, which process their fish on board. The large trawlers on the Grand Banks are from Portugal, France, Spain, and Italy: these can keep the sea (with their low-consumption diesel engines) for months at a time, and most of them still salt their cod aboard as the old barkentines and schooners used to do; but that is about their only resemblance to the old-timers.

There is still one fleet of sailing ships working the Grand Banks. These are the Portuguese hand-liners, the dory-carrying schooners and small motor ships out of Lisbon, Oporto, Aveiro, Viana do Castelo, and Figueira da Foz. In 1956 there were fifty such ships operating on the Banks, half of them sailing vessels. Nor were these poor old ships, eking out a miserable last few years in a hard trade—nothing of the kind. The schooner fleet includes a dozen vessels built or rebuilt since the war, most of them fine steel schooners of up to 700 tons. It has been the Portuguese policy to retain this method of fishing, in face of the increasing mechanization of fishing methods (and all else), for the simple reason that overmechanization means overfishing, and already some of the nearer banks are fished out, or nearly so. The hand-liner, taking his fish by hook and line, will always find good cod, because he fishes over foul ground where the draggers cannot tow their trawls, lest the rocks rip them to pieces. The hook-and-line method does not destroy the sea bed or the feeding grounds, or young stocks. All that gets in the way is swept into the great gaping trawls, regardless, and their destruction is dreadful, even on an area as huge as the Newfoundland Banks.

Today the draggers take smaller and smaller fish, and often have to shift ground all round the Arctic to get a fill—to West Greenland, East Greenland, Bear Island, the White Sea, to say nothing also of the trawlable grounds on the Grand Banks themselves. Meanwhile the hand-lining schooners, with their one-man dories, take better and better fish, and are bringing them home more quickly. In 1956 the whole Portuguese fleet, which sailed about Easter, was back before the end of September, bringing 40,000 tons of salted cod—all caught by hand by Portuguese working alone in 14-foot dories. There were something like 4,000 of these dorymen, and some of the ships carried eighty of them.

So many Portuguese fishermen operate for these long voyages on the Banks and off Greenland that their government keeps a special assistance ship in commission for them, called the *Gil Eannes* (after Prince Henry's navigator). There have been two such ships of that name, operating over the past thirty years. The current *Gil Eannes*, built in 1954, is a 4,000-ton motor ship which carries, among other things, a sixty-bed hospital and a fully equipped surgery with X-ray rooms and all the rest of it, a fishermen's chapel, a radio and radar of the very latest kind, to keep in touch with all the fleet and with shore stations. Nor are her services only for her own countrymen: the *Gil Eannes* works for all ships, and there are usually a hundred or so large fishermen on the Banks in the season, and many more off Greenland, including Eskimos, Danes, Faeroese, and Norwegians as well as the French, Italians, and Spanish and Portuguese.

I have made two voyages with these Banks fishermen, one in a four-masted steel schooner named *Argus*, the other in the new *Gil Eannes*. I was with the *Argus* on the whole six-months voyage of 1950, and in the *Gil Eannes* a year ago. Both were fascinating experiences. The *Argus* was a Lisbon schooner, built of steel in Holland just before World War II. She manned fifty-five dories and carried a crew of over seventy. She had refrigeration for her bait, and good auxiliary power to move about on the Banks and to navigate in ice, and she could stow some 14,000 quintals of salt cod. We sailed at the end of March and were back by the end of September, full ship. We fished the Grand Banks and Davis Straits, and we filled the ship until there was not room in her for another cod. We salted down tongues and cheeks, and made oil in a steam press from the cod livers, turning out the stuff by the ton. We had dorymen adrift on several occasions, and once one was lost for five days. But they always came back. A playful humpback whale overturned a dory one morning, to the disgust of the doryman; but he righted his dory again, retrieved such of his gear as the whale had not carried away, and got on with fishing. They were tough, magnificent men—grand sailormen and courageous, most skillful small-boat handlers—all this in addition to being wonderful fishermen, with nerves of iron, the endurance of bisons, and the hearts of lions.

It was a tough life indeed! The Grand Banks are a turbulent shallow area shaped roughly like a great egg, lying in the western part of the North Atlantic off Newfoundland and—in part—Nova Scotia. The cold and miserable Labrador Current, sweeping down from the Arctic, spills across the shallow, rocky sea bed, which abounds in food for bottom-feeding fish, like cod and haddock. Squid come there by the million, and squid is a T-bone steak to any codfish. Cod spawn and grow anywhere on the Banks—anywhere and everywhere.

Dory fishing is line fishing. The fishermen use the dories to set out their lines. They run out what they call "long" lines which drift to the bottom, and on these lines, attached by short lengths of tough cord called "snoods," are anything up to a thousand hooks. A doryman will lay out his long line three or perhaps four times a day. With fifty-five dorymen each working an average of 600 hooks, the bait requirements are enormous. Providing bait enough was far from being the only problem.

I wondered that men could still be found who would cheerfully take on such a job. The answer is that it is traditional. The dorymen of Portugal have been going to the Banks for so long that theirs is a way of life they not only accept but proudly return to, season after season. Villages of adult males go year after year in the same schooners, with the same captains—not only in the schooners now (the schooner fleet is dwindling) but also in the big new motor ships, which carry up to a hundred dories. The voyage is organized to the last detail, even to radio programs from the folk left at home, which are beamed across to the men on the Banks to help keep them happy, and such details as supplies of vitamin pills sufficient to give each doryman one a day to make up for deficiencies in diet.

I was back on the Banks again in the *Gil Eannes* a year ago. Somehow, again I found myself looking with astonishment at the first doryman I sighted. It was a gray, miserable morning, with the wind blustery and the sea lumpy and the big ship jumping. The frail little dory was leaping like the cockleshell she was. The schooner that the man had come from was not even in sight. Yet the doryman, red-faced and stalwart, turned and waved to us, up there on the high bridge. We passed close enough to see that he was a young man, smiling—a rough, chunky figure swathed in oilskins, with a black stocking cap on his head, and his feet, firmly planted in the bows of his dory, encased in big leather boots. He was standing up, hauling in his line, and flipping back the cod as they came in.

Soon we were among scores of the dorymen in their little red boats everywhere, rising and falling with the sea, each lying to a small anchor at the end of its long line. The doryman's job is to fill his dory, which will hold more than a ton of fresh fish even though its maximum beam is less than 6 feet and it is only about 14 feet long. He goes a long way from his schooner or motor ship. Every doryman is an individualist. They don't fish in groups. They sail for miles, each to his own piece of sea—there is room enough—and they get on with fishing. The wind was getting up as we cruised along in the comfortable *Gil Eannes*, and she rolled and jumped. What it was like riding one of those dories for a twelve-hour day I didn't like to think.

Late that same afternoon we were among a group of the schooners, three- and four-masters lying to single anchors there in the open sea. There was no sheltering coast within 200 miles of them. There were icebergs about, and it was pitilessly cold. All that late afternoon I watched the minute pin points of the triangular dory sails breaking the windy horizon as, the day's fishing done, the fish-laden little boats raced for their mother ships. They had no power—nothing but a pair of oars and a bit of a sail that the doryman's wife had sewn for him, at home in the winter. In each frail boat stood the oilskinned doryman, some young, some old, each with a skillful hand on his main sheet and the other hand on an oar which he was using as steering oar and leeboard simultaneously. With a roll of white water at the little bows, white water breaking everywhere, the small masts bent like whips (for they are mere sticks cut from small trees) and the colored sails straining, the dories leaped and raced along, surviving by a miracle. Each was as full as it could possibly be and still float, and I feared that the boiling seas would roll in on them and send them down. But they raced on—all of them; though the sea was ugly then and growing uglier, and I'd have hated to be out in it in a well-found liner's lifeboat. Yet the dorymen waved and smiled.

I watched them as they approached their schooners, dousing sail and dropping alongside the rolling hulls so simply that the dangerous maneuver was made to look easy, like going alongside a dock in a placid river, and I began to think that I was watching an exhibition of the most skillful and the most daring small-boat sailing left in the modern world.

Not long afterward we made for St. John's. The fleet needed to rebait for the Greenland campaign, and the *Gil Eannes* had brought an Image of Our Lady of Fatima to present to the cathedral at St. John's, as a gift from the fishermen. It was arranged that the Image should be landed while the fleet was taking fresh bait and all the schooners and motor ships were in from sea. The craterlike harbor of St. John's, usually a gray and somber haven from Atlantic storms, came to colorful life while the crowd of the white-hulled fishing ships lay there, with their nests of colored dories, drying their red and yellow sails. The 4,000 dorymen marched through the gray streets of St. John's carrying their Image—there were no bands, no choirs, no marshals, no organized procession, no organized anything, but just the dorymen led by their captains, marching upright and dignified. And yet the great concourse of those simple men streaming up from the lovely schooners, chanting in their strong, primitive voices, the reality of their faith evident upon their strong and rough but now ennobled faces, was greatly moving. The march was led by the deck boys, youngsters from the school of professional fishermen in Lisbon on their first voyage. They wore the checked woolen shirts, rough corduroy trousers, and sea boots which are the school "uniform." All the dorymen were dressed in brightly checked shirts, sea boots, rough wool or corduroy trousers.

Four captains carried the Image. I knew them all—old Lionheart Marquess, aged seventy-three, who had been a doryman himself and had not been a summer at home in Portugal since he was eight. His two sons, also captains, were marching near him. Abreast of the Lionheart was the slight figure of Captain Costa, a slim young man with a face like a priest's, and no discernible trace about him of the traditional seafarer. Yet I knew that Captain Costa, a year or two earlier, had lost his ship in a storm in the North Atlantic when he was homeward-bound from the Banks, not far from the Azores, and he and his seventy-five men had been flung out upon the mercy of the sea. Her radio was gone and the motor ship could send no S.O.S. She had no lifeboats, only her dories.

A week passed. In that week she should have arrived back at her home port, but she did not come in. For that whole week her men were adrift upon the sea in their dories, with no food, no water. The ship sank, the dories floated off, and the men jumped into them dressed as they were. The dories had been rigged down from the fishing and were without their gear. And yet, when chance brought the American steamer *Compass* near the place where the ship had gone down, a week afterward, there were the seventy dories still together in the wild sea with the seventy-five men still in them, held together by that slim young man with the face of a priest. There had been no breakdowns, physical or mental. Now all the seventy-five were marching there, too, in that procession at St. John's.

The other captains were veterans of lost ships in Atlantic storms, too. I knew that, among the four of them, they had spent a month adrift upon the North Atlantic in the spring or fall of the year, with or without dories. There was the young captain of the schooner *Maria das Flores*, for example. His previous schooner had burned out by night, and her dories had burned with her. Captain and crew had huddled on bits of wreckage all night in the cold, wild sea, and in the morning the other ships had found them there—not a man lost, not a man or a boy who did not go back to sea again. At least 500 of those 4,000 marching dorymen had been adrift at sea from eight lost ships, even in the intervening five years since I had last been on the Banks. Ice, fire, hurricane, the hazards of the sea had claimed their ships—the lovely schooners *Lousado, Senhora da Saude, Infante de Sagres, Rio Lima,* among them. From all those ships not a single doryman had been lost. Was this not a miracle, asked the people of St. John's? Indeed it was—a miracle of courage, of endurance, of superb seamanship, of the spirit of simple men, pitted against the sea in little open boats.

There was a great service in the cathedral and then, in the evening, having taken their bait, the ships went out to sea again—the pretty white ships with their decks stacked with dories. I watched them go from Telegraph Hill, overlooking the Narrows of St. John's harbor, and I thought what an epic all this was, in the mid-1950s—an epic based upon the nobility and simplicity of unspoiled men, sailing in unspoiled schooners. It was an inspiring thing, indeed, to find on the wild waters of the North Atlantic in the atomic age.

THE WONDERFUL RECORD OF THE PACKET SHIPS

14

AMONG the most beautiful ships which ever sailed the Atlantic or any other ocean were, without doubt, the big square-riggers—the packets, the clippers, the skysail-yard down-Easters, the glorious iron ships of Scotland and, before them, the humdrum little barks and ships, brigs, brigantines, and barkentines which carried on the trade of the world for centuries before the powered ship was invented and brought to perfection. They died hard, those wonderful wind-ships. It took two world wars in the twentieth century to put them out of existence, and the last big engineless Cape Horner was still carrying cargo in 1950. There had been steamships, then, for well over a century and a quarter. What a record!

In this story I am concerned mainly with those ships which sailed habitually in the North Atlantic, not the great ships which merely passed through that ocean on their way to more distant waters, like the glorious East Indiamen, the wonderful clippers which came later in the China and the Australian trades, and the Yankee racers which took the gold-seeking rush round the Horn to California. American ships undoubtedly took the lead in enterprise, almost immediately after the success of the Revolution. While Europe clung tenaciously to her stodgy, monopolistic ways or carried on endless stupid wars to the destruction of her commerce and the great benefit of neutrals (including the new Americans), the Stars and Stripes spread across the seas. The new flag flew from a fine Baltimore ship in the Canton River as early as 1785 and, not long afterward, Yankee ships were challenging the old European supremacy with an alert efficiency and seagoing effectiveness, matched by business enterprise and the fine qualities of their swift ships which, for a while at least, gave them the cream of the trade.

By 1788, a Captain Read, flying those same Stars and Stripes which spread so quickly over the maritime world, was racing his ship out to China by a new route, making easting along the whole length of the Southern Ocean beyond the Cape of Good Hope to the eastward of Australia, racing northward again there up through both Pacifics, clipping weeks off the outward run, and racing home again to Philadelphia with a rich and highly profitable cargo. Voyages such as these were a shock to Europe, where many shipowners were still mentally in the dark ages and seamen too often regarded prolonged voyages to distant seas as such arduous efforts of nautical skill that few could manage them, and those few only the most experienced. It was Europe's firm belief that such voyages could be made in safety, says the authority W. S. Lindsay, in his four-volume *History of Merchant Shipping*, "only by a few experienced commanders in the service of Spain, Portugal, Holland, and England, who had been accustomed to the navigation of those distant seas and were familiar with the routes and the prevailing periodical winds." Yet in a very short while Yankee shipmasters were storming round the world who were in their twenties, with mates of nineteen and second mates who were little more than lads.

Europe could do it, too, if the lads were given the chance, but it was the virile new country, backed by its abundant supply of splendid shipbuilding materials, its many fine harbors, and the maritime skills of its people (preeminent among whom were those of British stock) which got on with the job. As for knowledge of the "prevailing periodical winds," the famous oceanographer Lieutenant Maury got on with collating the study of these, too, and making the information generally available. Others had preceded him in such studies in Europe but, as so often was the American way, he injected action into the study—action and immediate use, not by a few but by all comers. At the turn of the nineteenth century, of a million tons of shipping on the American register, more than three-fourths of it was roaming the free ocean lanes of the world, north, south, east, and west, and the Stars and Stripes flew from more ships and were seen more widely than has ever been the case this century, apart from periods of war.

As the new country grew, a great and growing immigrant trade began to flourish. Soon this, along with almost the whole of the North Atlantic passenger business, was in the hands of American shipowners. It was they who first conceived the idea of running sailing ships to a schedule. This they began in 1818 and continued, with success, for more than the following half century, long after great steamship lines were established. Previously, sailing ships had sailed more or less when they felt like it, and going to sea was apt to be a leisurely and long-drawn-out business. A ship went on the loading berth at Liverpool, say, for Boston and New York, and it was not until she was filled with cargo and passengers that her owners thought of dispatching her. The passengers had to wait for the cargo, and so did the mails. But New York shipowners thought of a better idea. These delays were annoying to businessmen and to important passengers, even in those leisurely days. They put ships on loading berths and announced to the hour when they would leave, and they did leave then, regardless of wind and weather, state of loading, or anything else.

A generation used to airliners taking off from New York's airport "every hour on the hour" for Chicago, Washington, and almost as often for Europe may think this strange, but the whole idea of keeping to a schedule then was completely new. How many such ships must an owner build or charter to maintain a scheduled ocean service that was of any use? Until then, westward passages across the North Atlantic often took more than two months. Eastward, a month was considered good going. If an owner sailed his ships on schedule from New York, how could he ever be certain that he would get them back again from the round voyage in time to maintain the schedule? Schedules, to be of use, had to be announced well ahead.

The answer was good ships, good masters, good crews, hard driving: and the answer was provided in all these matters. The North Atlantic began to know a new breed of ships—not the clippers (which were different) but the hard-driving and hard-driven square-riggers of the liner class, packets which kept their sailing dates precisely and their arrival dates roughly, and beat to the westward over the grim Atlantic summer and winter, and ran to the eastward with a regularity not before dreamed possible. They were liners because they ran a "line" service, from one definite port to another definite port, regularly, and did not just go where and when good cargoes offered. These were all American ships. Europe, left behind in the race at the start, never seriously entered the competition. (British competition took a different shape, and it was effective in the end—very effective.)

Soon there were several world-famous lines of these American packet ships, amongst which the Black Ball Line was preeminent. Even when I was first at sea at the end of World War I, there was still a living tradition of this line and the sailors sang chanteys about Black Ball ships and captains with a curious show of real feeling—especially Liverpool sailors. The Black Ball liners had been gone from the seas for half a century then, but tradition under sail was a strong thing, and the term "Liverpool packet rat" was applied with some feeling even then. It was not meant as praise.

Black Ball, Red Star, Swallowtail, Black X, and Black Star were some of the lines which maintained, among them, a steady sailing both ways weekly, summer and winter. They carried the best passengers and the cargoes, the specie and the news. Liverpool, London, and Le Havre were their terminal ports in Europe, and the waterfronts there and along the famous South Street in New York were lined with the taut, proud jibbooms. The ships were never big, the most famous of them being something over a thousand register tons. They were fitted with spacious cabins in a long poop which often extended to the mainmast, but the immigrants were crowded into the dark 'tween-decks as they were in the *Mayflower*, and sometimes they were even more crowded than the Pilgrim Fathers had been.

The miseries of a westbound winter crossing in a Black Ball or any other packet liner are now incredible. Except that they were unfettered and had more or less individual shelves to lie upon, in bad weather the poor immigrants were little better off than slaves. What they lived on depended upon themselves entirely, for they had to bring their victuals with them and cook them. Men, women, and children were all tumbled into the 'tween-decks together and left to sort themselves out. Many immigrants were lousy, literally, and when some were in such a state, all very quickly became so. The stench and general noisomeness down below were awful. When gales blew, which was all too often, hatches were battened down and the wretched people took their chances of survival. Ship fever, smallpox, and other contagious diseases were common, and sometimes packet ships came in with dead by the score. Rations, when they were provided at all, were dished out once weekly (as required by later British law) and food issued was the bare minimum to avoid death from starvation. Where there was so much seasickness, the food was often more than sufficient. Rates for a passage varied between £3-10 and £5 a head. In the cabins where a berth cost £25 (with wines extra), conditions were vastly different, and Charles Dickens himself, who wrote nasty things about the steamship he crossed the Atlantic in, chose to go back to England in a packet named the *George Washington* where he considered that he had every comfort.

There were no immigrants on the eastbound crossing, naturally, and conditions then were very much better. The 'tween-decks where the immigrants had to live were then crammed full with cargo. The officers, crews, and the cabin passengers were well fed, though the crews were not well paid and their life was always hard. Packet ships were hard ships, like all hard-driven sailers. The sails, gear, masts and yards were of the best, as they had to be when they had to stand up to so much hard and constant use. A weak ship could never keep schedule on the North Atlantic! Sail was carried to the last moment, and American sails were sewn from the best of tough cotton canvas. The snowy-white appearance of this was beautiful, but it was absolute hell on the hands, and the Cape Horn seamen even in my day dreaded the stuff. We had some sails of it in a bark I was in, and they were hated. They ripped out far more fingernails than all the other sails (sewn from good Scots flax) put together, and they were always most difficult to secure when they were wet, and heavy enough when dry.

Typical of the packet days was the ship *Dreadnought*—the "wild ship of the Western Ocean" as sailors called her—and her colorful captain, Samuel Samuels. The *Dreadnought* was not a Black Ball but a Red Cross liner, built of wood in 1853, a comparatively large vessel of 1,400 tons displacement which drew 22 feet when loaded. She was not a clipper in the true sense of that word (meaning that she could have had even faster lines and have sailed faster, if that were all that would ever be required of her: but a packet had to be able to fight to windward in a gale, too, and keep on fighting). Her rig was big and square, her mainyard being almost 80 feet long. It was her captain who made her. Captain Samuels belonged to the days when famous ships had famous masters who—since they were not near the end of their careers but at the height of them when appointed, and also because the captains very much made or marred the individual reputations of their commands—were often as famous or even more well-known than their ships. Their reputations were worldwide, not only among seafaring circles.

Samuels was a colorful character who has left behind an autobiography, which was very probably written for him. In this he records how he ran away to sea at the age of eleven, had been shanghaied (kidnapped) out of a Coast Guard cutter, chased by pirates, a seaman in the Texas Navy and chief mate in the British merchant service, had refused the post of admiral in the Turkish Navy and had rescued a good-looking young Christian woman from an Eastern harem—all before he was twenty! Such colorful careers were available to the adventurous in those days. He soon showed himself to be an outstanding and supremely capable young master mariner when he was given his first command at twenty-one. From that time onward he had his adventures in driving worthy ships, at which art he quickly showed that he was an expert of experts. On her very first westbound passage Samuels drove the *Dreadnought* from Liverpool to Sandy Hook in better than Cunard time, for the Cunarder *Canada* had sailed a day ahead of him and arrived at Boston at the same time. (Perhaps she had defective boilers on that voyage; at any rate, this particular episode in Captain Samuels's career has been disputed, but the fact remains that the packet made the round voyage in less than two months, and the owners pocketed a profit of $40,000 on it.)

Whether he could outsail westbound Cunarders regularly or not—and it was a fact that sailing ships could never hope to do such a thing, which in the end put them out of the business—Samuels soon had made a great reputation for the new packet and himself. Eastbound and westbound, he drove her along, and she could stand the driving. One run she made from Liverpool westward in 1859 was clocked as only 13 days 8 hours, which is a wonderful performance. The passage was of more than 3,500 miles, every mile of it against the prevailing winds and a great deal of it against the Gulf Stream Drift. Captain Samuels was able to make a passage like that, and to go on making good passages, because he was not only a sailing-ship master but also a master student of the ocean winds. One advantage the packet captains had, and that was that they spent their adult lives in the same trade. No one ever knew more about the practical use of North Atlantic winds than they did. The winds blow the same for all men and all ships. It is what a master does with them that counts, and with a square-rigged ship his choice was vital. Like Robert Hilgendorf in the great German nitrate sailers half a century later, Captain Samuels seemed to be able to outguess the wind, to foresee how it would change, and to know ahead where the best sailing breezes were to be found. It was this knowledge, coupled with his tremendous ability to get the best out of a strong and able ship, which made him outstanding: the Turkish Navy's loss was the packet ships' gain, and the fame of the *Dreadnought* and her master spread round the world. News of a record-breaking passage by a ship like that was, in those days, like the report of a new water speed record of today, except that its impact lasted longer and so did the record. The very fact that records meant so much both to line and captain's reputations was, to say the least, a pretty strong temptation to produce them, regardless, and not all that have been claimed will stand the light of investigation.

Captain Samuels sailed his *Dreadnought* successfully for ten years, so much so that his owners offered freight rebates if they did not deliver their cargoes within a stipulated time. Despite the growing and ever more effective competition of the Cunard and other steamers, on several occasions the famous sailing ship brought in the first tidings of important news. Samuels himself attributed his long success not so much to the innate speed of his ship (and in that he was right) but to the iron discipline which he maintained, and the fact that he drove her for all she was worth all the time, *night and day*. The *Cutty Sark*, in all probability, could have outsailed the *Dreadnought;* but that is not the point. The *Cutty Sark* was designed for a totally different trade. The *Dreadnought* claimed at least one run of 387 miles in a twenty-four-hour day, which was better than anything the *Cutty Sark* ever claimed. But those enormous day's runs were always dependent upon the captain's ability to fix his ship's position with precision, and the wet decks of a reeling, rolling little sailing ship in a North Atlantic gale were hardly the place to expect precision with a sextant, some odd tables, and a batch of three chronometers.

Captain Samuels made sure that he knew what was going on aboard his ship, at all hours, by his habit of never stretching out properly for a sleep at sea, in order that he would always wake easily. He had a shelflike bunk built into the companionway on the poop, and kept it deliberately half a foot shorter than he was. It is probable that neither he nor any other good packet captain really needed such an aid: a good sailing-ship master slept with his ship, and waked when she needed him. The slightest difference in the shipboard sounds, a different hum or howl in the rigging, the flapping of a sail or the throwing down of a coil of rope, a slightly increased list or a lurch in a squall, and he was on deck in an instant —on deck and in charge. He was the brains of his ship, and he alone sailed her. He was the maker of all decisions, once port was left behind. He had powers over men's lives and, indeed, could summarily execute any who by disobedience threatened—in his opinion—the safety of his ship and those on board her. This was a right not infrequently exercised, in the later days of American sailing ships, and toward the end of the packet era, when the ships were struggling hopelessly against increasing steam competition but would not give up, there was more than enough brutality. Those were the days of bucko mates who were no fiction, and of packet "rats" who suffered hard, and fought back viciously if they could. By that stage good crews went in more easily run ships where the life was better: the Western Ocean packet service offered the hardest deep-sea sailing ship there was. Though the ships were American, many of the crews were English, among whom the Liverpool Irish predominated. Those Liverpool Irish seamen were tough, too, but they could respect a man and they knew one when they saw one.

There were plenty of accidents and losses. The *Dreadnought* herself lost her rudder on one occasion, and the remarkable Samuels then sailed her stern first nearly 300 miles into a port of refuge in the Azores—this despite the fact that his leg had been badly broken by a sea and worse set by a couple of the mates and the ship's carpenter, using a block and tackle. The leg caused the unfortunate man such pain that he wanted to cut it off, and proposed to perform this operation himself, but he was deterred from this on the grounds that it was better to have a painful leg, even in broken pieces, than to bleed to death. He saved his ship, but it took him a twelvemonth afterward to save his leg with the best of surgery and attention. Because of that Captain Samuels had to turn his beloved ship over to another master. Perhaps resenting the change, the *Dreadnought* knocked her new captain down with a heavy sea on his first voyage with her, and killed him. After that she was taken off the packet service and sent out round the Horn to San Francisco, but she did not like that and, after a voyage or two, she drifted up on the rocks of Tierra del Fuego in an unusual calm and went to pieces. She was a great ship, ably sailed, and she has left a great record.

One sees her in one's mind's eye now though she has been gone almost a hundred years—a stately, graceful ship, a creation of well-hewn pieces of wood, and spars and cordage and canvas, the whole brought to a lovely perfection by the builder's art and to even greater beauty and greater perfection by the sea wizardry of a genius. Never again will such ships thrash to windward in the great sea, taut and trim and beautiful, their whole being in the competent hands of a single man, master of his craft and science and art, the driving force, brains, heart, and character of the creation he commanded! Great masts whip in the violent gale and the cold spray thunders over the exposed seamen as the sharp cutwater cleaves cleanly through the sea, and it is no thudding screw that churns the water white for miles astern. Now such ships are wraiths, and their masters, mates, and seamen with them. The packet ship had no hope, really, against steam, and those who clung to her suffered for their constancy. Efficient steamship lines thrust the sailing ship aside at the period of her greatest perfection, and henceforth, while it lived, the sailer was condemned to the lowliest of cargo trades.

At least one packet ship went missing with 600 passengers aboard, most of them immigrants, and her last moments defy the imagination. But, on the whole, the packets had a good safety record. Making the land at either end of their journeys was the most dangerous time for them, and the official statistics show that, over the years, one packet in six was wrecked. This seems a lot, but considered against the figures for sailing-ship casualties generally the packet record was extremely good. It was computed, from the records, that only one passenger in every 17,000 carried by the New York packets was doomed to lose his life by accidents at sea. Yet there were horrible accidents enough. Several famous packets piled themselves up on the coast of Ireland, including the *Stephen Whitney*, which flung herself so effectively against the rocks not far from Cape Clear that, within hours of her striking, nothing of her remained except pieces of canvas and timber, none of which was more than 4 feet long. Two of her mates and a handful of seamen succeeded in jumping on the rocks and clambering up them, but everyone else aboard perished. There were more than a hundred.

The packet *Liverpool* was lost on her maiden voyage, and the *United States*, *Crisis*, and *England* all were posted missing. But it was not the inability of a few to keep off Irish rocks, or the tendency of fewer to go missing, that ran the packets off the sea.

Before the packets died and while the steam menace was constantly growing, the Atlantic briefly knew the greatest days of the oceangoing sailing ship. This was the period of the wonderful ships called clippers, whose time was brief but whose careers were glorious. The discovery of gold in California in 1849 (and the fact that, being coastwise, all voyages from east coast to west coast of the United States were strictly reserved to American ships, though they involved 15,000 miles of ocean sailing) gave a great stimulus to the demand for fast ships. Steamships might be all very well on the comparatively short haul across the North Atlantic, but on longer runs their inefficient engines and boilers required so much coal that they could not carry anything useful and have coal enough to steam with as well. So a few steamships took people to the Isthmus of Panama, across which they got themselves in the best way they could, and then other steamships and sailing ships staggered up the west coast toward San Francisco. For sailing ships this was through a great deal of calm, their greatest curse, and it was a mighty long way for steamships. It was better and generally faster to go the whole long way around Cape Horn.

To continue in that kind of voyage, sailing ships had to be *good*, and this they were. The grim headland at America's near-Antarctic tip then saw such ships as the world had never known—creations of beauty with wondrous names. *Glory of the Seas*, *Sea Witch*, *Sovereign of the Seas*, *Flying Cloud*, *Crest of the Wave*—lovely, high-sounding names for lovely, high-sailing ships! Many of these most wonderful ships were the creation of one man, the brilliant and inspired Donald McKay. Donald McKay had built ships for the packet service, too, especially for the Boston packets run by Enoch Train. But it was his larger ships that made his reputation—not only the golden clippers for the California trade but a succession of great wooden beauties built to British order for the Australian trade, ships like the *James Baines* and the *Lightning*, which stormed across the Atlantic from their New England building ports to Liverpool, to carry passengers and migrants from there on the 15,000-mile run round Good Hope to Australia, and home again around the Horn with more passengers and gold, and the richest of freights.

There were other clippers, and lovely ones—the little Scots and the Americans of the tea trade and, later, the Scots and English beauties in the wool trade from Australia. None of these ships sailed in their prime in the Atlantic trade, as such: the true clipper was designed for longer hauls, where the trade winds blew and where a spell of great westerlies would send her winging for Cape Horn, or fleeting at 17 knots along the rolling road that stretches 5,000 miles from south of Good Hope toward Australia. The North Atlantic produced the ships and produced the men to sail them, too; in their last days, some clippers came back to the ocean of their birth. But it was a return to carry undistinguished cargoes, to engage in lowly trades, cut-down ships with insufficient crews, known only for the grace of beauteous lines that never could be removed from them—not even when one or two became strained and sagged, or broke their backs.

The clippers filled a need while the steamship engine developed to catch up with them, and, having once caught up, it was the engine which went on to command the seagoing commerce of the modern world—the engine, and the steamship (and later motor ship) which used it. Not content with the good progress of his powered monsters, restless man determined to create two new exits to the North Atlantic, the better to speed his engine-driven commerce—the canal at Suez which, though at the Mediterranean's eastern end, was designed primarily as a way between the Atlantic and the Indian oceans, and, 10,000 miles from the Egyptian sand, the sterner, rockier, mountainous barrier of Panama was also burst asunder. When he dug through Suez he spelled the end of sail in the Eastern trade; when he cut through Panama, it was a powered world.

But the sailing ships fought back for almost a hundred years. The great fleets of coastwise schooners, economic until the day of the heavy diesel truck; the big down-Easters from Maine and the fine wooden full-rigged ships and barks of New Brunswick and Nova Scotia; the wonderful iron and steel four-masters of France and Germany, Italy, and—above all—Britain, which were still being built in fleets as late as the 1890s—all fought for a share of the world's abundant and growing trade and, in time, all lost. It was of no use to be able to run a swift 400 miles in the twenty-four hours, if such a twenty-four-hour run came once only in the course of years. If the fast square-rigger was capable of 350 miles and more upon her day (as few of the more modern were), the slower steamer disposed of her 200 always, and the dates of her arrivals and departures could be known in advance for sure. She took the liner trades and, in time, the bulk trades too. Today the only square-rigged ships to be seen upon the Atlantic or any other ocean (apart from a lone brigantine in the Maldive Islands) are sailing school ships, like the U.S. Coast Guard bark *Eagle*, and their purpose is the excellent one of training boys.

There is still one packet line—one last little sailing ship on a packet run out of a port in America. She is the brigantine *Madalan*, of the Cape Verde Islands. I saw her lying at Providence, Rhode Island, upon a late November day in '56, taking in cargo and making ready to embark passengers for St. Vincent in her home islands. She is a former yacht still with some luxury-yacht accommodation, and a large diesel engine, and the only resemblance she bears to the real packet ship is that she still can set square sail.

THE ATLANTIC FERRY

15

SAILING SHIPS look delightful on Christmas cards and calendars and they could be inspiring to those who had the good fortune to serve in them, but they had impossible disadvantages. When it came to so highly competitive a branch of maritime activity as the carriage of passengers between the United States and Europe, they just had to go out of business. As the vast continent of the U.S.A. prospered, and those who migrated with little or nothing fought their way to fortune, there was an increasing traffic—westbound, of migrants, mainly; eastbound, of the prosperous, returning briefly to visit their homelands or to spend their retiring days there, and, with these, businessmen, diplomats, and just plain wanderers—which soon attracted the attention of shipowners in Europe.

Enterprise was no Yankee monopoly: it simply flourished earlier and much more generally in the United States, where there was more room for it. When European shipowners began to provide an adequate North Atlantic powered ferry, they soon made such a success of it that the Yankee packets were swept off the sea. Sailing ships had open decks which had necessarily to remain open, because that was where the ship's work was done. All the gear from the sails and yards led there and was handled there, and the crew had to have priority in the arrangements of the ship or she could not be sailed at all. This meant that passengers had to live in the hull, where only a favored few could have reasonable light and air. The steamship put her engines in the hull and her passengers in a superstructure, built up on and outside the hull, and as the years passed and steamships were able, with better and better engines, to give up the web of auxiliary masts and yards which once cursed them, these superstructures became larger, more comfortable, and more palatial. All the passengers could be accommodated above the waterline, and there was plenty of room for valuable cargoes as well.

Moreover, steamship schedules could be planned ahead with a much greater degree of reliability than the square-riggers could. Although the best of the New York and Boston packets offered a splendid and well-maintained service, there could never be any real assurance as to how long the ships might be at sea. Westbound winter passages of more than two months were all too usual, right to the end of the packet era. Eastbound, the odd "crack" and most fortunate vessel *might* be 10 or 12 days, but she stood a much greater chance of being 20 or 30. The fastest westbound passage over a period of thirty years was 18 days, and the slowest 83, but in all the nearly 3,000 packet crossings made in that time, only five westbound trips were made in less than 20 days. The average was about 36 days. For the eastbound passage, it was 24 days.

As soon as steamships became anything better than weakly powered auxiliary sailing ships, it was easy to better both averages, and never to have a ghastly long passage at all. Very soon the steamers were awarded the mail contracts, and it was they which brought the news. When a lucky packet, by slipping in after a quick run between steamship schedules, succeeded in being first with some important news, that fact was news too. Yet it is extraordinary how long it took many sailing-ship owners to realize that they were pinning their faith and capital to an outmoded service.

It was the Americans who first sent a vessel with a steam engine across the North Atlantic, but then, perhaps horrified at the unsporting nature of the foul and expensive auxiliary, they sold the ship and gave the idea up. This was a wooden vessel, built at New York in 1818 for the packet service to Le Havre, but sold on the stocks to the Savannah Steamship Company, which gave her the line name of *Savannah*. At that time, the steam engine had been successfully adapted to inland navigation, and the great rivers of North America already had their steamship lines. There was a vast difference, however, between a big shallow-draft raft of a vessel which could be pushed along a flat river by means of a steam-propelled stern wheel or a pair of paddles, and a vessel fit to make an ocean crossing under power.

The *Savannah* was essentially a sailing ship with a couple of small paddles made to fold up like fans, one on each side of her amidships. She waddled across with these things in brief use, now and again, and she made such a power-assisted passage only once. For the greater part of this passage, she was under sail. But she led the way. Her crossing, made in 27 days at an average speed of about 6 knots, was in 1819. She carried no passengers, though she had berths for 32, and, though she made for Liverpool, she was taken on to St. Petersburg in Russia and offered there for sale. There were no buyers, apparently, so she sailed back to Savannah, where the paddles and the 90-horsepower engine were taken out of her. She became a plain sailing packet in coastwise service; apparently disgusted with her poor showing, she wrecked herself on Long Island the very next year, and that was that. The *Savannah* was 320 tons gross register with a net tonnage of 170 (that is, a little smaller than my old ship, the *Joseph Conrad*, which can be seen at Mystic). Like all sailing ships, she was deep-hulled, drawing 13 feet of water, though only 99 feet between perpendiculars, with a maximum beam of less than 26 feet.

After her, America retired from the pioneering scene as far as the Atlantic service went. Perhaps the frightful boiler explosions in one or two of the famous inland river steamers helped to defer oceanic steamship development. Perhaps the Yankee genius showed itself at its best in the development of the lovely sailing ships. Or, more likely, American concentration on the development of the land, together with the great industrial revolution which was already then under pulsing way in Britain, laid the foundations of British supremacy at sea. British shipowners, quickly sensing the real possibilities of the application of power to the propulsion of ships at sea, began at once to establish a lead which they kept. In 1820 and in 1830 too, American deep-sea shipping was under sail almost to a ship, and they were better sailing ships than any other country was then capable of producing. But American shipping interests made the fatal error of leaving the development of power to the lake and river craft, which did very well but did not go and could not go to sea. There were other factors tending to obscure the need for a continuously good American merchant marine, chief among which was the tremendous and apparently limitless internal development. When the greater part of a vast, rich continent was crying out for development, who would hear the call of the sea? Overseas trade became subservient to internal; as Britain developed better and better steamships, she captured the carrying trade for ocean voyages, and she could keep it.

The American sailing-ship seamen, like their ships, were undoubtedly then the best in the world: it was lack of support ashore that defeated them. In 1843, when there was some alarm in responsible quarters in London about the general competence, status, and standards of the British seamen, a report was called for from all British consular agents abroad. These officials, who might be thought to take as good a view of British seamen as anyone—though perhaps not, since they had to deal with a good many quarrels among them—were practically unanimous in their opinion that both the men and their officers were just about the most drunken and riotous lot who came into their ports, and both their technical competence and standard of education were markedly inferior to the Americans'.

Yet British shipping prospered and American did not, almost from that time onward. Britain had abundant coal and iron, and the men who could work them. Britain developed the steam engine, particularly in Scotland. The British seafarer early took to power in his ships, though there were just as many Britishers as

Americans—if not more—who sneered at the "steam kettles," and expected steamships to blow up or, at best, to break down. The London General Steam Navigation Company was founded well over a century and a quarter ago, and it has been using powered vessels successfully ever since. Many of the greatest British shipping lines have celebrated a centenary of progress, long ago.

If America had the half of a continent to develop and exploit, Britain had an empire which was—then—constantly expanding, and ships were necessary to serve it. Britain manufactured and carried goods and commodities, not only for its own empire. Textiles, iron, steel, coal, and ten thousand consumer items all flowed outward from the little island off the coast of France. London became the financial center of the world, the merchandise mart, the merchants' center, the insurance center. A great and steadily increasing shipbuilding, ship-repairing, and shipping industry grew up, at first slowly but soon by leaps and bounds. All this very quickly gave the British shipowners, shipbuilders, and seamen, indifferent as they had appeared even to their own consuls in the mid-century, the greatest store of maritime "know-how" in the modern world. Their flying start in steam power was at the root of this.

There were Americans who were just as farsighted and enterprising, but they were handicapped in their efforts to compete. Seeing the early success, for instance, of the Cunard Line (known then by the unwieldy title of The British and North American Royal Mail Steam Packet Co.), an enterprising New Englander named Edward Knight Collins declared in 1840, "I will build steamers that will make the passage from New York to Europe in ten days or less," and he did. But steamers cost a great deal more both to build and to run than sailing ships did. Collins could manage his brief success only with considerable subsidies which had to be voted by Congress, and Congress (very foolishly) tired of voting such enormous sums, which many Southerners regarded as being exclusively for the benefit of a few inhabitants in a small strip of the Northern seacoast of their great country which was antagonistic to them. After some unfortunate losses, the subsidy stopped and the Collins Line went out of business. But the Cunard Line stayed, and prospered.

Indeed the story of the Atlantic powered ferry is, very largely, the story of the Cunard Line and Mr. Samuel Cunard, who started it all. He was a Nova Scotian, like Donald McKay and so many other illustrious figures in the story of shipping. If Samuel Cunard, like them, had moved to Boston and not across the Atlantic to Great Britain, one wonders whether it would have made much difference to British supremacy in the field. Perhaps not, for if he had done so, it is highly probable that Cunard would have foreseen the impossible difficulties which brought the Collins enterprise to nothing and have transferred his efforts anyway. In the beginning, he was as interested, if not more interested, in the steamship trade to Canadian ports as to the United States, and he was a successful merchant in Halifax before he became a transatlantic shipowner. Nor was Cunard the only pioneer in the British service. Not long after the little *Savannah* had managed to waddle smokily across, that extraordinary and capable figure, Lord Cochrane—a sort of fiery cross between John Smith and Lord Nelson, with a large dash of Benjamin Franklin thrown in—had built the paddle steamer *Rising Star*, which was the first steamer ever to use power westbound on the North Atlantic. After his *Rising Star* (428 tons) came the French *Caroline*, which with the Dutch *Curaçao* (built at Dover), the British Navy's paddle ship *Rhadamanthus*, the Canadian paddler *Royal William*, the minute *Sirius* (built in 1837 for the service between London and Cork, and pressed into the Atlantic service), and Isambard Kingdom Brunel's 1,300-tonner *Great Western* had all seen some sort of service before there was a Cunard Line.

The *Sirius*, which was a little wooden ship with a great high funnel like an upended cigarette and a couple of masts carrying brigantine rig, was the first vessel ever to cross the Atlantic under continuous steam power, and command of her for the job was given to a Royal Navy lieutenant. She was 18 days, 10 hours making the westward crossing to New York from Cork in Ireland, but she made only two Atlantic voyages. The *Great Western's* was a different story. With any luck, she would have beaten the *Sirius* into New York, for she was held up by bad weather in the Bristol Channel and reached Manhattan only a few hours after the smaller vessel. The *Great Western* was the first really successful liner in the transatlantic service, running regular voyages. She crossed that ocean sixty-four times before she was sold, to run a further decade for the Royal Mail Line, to the West Indies. There were other pioneering steamships, most of which wandered across a voyage or two and then retired to shorter hauls, where their rapacity for coal gave them a better chance of earning something. It was 1840 before the Cunard Line could make a real beginning. But, having begun, it stayed.

It was an Admiralty mail contract that started them, and it was Samuel Cunard's business perspicacity that landed the contract. At the time, the general feeling was that the Great Western Company would carry it off. After all, they already had a good ship in service when the bids were called. But Cunard had good Scots backing, and his new line had four fine ships building. He put in the best bid and he got the job. His ships were the *Britannia*, built at Greenock and launched in February, 1840, the *Acadia*, *Caledonia*, and *Columbia*. They were not for the New York trade but sailed to Boston via Halifax; it was not until 1847 that Cunarders began to call at New York. By that time, they had managed to run most of their early competitors out of the business. There was room on the North Atlantic service, then, for only one Royal Mail line, and that was Cunard. The first mail subsidy (which is the wrong word really: the word should be payment, for the ships were not subsidized, but underpaid for a difficult job) was £55,000 for a bimonthly service from Liverpool.

This sum was far from sufficient. Mr. Cunard had made his estimates too low and, when he learned that the government intended to insist that British naval officers should command his steamers, he was worried. Naval officers, though extremely competent, are expensive luxuries in merchant ships, for the trend of their training is different; nor did Liverpool crews take any more kindly a view than their owners did of shipping under

Royal Navy commanders. If Liverpool could man the packets and a thousand other hard-run ships, surely she could man and officer her own liners. The government offered and increased mail payment, still keeping the R.N. officers. Mr. Cunard said he would take the lower subsidy and his own officers, which he did.

His line began at once to build up that state of efficiency and good discipline which, then a somewhat new idea in the merchant service (apart from the East Indiamen and a few others), has continued right down the years until today. It is that which is the keystone of Cunard success. The sailing-ship outlook had to be changed before fast and regular line steamers could be run successfully. A sailing ship voyaged under God and so did a steamship, but if the steamer were to keep her schedule and earn dividends, man had to take an increasing hand in her affairs. Sailing ships made port as and when they could, and performed their voyages in much the same manner. The idea of knowing precisely where his ship was all the time she was at sea was something novel to the general run of sailing-ship master. But a steamship had to be navigated, throughout her passage, with precision. She had to make pinpoint landfalls, on schedule. For her, to miss even one tide could be an expensive thing, and to waste fuel dodging unnecessarily about the ocean was not to be tolerated.

Nor was poor discipline in the ship. In the sailing ship the afterguard had to be prepared to do physical battle with the forecastle hands to accomplish the working of the vessel. Even the redoubtable Captain Samuels had to fight his way across the North Atlantic at least once, personally knocking out a mutinous helmsman and, almost singlehanded, wearing down a thoroughly recalcitrant and semimutinous crew. There had to be a different spirit in the steamships, and Cunard built it. If he had thrown the R.N. officers ashore, he kept their discipline. It was the Cunard Line, too, which introduced the idea of using defined liner lanes for safer North Atlantic navigation. It was Cunard which pioneered in seagoing safety in every way. For the first thirty-five years of their existence, the Cunard steamers never lost a single life or a letter entrusted to their care. They lost two steamships, but all on board survived.

This was because of the high standard of discipline and the good training of the crews. Safety, efficiency, punctuality could alike be achieved in no slipshod manner: the Cunard ships were well run *all the time.*

Other lines were in the habit of presenting their masters with a list of standing orders, for their guidance, but the Cunard instructions were most thorough and they were also rigidly enforced. *You cannot fool with the sea:* that was the first lesson, and it was a lesson thoroughly well understood by tough Nova Scotians like Samuel Cunard. Here are his standing orders to captains in the Cunard Line:

> We rely on your keeping every person attached to the ship, both officers and people throughout the several departments, up to the high standard of discipline and efficiency which we expect in the service. Your own practical knowledge may be your best guide, but we will allude to the following things:
>
> The charge of the ship, in all departments, is put under the command of the captain.
>
> The departments on board are classed under three heads—sailing; engineers; stewards and servants.
>
> The captain is to divide the sailors into two watches only, so that two officers may be always on deck.
>
> Keep good look-outs. The trust of so many lives under the captain's charge is a great responsibility, requiring vigilance night and day.
>
> Be most careful regarding fire and the use of naked lights. See the rules in cabin regulations on this point are attended to.
>
> Good steering is of great value. Pick the best helmsmen for this duty.
>
> We beg your especial care to the drawing-off of spirits. The spirit-room should, if possible, be entered during the day *only*. See the instructions to the purser under this head, and enforce them.
>
> Avoid familiarity with any particular set or portion of your passengers. Avoid national observations yourself and discourage them in others. Keep yourself always a disinterested party ready to reconcile differences. Be civil and kind to all your passengers—*recollect they will value your services on deck looking after their safety more than talking with them in the saloons.*
>
> The engine store-room (where waste and oil are kept) should

have the engineers' close attention, so as to prevent fire or even the alarm of it, not only on passage but in port.

It is to be borne in mind that every bit of the coast-board of England and Ireland can be read off by the lead and, on making the land, you should never omit to verify your position by soundings. Rather lose time in heaving-to than run the risk of losing the vessel and all the lives on board.

You are to understand that you have a peremptory order that, in fog or snow-storm, or in such state of the weather as appears attendant with risk on sailing, you are on no account whatever to move the vessel under your command out of port or wherever she may be lying in safety, if there exists in your mind a doubt as to the propriety of proceeding: and, at the same time, you are particularly warned against being influenced by the actions of other captains who may venture to sail their vessels in such weather.

In any case when, in sailing, you are overtaken by thick weather, fog, or snow-storm, the most extreme caution is to be exercised, and you are not to be actuated by any desire to complete the voyage, your sole consideration being the safety of your ship and those under your charge....

In the navigating of our vessels generally we have entire confidence in the ability of our captains, and full reliance upon their judgment and discretion...but, in the matter of fog, the best of officers become infatuated, and often attempt to push through when common sense and prudence would teach them to exercise patience.

You will bear in mind that we are now impressing upon you stringent rules, long laid down by us for the guidance of our captains, the terms of which are plain and inmistakable....

These regulations were drawn up over a century ago. If they had been strictly applied in a recent terrible collision between two big liners (not Cunarders) not far outside New York, it is probable that the collision would never have happened. Nor were these orders prepared merely to be hung on sundry shipboard bulkheads, or to be produced at some court of inquiry after an unfortunate accident. They were real orders, rigidly enforced. The Cunard Line were hard taskmasters: it paid. Before long, they were running a great fleet of steel steamships, carrying the cream of the Atlantic trade. Their success bred rivals, naturally: they have never had the field entirely to themselves. The Collins Line ran faster and more luxurious steamers for a while, for instance; but it was the Collins Line that went out of business.

E. K. Collins was an enterprising New Englander who had been running sailing packets, and he built some magnificent steamers. His steamers were easily the best of their time, but they achieved their superiority at the expense of the American taxpayer who, before very long, being mainly a landlubber, decided that he could do without them. Their subsidy ceased; this was after the line had suffered two grievous losses, and the effect was fatal. Apart from the Cunard Line, the mortality rate among the early steamships in the North Atlantic service was high. The Collins Line lost two splendid steamships, the *Arctic* and the *Pacific*, one missing and the other foundered in tragic circumstances, taking 350 persons to the bottom. Among these were Collins's own wife and children. The *Arctic* collided with a French steamer off Cape Race, which was the greater tragedy since the American crew feared for the other vessel more than for their own, and got on with rescuing the French people. Doing this, they did not look sufficiently after themselves. It was their ship that went down: the Frenchman managed to stagger back to port. When the Collins line's S.S. *Pacific* sailed from Liverpool a little later with nearly 300 people aboard, and never was seen or heard of again—not as much as a piece of wood from the ship nor the floating corpse of a single person—the blow was heavy. In 1858 Congress, though not frightened by the accidents, would have no more of it. It was not the sea and it was not Cunard which defeated poor Collins. It was his own landlubber countrymen, and the hard core of Southern influence in Washington, which was not anti-shipping but was anti-Northerner.

Britain had lost ships, too, swallowed up in the North Atlantic as the *Pacific* had been, or ground down in collisions, or driven ashore; but the British lines carried on. The *Pacific*, *Tempest*, *United Kingdom*, *City of Boston* all went missing with every soul aboard. There was no wireless in those days, and there was no Atlantic cable either. The anxiety of waiting for news of a ship which did not come in, of hope deferred and steady heart-sickening, must have been dreadful.

There were some odd ventures now and again, such as that of the ambitious Galway Line, otherwise known as the Atlantic Royal Mail Steam Navigation Company, which undertook in 1859 to maintain a regular service between Ireland and St. John's, Newfoundland, with 20-knot steamers, for a subsidy of £3,000 a voyage. They built only two ships, the first of which (the *Connaught*) managed an unsteady 13 knots and burned out on her second voyage, and the second (called *Hibernia*) took such a battering from the sea when on her way from the Tyne to Galway to begin her maiden voyage that she never entered the Atlantic service at all.

The Atlantic, though not often its expensive and highly competitive ferry service, was the testing ground for some curious vessels, none stranger than the mighty *Great Eastern.* The *Great Eastern* was intended as a wonder ship which would revolutionize much of the sea transport industry. Her designer, Isambard Kingdom Brunel, had already designed the successful *Great Western* and *Great Britain,* and in 1843 his *Great Britain* was the first screw-propelled iron steamship to go into Atlantic service. She was built (at Bristol) so well that she is still in existence, after a wonderful career first as a steamer, then as a sailing ship in the Australian trade, finishing up as a storage hulk at Port Stanley in the Falkland Islands.

The *Great Eastern* came fifteen years later, a great swollen hulk of a premature leviathan which staggered about for a year or two, inadequately powered (though she had a giant propeller, enormous paddle wheels, and six great masts spreading sails), inadequately employed, and altogether unable to get out of her own way—from either the business point of view or the practical. Whatever a ship could have, the *Great Eastern* had more of it than any other vessel—six masts, six funnels, acres of main deck, two hulls (one inside the other), her own tugboat at enormous davits to assist in docking (at least, such an acquisition was intended), a cast-iron four-bladed propeller 24 feet in diameter with a 37-foot pitch, which had its own engines of 1,600 horsepower, constructed by James Watt and Co. of Birmingham, and gave the giantess a speed of 9 knots on trials. The two enormous paddle wheels could give her 7¼ knots, without the aid of the screw. But under sail alone she was unmanageable. Her hull was altogether too big. It had need to be enormous, for she had bunker space for 12,000 tons of coal, and (without any superstructure to speak of, for her decks were needed to work the gear of her sails) she was supposed to be capable of carrying 10,000 troops or 4,000 passengers, and 6,000 tons of cargo besides. Yet the *Great Eastern* was not really so enormous, judged by today's standards. She displaced 32,000 tons (which a medium-sized oil tanker often does today) and was less than 700 feet long, with a beam of 82.7 feet and a 48.2-foot depth of hold. Today she would merely be an odd monstrosity because of her tremendous hull and lack of superstructure, but to the Victorians she was a seagoing mountain.

Unfortunately, she began her career by being about as easy as a land-bound mountain to launch, and the optimistic company which had financed her building went bankrupt trying to get her in the water. She was built at London in 1858, and it took three months to push, slide, shove, and otherwise cajole her into the river. In the end an unusually high tide floated her off by surprise, and she was off on her own, to the great consternation of all the other shipping in the Thames. Thus begun, her career was dogged by consistent and ill-deserved misfortune. Poor Brunel, who had been four years building her and had had to overcome far more difficulties than either he or anyone else had bargained on, had a stroke when visiting the ship on the eve of her sailing, and died; her funnel blew up in the Channel on her first trip to sea; the skeleton of a riveter was found inside her double skin when she was broken up, where the unfortunate man had been imprisoned while she was building, and built in (the presence of this skeleton was what brought the bad luck, said the old salts); she lost both rudder and paddle wheels in a gale, stove her bottom in on an uncharted rock off Montauk Point, collided with and sank or seriously damaged at least ten other vessels, drowned her first captain, never had more than 200 passengers in first class instead of the anticipated 2,000, and brought those who financed her to their ruin.

All these dreadful things are true enough; but the *Great Eastern* was a great ship and a great idea, for all that. She was before her time, built before there was a traveling public to appreciate her, even if she had been thoroughly efficient. There were no adequate tugboats to handle her in port, and, at sea, she had not really power enough, even with her variety of engines, to make her manageable. There was no dry dock capable of taking her, and she had no consort to share the ferry service. One great ship is of little use: there must be two. Hence the Cunard conception of the *Queens* —two great ships can carry on an effective New York–to–Europe ferry service on a weekly basis, but one is just a swollen oddity.

The *Great Eastern* sailed from Southampton in mid-June, 1860, on her first run to New York, and averaged 14 knots on the way across. She was never a success, except to ship-viewers at 5 shillings a head: for much of her career she was without employment. She ate her head off in overhead and her running costs were as outsize as she was, without leading to any proportionate return. The traveling public, probably alarmed by the series of misfortunes which dogged the ship, would have none of her, except to look at her with wonder in port. In the end she did splendid service in an unusual branch of maritime activity which her designer and builders had probably never thought of. The *Great Eastern* not only successfully laid the first effective transatlantic cable; she made such a cable possible.

In 1858, while attempts were being frantically made to shove her reluctant great bulk into the gray old Thames, two ships were trying to lay the first transatlantic cable. One ship was American and the other British. After the first abortive attempt they decided to meet halfway in the sea, each with her holds full of the expensive cable. At the meeting place they spliced their two cable-ends carefully together, then each turned and headed back for her own coast, the American *Niagara* for Newfoundland and the

British *Agamemnon* toward the coast of Ireland. But they had not made 40 miles before the cable broke. Again they spliced it, having fished for the ends; again it broke. This time it stayed on the bottom, and the ships went back for better gear to fish for the broken ends, and splice them again. This they did, and at last the cable was successfully laid. Sailors from the *Niagara* paraded up Broadway, Queen Victoria and President Buchanan exchanged greetings, and optimists on both sides of the Atlantic forecast an era of vastly improved relations. But the cable broke again, or wore through on a rock, or something. At any rate, it went dead and had to be entirely relaid.

This time some genius hit upon the idea of employing the *Great Eastern.* She was five or six times larger than any other vessel in the world. She alone could carry all the cable necessary, and more, in her enormous holds, and her ball field of a main deck gave ample room to work on. So the *Great Eastern* did the job, in 1866, so successfully that she was chartered after that to lay several more cables. There was a finality about that job, however, which put her the more effectively out of future employment the better she was at it: the costly business of laying ocean cables came to an end, and the ship finished her days as a fun-fair on the River Mersey, in England. In 1888 she was sold for scrap, but she was built so solidly that it took the following three years to break her up.

It was not until the end of the century that a larger ship was built. By then there was adequate power for her, and there were docks and tugs and all the other things she needed, far from the least of which was a properly educated and appreciative traveling public. The poor *Great Eastern* was gone by then, but it was she who began the education. Disastrous speculation, expensive folly, gigantic waste of good metal and better workmanship, cumbrous and bloated great unnecessary showboat she might have been, depending upon how one looks at the experiment. But after all, she *was* an experiment, conceived by brilliant men who had the misfortune to be far ahead of their time and who, at vast expense, provided something the market was not ready for. In the true sense, the *Great Eastern* set a tremendous precedent. In every way she was the ancestor of the huge, smooth-running liners which today crisscross the North Atlantic with a comfort and success that is taken for granted, and make the New York–Europe run a ferry service indeed.

Others have helped, of course. Not a single maritime nation whose coastline borders the North Atlantic anywhere but has provided, at some time or other, the best of her merchant shipping —the biggest, the fastest, the safest, the best designed—for the New York–to–Europe run. Germany, with a succession of magnificent huge ships; France (above all with the revolutionary *Normandie*); Italy, with a fleet of fine vessels; Holland, Norway, Sweden, Belgium, Denmark, Greece, Portgual, Spain—all have made and continue to make notable contributions. Today's transatlantic passenger is offered the choice of more than a score of fleets, all run by splendid shipping lines. In 1956 over one million passengers traveled by sea between Europe and the United States, which is the largest number since the war: these are not immigrants, packed into ships, but in every case fare-paying passengers traveling in comfort which, even in the cheapest classes, was undreamed-of fifty years ago. In June alone, 137,000 passengers were at sea on the North Atlantic, either eastbound or westbound. The Cunard liner *Queen Elizabeth*, throughout the entire year, averaged 1,750 passengers on each crossing she made, and she made nearly fifty. The magnificent liner *United States* runs 95 per cent full to capacity on the fastest schedule in the North Atlantic, month after month. Splendid new ships have entered the service, whose safety record (apart from the unfortunate incident of the collision between an Italian and a Swedish liner) is unblemished.

Such success is not gained easily, and the experiment of the *Great Eastern* helped to pave the way—she, and the Collins ships, the early Cunarders, and all the rest; and, too, the standards of good discipline and good seamanship set by that outstanding shipowner, Samuel Cunard.

"DROWNED FROM OUR BRIG, *MARY CELESTE*"

16

THERE ARE many ships missing in the North Atlantic, lost there without a trace—big ships and small ships, sailing ships and steamships, motor ships and yachts; ships, for example, like the U.S.S. *Cyclops*, a 10,000-ton collier, the new German motor ship *Melanie Schulte*, of 9,000 tons, the old Brazilian battleship *São Paulo*, 20,000 tons, the British tramps *Hopestar*, *Samkey*, and *Anglo-Australian*, which were all big vessels. No one knows where these ships are, except that obviously they must be somewhere on the bottom of the Atlantic. They sailed in good order, and sent their routine wireless messages, and then they just suddenly disappeared—all of them, and a great many more. The three big Britishers and the new German have gone missing in recent years, all of them since the end of World War II.

The U.S.S. *Cyclops*' story is typical of them all. She was a fine vessel, well manned—indeed more than well manned, for, being a navy auxiliary, she was crowded with 15 officers and 236 men, to say nothing of 72 passengers and a United States consul coming home from Brazil—and in the best of condition. A twin-screw steamship, launched at Philadelphia in 1910, she was only eight years old in 1918 when she went missing. The *Cyclops* sailed from Rio de Janeiro with a cargo of 10,800 tons of manganese ore, bound for Baltimore by way of Barbados in the West Indies. She duly called at Barbados, having done so well that she was there ahead of her schedule. She bunkered and sailed on March 4, 1918: and that was the last ever seen or heard of that big steel ship, with all her men.

Ever so often throughout the years since, some "evidence" comes up or some yarn is told purporting to throw light on the fate of the *Cyclops*, but not a single matter ever brought forward has stood up to any sort of examination. Mutiny, piracy, giant waterspouts, sabotage, enemy agents, explosion have all been brought forward as reasons for the big ship's disappearance, and some have been argued at length by "experts" who did not even have their dates right. As late as 1956, the *Cyclops* was reported as having been seen to blow up in the Florida Straits "just before Easter Sunday in 1918," though why the report had been withheld through all the intervening years was not explained. Perhaps the fact that the ship would have had to steam 500 miles out of her course in order to be seen in the Straits of Florida, on the run from Barbados to Baltimore, may have had something to do with it, to say nothing of the fact that had the *Cyclops* still been afloat by Easter, 1918, she would have arrived long since at Baltimore, for she was a 14-knot ship and she had left the West Indies port early in March. If engine breakdown had been the cause of such a delay, where had she been drifting for those three weeks?

The most probable cause of her complete disappearance was that her ore cargo shifted, she shipped water, and rolled right over so quickly that her enormous crew had time scarcely to cry out. There was some evidence of two highly significant things to account for such an accident. The first: weather records showed that on March 8 a front was quickly developing right in the *Cyclops*' path, which would have brought up a high sea and very strong wind; the second: an officer who had sailed on the ship said that, though everything else was lashed down securely, it was the practice to leave the topside manhole covers off for ventilation.

It is not a ship that is missing but one which was found that is commonly regarded as the Atlantic's greatest mystery. Her name was the *Mary Celeste*, and she was an undistinguished little brigantine, built of wood in Nova Scotia in 1861. More articles, books, broadcasts, radio plays, and general nonsense have been written about this vessel than any other that ever sailed the seas (not forgetting the *Titanic* and the *Great Eastern*), and more than enough stupid theories, false explanations, and downright fabrications have accrued to the poor little ship's name. It is the fiction, not the facts, which have made this name of the *Mary Celeste* so famed and it is the fiction, of course, which has swamped the imagination of the general public. Yet the facts of themselves are startling enough, for the *Mary Celeste*, a good ship well found and in good order, was come upon abandoned at sea for no discoverable reason off the Azores eighty-five years ago, and no trace of her crew has ever been found.

When she was sighted in this extraordinary crewless condition she was under very short sail—*not* the full sail most writers have credited her with—and, though under way, she was yawing about in a curious manner. The only square sail which was properly set was the fore lower topsail. The upper topsail and the foresail were both blown out, and pieces of their canvas flapped from the yards. The ship was also setting two headsails, which were the fore topmast staysail and the inner jib. These were sheeted on the starboard tack, but the square yards were more or less trimmed on the other tack. (Some of the braces were carried away, which may have accounted for this mixup.) The main staysail was run down and lay loose on its hanks on the forward house. All the other sails had been properly secured, as if it had been blowing hard.

The ship which found her was the *Dei Gratia*, another Nova Scotian brigantine very similar to the *Mary Celeste* and in the same trade. Captain Morehouse of the *Dei Gratia* recognized the *Mary Celeste*, for the two ships had loaded together in New York and Captain Briggs was a friend of his. The *Dei Gratia* had sailed a few days after the *Mary Celeste*, being bound for Gibraltar for orders with a cargo of barreled petroleum. Captain Morehouse at once sent his mate, an experienced seaman named Oliver Deveau, across to investigate. In view of the many incorrect statements and generally misleading descriptions which have been circulated

Anne Bonney,
woman pirate

The *Prince Frederick*
and *Duke*, privateers

I sailed the *Joseph Conrad* in Columbus's tracks

The American whaler *California*, built at New Bedford, Massachusetts, in 1842. She was afloat when seventy years old.

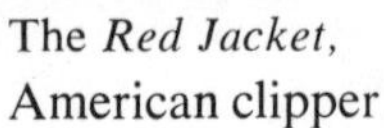

The *Red Jacket*, American clipper

Donald McKay

Ships like this Indiaman carried on the world's trade — such as it was — for centuries

Typical West Indiamen

Great Eastern

Model of the *Sirius*

Portuguese fishermen on an Atlantic beach

Becalmed in the Sargasso Sea

Whaling is an ancient business

for years as to just what Mate Deveau found (one writer copying from another and adding further imagined details of his own), I will recount the fiction and the fact, as stated on oath before the Court of Admiralty at Gibraltar by Mr. Deveau himself, and corroborated by his captain.

Fiction: *The* Mary Celeste *was in perfect order under all sail.*

Fact: As already stated, the *Mary Celeste* was under very short sail, and her running rigging was damaged. The peak halliards (a long length of rope used, with another tackle called the throat halliards, to haul the main gaff aloft and so to set the mainsail) were cut adrift and gone. Some of the braces (the important tackles which swing the yards, and so trim the sails to the wind) were carried away. So was the running gear on the foresail. The ship had about three feet of water in the hold, and the small deckhouse, used as a galley, had water in it, swishing about as high as the foot-high coaming. One of the forward hatches was off.

Fiction: *Some superhuman agency kept the ship on her course, and the* Dei Gratia *had to chase her for some time before overhauling her.*

Fact: The *Mary Celeste,* when first seen, was on the *starboard* tack to a northerly wind, and was heading west, back toward New York. The *Dei Gratia* had no difficulty in intercepting her.

Fiction: *There were the remains of a meal on the cabin table, with all the signs of the occupants' having hurriedly left while they were at their breakfast that very morning.*

Fact: There were no remains of breakfast or of any other meal on the cabin table, or in the galley or the forecastle. The dishes were all clean, and properly stowed. The ship's slate log showed entries to the morning of November 25—nine days before the *Mary Celeste* was discovered—and the chart showed her noon positions only up to November 24.

Fiction: *The cabin was in perfect order.*

Fact: The cabin was sodden with sea water, which had probably broken in through the skylight. The bunks, clothes, and everything else was wet through.

Fiction: *The ship's boats were still aboard.*

Fact: There was no boat aboard the *Mary Celeste.* That voyage she had carried one boat only, and the manner in which this had been carried and secured, on top of the main hatch, could clearly be seen. She had had no boat at her only davits, which were aft, across the square stern. The manner in which these davits were lashed showed that no boat had been carried there that voyage.

Fiction: *A blood-stained sword was lying on the deck, on which there were also bloodstains.*

Fact: An old rusty sword, in a scabbard, was among the trinkets found in sundry places where they were kept in the cabin. Captain Briggs was known to possess such a sword and to keep it aboard as a curio. There were no bloodstains on it, or on the deck. (These allegations are dealt with at greater length later in this chapter).

Fiction: *The alcohol cargo had been tampered with.*

Fact: The cargo had not been broached. Fifty barrels were swung ashore at Gibraltar for examination. All were in order, and so was all the rest of the cargo which was then in sight. Subsequent discharge showed less than the ordinary wastage.

Fiction: *There were cuts made on both bows, above the waterline, obviously cut in with a sharp instrument, to give the impression of collision or other damage which would account for an arranged abandonment of the ship, with criminal intent.*

Fact: There were two such slight marks, not structurally damaging to the ship and of no importance whatever, in the view of responsible and experienced seamen who examined the *Mary Celeste* at Gibraltar. Capt. R. W. Shufeldt, U.S.N., of the U.S.S. *Plymouth,* for example, gave the opinion, after careful study of these marks, that they amounted to "nothing more than splinters made in the bending of the planks which were afterwards forced off by the action of the sea." (The *Mary Celeste* had very recently been extensively overhauled.)

Fiction: *There was a sharp axe-cut or saber-cut on the vessel's rail.*

Fact: There was such a cut—at Gibraltar—but Mate Deveau said there had been no such cut there when he boarded the ship, nor had he or his men made it when sailing the vessel to Gibraltar. There was no sharp axe aboard.

Fiction: *There was criminal connivance between Captains Briggs and Morehouse to arrange the apparent abandonment of the* Mary Celeste *for the sake of the insurance and salvage, which both captains were subsequently to share.*

Fact: No evidence whatever in support of this or any other such theory was brought forward in the exhaustive inquiry at Gibraltar, nor has any such evidence come out since. The *Mary Celeste* was a paying proposition. Captain Briggs would have thrown his career away, for very small temporary benefit, if he had ever been so dishonest and incredibly foolish to try to arrange any form of barratry or fraud whatever. If he had been a party to any such stupid idea, he would at least have taken steps to survive the deed.

Fiction: *The principal owner, Captain Winchester, had arranged with the crew to murder Captain Briggs, his wife and child, and then to lose the ship; these arrangements the crew bungled.*

Fact: No evidence whatever supports so stupid an idea, which was not put forward in Captain Winchester's lifetime. He was a respected merchant, with everything to lose by criminal acts of such folly. He went at once to Gibraltar to attend the inquiry.

Fiction: *The crew were scum, scourings of New York's waterfront, cutthroats, desperadoes.*

Fact: The crew were quiet Germans, good seamen and good citizens—an exceptionally able lot. Mrs. Briggs, who knew seamen, had written home very good reports of the crew. Both mates and the cook-steward were respectable family men. It was the big Yankee ships which had to scour the waterfront for crew: the small ships, provided they were known along South Street as well run, could get good seamen who were glad to serve in them. This matter of crew is important as disposing of all allegations regarding the reputation of the *Mary Celeste*, and will be dealt with later.

The known facts are sufficiently intriguing, without imagining any. When the abandoned *Mary Celeste* was boarded by Mate Deveau and two seamen from the *Dei Gratia*, they found the ship well provisioned and, as they said, "fit to go round the world with a good crew and good sails." The pumps were in order, and after they had pumped her out she did not leak any more than the normal well-built wooden ship, for the water had come in from above, not below. It took the mate and his scratch crew of two (these were all the men that Captain Morehouse could spare him) three or four days to get the ship to rights. They had sails to shift, gear to prepare and reeve off, and with so few, watch-keeping of itself was work enough. The brigantine's wheel was loose, not lashed, but the steering gear was undamaged. The wooden binnacle had been knocked down—they thought by the sea—and the compass card inside it was destroyed. It took time to air and dry the bedding in the cabin (the captain's bed was unmade, and there was the imprint of a child's body upon it) and in the forecastle. The salvage crew got on with the practical work of sailing the ship, while they wondered about the possible causes of the mystery. Whatever it was, the ship had been abandoned in such great haste that the sailors had not even had time to pick up their pipes, the last things they would intentionally abandon.

What *had* happened? The mate of the *Dei Gratia* pondered the problem. Had the ship been drifting toward some rocks on the island of Santa Maria, forcing the captain and all hands to jump for their lives into their only boat and pull away rather than be drowned in the breakers? Maybe; but it was unlikely. The slate log, which was used for recording the navigational data of the voyage, day by day, showed no entries even hinting that such a thing could have happened. The relevant entry, indeed, showed the ship to be an estimated 6 miles off the land—though she might, of course, have drifted after that. Then what? A waterspout? Not in those seas. A submarine turbulence sufficient to alarm all hands? Maybe—but there was no evidence of any such thing. All the evidence was against it. If the *Mary Celeste*, through shift of cargo, or going on her beam ends in a squall, or being violently flung about by some underwater turbulence, had been subjected to unusual motion, her gear and cargo would have shown some evidence of it—plates tossed out of racks, open provision barrels overturned, under-bunk drawers fallen open, and so on. The open barrels, the plates in their racks, the fuel in the small galley bunkers, the tiers of full barrels in the cargo—all were in order.

Mate Deveau wondered why the long rope of the peak halliard was gone and, at the same time, the small lazarette hatch had been taken off. This hatch led to the ship's stores, such as her stock of spare coils of rope, spare sails, and so forth, but as far as he could see no such things had been taken. His seaman's sense led him to deduce, then, that the ship had been abandoned only *temporarily*—at least, that was the intention—and the missing length of the peak halliards had been unreeved and used as a line on which the boat could hang astern, while those in it waited either for some danger to pass (when they would haul themselves along the line and climb aboard again), or for whatever accident or calamity it was they feared actually to happen. Then at least they could escape in the boat. But then why was there no such line trailing over the stern? If it had been so used, why hadn't the crew recovered their ship again, since obviously she had avoided the calamity? Where was the line? In the excitement perhaps it was made fast with a slippery hitch, which slipped of its own accord when a strain came on it; and then the breeze got up, and the ship sailed away from her people, who could not catch her up again. She had had more sail set then, for two sails had blown out. Perhaps, ruminated Mate Deveau, the boat would still turn up. The weather had been bad, but not hopelessly so. Maybe the boat full of the *Mary Celeste's* crew had already arrived in the Azores, or somewhere on the coast of Portugal. Both places were comparatively close by.

In that the mate was wrong, but he did not know that then. He had no means of knowing that the *Mary Celeste's* boat and people would never be seen again.

He never gave a thought to mutiny, or murder, or drunken orgies leading to chaos and fatality. He left that kind of thing to lurid imaginations ashore, where they abounded, and got on with the job of bringing the little, woefully undermanned ship into port.

This he did so well that he was sailing her into Gibraltar a few days later. She came nosing in from sea, among the crowded ships at the anchorage, and the seamen aboard those ships looked at her curiously. Already something of her story was known, for the *Dei Gratia* had arrived before her.

In Gibraltar, as it turned out, there were some exceptionally lurid imaginations. The story-seekers got to work, for here was something—just what, they didn't know. Ghost ship, Flying Dutchman, silent survivor of midocean mutiny and murder—or just plain hard-working little brigantine, which had been abandoned by good seamen for what appeared to them good cause and then, in her turn, had chosen to abandon them? The odds, in Gibraltar, were on any of the former. After all, any of them was so much the better story.

Let us take a quiet look at this much publicized vessel and her crew, the better to appraise the real chances of bloody fate having overtaken them. The *Mary Celeste*, called variously brig, brigantine, hermaphrodite brig, and even sometimes barkentine or schooner, was a two-masted vessel square-rigged on the fore and fore-and-aft on the main. This is the rig which is commonly regarded in Europe as that of a brigantine, but minor variations caused different names to be used in America, such as half-brig. She was built by Joshua Dewis at Spencer's Island, Nova Scotia, and launched there in the spring of 1861 under the name of *Amazon*. She was extremely well built of the local woods—birch, beech, and maple underwater, with upper sides of best spruce and decks of pine. She was 99.3 feet long by 25.5 feet beam and 11.7 feet deep, giving her a gross tonnage (as first measured and registered) of just under 200 tons. Later she was rebuilt, to some extent, and her tonnage increased slightly, when she was under American registration. She was carvel-built with a billethead (no figurehead) and a square stern. At first she was just another trim little Bluenose brigantine, engaging in the hauling trades, deep-sea and coastal, as opportunity offered—now coals out of Sydney, Nova Scotia, now dried cod from some port in Newfoundland down to

Puerto Rico or somewhere else in the West Indies, and salt back, or maybe lumber coastwise or across to Europe, or petroleum in barrels from Philadelphia or Hoboken for anywhere round the Atlantic or Mediterranean seaboard. The *Amazon* was a stout ship and she did well, but she did not always make much money and she had the inevitable accident or two. She was thrown ashore once, but came off without vital damage.

In due course, after changing hands several times, new owners gave her a new name, *Mary Celeste.* (Her name was not *Marie Celeste,* as she has been often called.) She then belonged to Messrs. Winchester and Co. of New York. Her national flag was changed in 1868, four years before her historic voyage. A half share in her was owned by James H. Winchester, and a third by her master, one Capt. Benjamin S. Briggs, of Marion, Massachusetts. A few shares were held by two other gentlemen. Mr. Winchester was a highly respected New York merchant and an experienced shipowner. He thought well enough of his new ship to have extensive repairs made to her, and the deep single topsail, which had been rigged on her when first built, was changed to the modern form of double topsails. This made her easier to handle and possibly saved the wages of a man or two before the mast.

On November 7, 1872, the small vessel undocked quietly from Pier 50 on the East River in New York City, with a full cargo of alcohol in barrels—1,701 of them—bound for Genoa. The cargo was well stowed and properly secured, as such a cargo had to be. Like many other sailing ships then engaged in the same business, the *Mary Celeste* was not especially fitted for the carriage of liquids. Her hold had no ventilation beyond that which could be arranged by removing a hatch: but the barrels were jammed in by stevedores who knew their business, and wedges of wood here and there helped further to prevent them from moving. This alcohol was required in Genoa for the fortification of Italian wines, and is not to be confused with spirituous liquor. Since it was late fall, which is usually a rough time on the North Atlantic, the hatches were well battened down and everything well secured.

Captain Briggs, who had his wife and small daughter with him, was in command, and the ship carried two mates, a steward-cook, and four seamen—a small crew even for a vessel no larger than she was. But if it was small, it was adequate. Similar ships under many flags in Europe would have dispensed with the cook and the second mate, and probably with one of the seamen as well. None of the brigantine's gear was heavy. In small ships, it was the practice for all the crew to help work the ship and to help with the ship's work—these employments are different—as the occasion might demand it. Mates worked with the seamen, and the steward-cook had defined tasks in all-hands maneuvers, such as tending the foresheet (just outside his galley) when the ship was being tacked. Both mates were expected to be sailmakers and rough carpenters as well, at least with competence sufficient to cope with the day-to-day needs of the ship.

In view of the many baseless accusations made against all hands aboard, from Captain Briggs to his youngest seaman, it is worth taking a look at the facts of their lives and characters. Captain Briggs was aged thirty-eight, and he had been a sailing-ship master since he was twenty-one. The son of a respected shipmaster who was also known as something of a poet-philosopher, he was properly educated before going to sea. Three of his four brothers also were respected shipmasters. At the age of twenty-seven he had married a twenty-year-old girl named Sarah Elizabeth Cobb, at Marion, and she had been his boyhood friend and first sweetheart. Mrs. Briggs (against whom also there are many baseless accusations) was the daughter of a clergyman, the Reverend Leander Cobb of the Congregational Church at Marion, and it was he who performed the marriage service.

Like all good Yankee shipmasters' wives, the young Mrs. Briggs went with her husband straightaway to sea, and their honeymoon was a voyage to the Mediterranean in a schooner named the *Forest King*. This was in 1862, and the pair had sailed together almost ever since. It was Mrs. Briggs's habit to take a melodeon to sea with her, for relaxation. Looking after her two-year-old daughter and her husband kept her busily occupied. These New England wives who went with their menfolk to sea had as real a tradition of seafaring as the men themselves, and they were usually assets to the ships they sailed in. As for Captain Briggs, Horatio Sprague, the American Consul at Gibraltar—who had a great deal to do with the *Mary Celeste*—described him as a man who "bore the highest character for seamanship and correctness." Mr. Sprague had known Captain Briggs personally. Had there been any blemish on his record it would have been known. Shipmasters' records were closely watched in those days (and afterward) as affecting the rates charged for their ships' insurance.

The mate of the *Mary Celeste* was a good Brooklyn seaman named Albert G. Richardson, who came originally from that fine homeland of good sailing-ship men, the state of Maine. He had been much at sea, had served in the Coast Guard (which made him a veteran, and when he died his widow was paid a government pension until her death in Brooklyn in 1937) and was aged twenty-eight when he signed on for his last voyage. The second mate was a young Dane of twenty-five and, like the mate, was known as a competent seaman of good character. Although he had not sailed before with Captain Briggs (as the mate had done), his captain was known to be well pleased with him.

The captain of a small ship, with his wife and family aboard, was particular about his mates and about his cook-steward, too. This functionary's name was Head—Edward William Head, aged twenty-three years, born and bred in New York—and there was no other cook. (Some years ago I was sent to Liverpool to see a fellow who claimed that he had been cook of the *Mary Celeste,* and could tell her story. His name was not Head. He was an old fool who could not even name the brigantine's crew correctly, and I doubt whether he had ever been in any sailing ship throughout his useless life. Yet his "story" was seized upon avidly, and printed in a national newspaper, and later in a book. Anyone who took the time to consult the records would know that the cook-steward, or steward-cook, was Head, for there was correspondence regarding him in the files of the U.S. Consulate at Gibraltar, when his widow wrote to Consul Sprague to ask for the return to her of her dead husband's effects.)

The foremast hands, four in number, were all "Dutchmen," in the seafaring vernacular. Two were the brothers Lorenzen, young fellows from a small island in the Baltic, whence naturally they had taken early to the sea. These shared the same sea chest, and this chest was standing in the wet little forecastle of the ship when she was found, still packed carefully with their pathetic few possessions and their sailors' gear. The other two were young fellows by name Arian Martens and Gottlieb Goodschall, both of whom also had been Baltic seamen. Any seaman from Baltic coasters would know that he was well off in the *Mary Celeste.*

So much for ship and crew. Her career, after she was found abandoned, is as shipshape and straightforward. Mate Deveau sailed her to Gibraltar. There Captain Morehouse claimed his salvage, to which he was perfectly entitled. (He had spared his best officer and practically half his crew to bring in a crewless but cargo-laden vessel from the sea where he had found her: he had taken risks and performed a service.) But he reckoned without the shore authorities. As a derelict brought in from sea, the *Mary Celeste* came under the Admiralty Court and, with that, the Attorney General of the Colony of Gibraltar, a nosy, suspicious character named Flood. It was Flood who found the blood, and it was Flood who kept on finding more blood, and more bloody reasons for the indefinite delay of both ships. Becoming, in time, a little tired of all this, and having the care of his own ship as his first charge, Captain Morehouse sent the *Dei Gratia* on to the port of discharge where she was ordered, under the command of his mate, remaining in Gibraltar to watch the case and collect—he hoped—the salvage.

By this time Attorney General Flood, insisting that he had a murder mystery to solve, was well on his unnecessary warpath, and he censured Captain Morehouse for letting his mate take the ship when it was the mate who had boarded the *Mary Celeste* and knew most about her. But the mate had already been before the court for days, and had said all he knew. Mr. Flood had found the sword—bloodstained, of course—and the axe marks, and the "sinister" markings at the bows; and Mr. Flood seemed to be after more blood—anybody's. The theories of foul play seem all to have stemmed from him.

"The crew got at the alcohol, and in the fury of drunkenness, murdered the master and his wife and child, and the chief mate," wrote Mr. Flood, theorizing in a letter for the benefit of the Board of Trade in London, requesting them to take all appropriate action to trace the fate of these persons and the rest of the ship's company.

In the meanwhile, he hung on to the brigantine. The sword was regarded by him as a "clue" of the utmost importance. "It appeared to me to exhibit traces of blood, and to have been wiped before being returned into the scabbard," he told the board. Blood? He could not tell blood from rust. Wiped? Weeks after the sword had first been noted briefly by Mate Deveau and disregarded as of no importance, a man in Gibraltar could find evidence that it had been *wiped?* It is very odd. What is more odd, and even sinister, is that Mr. Flood called for an analyst's report on the stains on this famous sword, yet when he received the report he refused to divulge its contents. Years afterward, the reason was found. The analyst had made certain that those stains were rust.

Even then, Mr. Flood refused to be beaten—even with that suppressed evidence. The sword had not just been wiped off, he said in court, but wiped off *with a lemon,* used "to destroy and disguise the original marks of the blood which were once there." There was a minor sensation in the courtroom when the Attorney General delivered himself of this curious and completely baseless accusation, but Mate Deveau (whom he seemed to suspect as the arch-murderer) looked back at him unperturbed, wondering no doubt whatever it was that was ailing the man.

"I saw the sword aboard the *Mary Celeste,*" said the mate. "I found the sword under the captain's berth. I took it out from there. I looked at it—drew it out from its sheath. There was nothing remarkable on it. I think I put it back where I found it, or somewhere near there." These straightforward words of the mate disposed of the sword as far as he was concerned, and he stood by his statements.

Then there was the blood on deck. What blood? More of Mr. Flood's blood.

"I saw no marks of blood on the deck," said Mate Deveau, who was the first to look. "I noticed no marks or traces of blood on the deck. We never washed the decks, nor scraped them. We had not men enough for that. The sea washed the decks."

Sea water contains chloric acid which would dissolve the blood, said Mr. Flood.

"It did not occur to me that there had been any act of violence," the mate concluded his evidence and cross-examination. "There was nothing to induce one to believe or to show that there had been any violence."

Mr. Flood would have had the cargo tampered with, too, but again, it seemed to be only he who saw evidence of that. When it comes to matters to do with ships, I prefer the word of seamen. It appears that the Attorney General was a man notorious in Gibraltar for his lurid imagination. Captain Winchester, who came from New York to look after his interests, left again after some time. He had heard a report, among other alarming statements, that his arrest for conspiracy was not outside the bounds of possibility. It was expensive and largely useless to wait in Gibraltar until the long-winded court at last made up its mind, for Mr. Flood was determined to find a victim.

He never did: at last, after many weeks, the *Mary Celeste* was released to go on to Genoa with her cargo, and the *Dei Gratia* received her salvage award. It was a miserable one, in the circumstances—not a fifth of the value of ship and cargo saved. And, as a crowning meanness, Captain Morehouse was charged with the costs of analyzing the "blood" on the sword, the blood that was not blood, the analysis which remained filed away in legal secrecy for the following fourteen years.

Frederick Flood, it seems, was that abomination in the legal or any other profession, a little frog in a little pond who thought he saw a chance to puff himself out big, and flogged that chance *ad nauseam*. It was he who started the ball rolling which built up the endless mystery of the *Mary Celeste*, and not those who had found the ship. Then a man named Conan Doyle heard his story and went on from there, and the thing has been snowballing ever since. We know enough, I think, about the *Mary Celeste* to have a shrewd idea of the solution of her mystery. What I would like to know is some more about Mr. Flood.

As for the mystery, I think the solution lies in that cargo, and the significant fact that the forehatch was open. The inference is that it was fumes from the cargo which so alarmed Captain Briggs and his crew that they hastily took to the boat. Either rumbling noises down below were the sign that caused them to throw the fore hatch off, or it blew off. Fearing an explosion which would blow them all sky-high, naturally they rushed for the boat, pulled it from its temporary stowage and pushed it over the side, throwing in a few provisions, the chronometer, sextant, and the ship's papers (which were all missing), and jumped in the boat themselves. At the same time, somebody was trying to break out a coil of line from the lazarette to act as towline for the boat, in the case the ship did not blow up (Captain Briggs was part owner of her, and Yankee instinct, if nothing else, would never permit him finally to abandon his property if there were a chance of its survival). At the same time, another crew member—possibly the mate—thought of the better idea of using the peak halliards. Down they came, quickly unrove. Stand from under, there! Down swished the halliards on deck. Out rushed the captain, with his wife and child and handful of chronometer, papers, and so forth. Along came the cook-steward with the provisions. More rumblings from the gases in the hold. Hurry, hurry! Over the side!

Mr. Mate now, catch a turn with that line on the pin there! Throw the bight overboard! Into the boat, all hands! Shove off! Lively, now!

And, in the haste, not just the bight of the halliards went, but all of it, for the vital turn around the pin was overlooked. So the boat dropped astern and kept on dropping astern. The wind got up, and the sea with it. The ship sailed on, and the boat—with the captain, the mates, the cook-steward, Mrs. Briggs and the little Miss Briggs, the German brothers, and the rest of them—was left to fight it out with the sea. And lost.

The loss of a boat full of people, after all, is commonplace enough, in the North Atlantic or any other ocean. Who could find ten bodies, tossed about in the sea, or identify pieces of wood from a small ship's boat?

"Albert G. Richardson sailed in our employ for about two years and the said Albert G. Richardson was lost, drowned from our brig *Mary Celeste* on or about Nov. 24, 1872. . . ." So read the affidavit of Messrs. Winchester and Co., the evidence of death which gained Widow Richardson her pension. Drowned from our brig—no bloodcurdling mysteries, no wild outbreak of drunken mutineers flailing a rusty old sword. That was the seaman's view of the *Mary Celeste* mystery at the time; and it still is.

In spite of that, I don't doubt in the least that *Titanics*, *Lusitanias*, and *Andrea Dorias* may come and go, but the "*Marie Celeste*" will sail on forever, still with that uneaten breakfast on the saloon table, the boats at the davits, the warm impress of live bodies in the bunks, and with murderers swinging swords and axes as her crew.

SOME ADVENTURERS

17

AT any one time, at least a dozen small yachts or craft of one sort or another are crossing, or have just completed crossing, or are about to cross, the North Atlantic Ocean. In summer the number could well be fifty and at times, when a transatlantic yacht race is in progress, as many as a hundred. Ever since that tough old Cape Horner, Captain Joshua Slocum, showed the modern way, when in 1895 he took his cockleshell of a *Spray* across from Gloucester, Massachusetts, by way of the Azores to Gibraltar on a trial run prior to sailing round the world, the yachtsmen, the globe wanderers, the retired shipmasters, schoolmasters, and masters of no trade at all have been following in his tracks, or trying to. Captain Slocum was a Nova Scotian, like so many good sailors, and he knew what he was doing. His ship was staunch and seaworthy though small, and he was an experienced sailing-ship seafarer.

Some of the others have been nothing of the kind, and their ships have varied from catamarans through rubber rafts to 18-foot sloops, some seaworthy, some not. Many of these voyagers have not been yachtsmen in the true sense of that word at all. By yachtsman (which is a very wide term) one should understand the meaning to be a man, or a woman, really interested and competent in the splendid sport of sailing—it may be as crew member in some ocean racer anywhere from 22 to 82 feet long; or maybe in a 12-foot dinghy, either as helmsman or as crew. It is not yachtsmen who attempt what the seafarer may regard as foolish things with ships. There is an increasing sense of responsibility among the fraternity, which, by the very exercise of its thrilling sport, learns very quickly the abiding lesson of the power of the elements. These odd navigators usually fly some yacht-club burgee, if for no other reason because it is required that they have been accepted by some club somewhere in order to be granted proper documentation for their craft. Some of them have indeed been odd fellows, but they have made their passages, and most have survived at least to write a book about it.

The Atlantic has been crossed by a man alone in a small rubber dinghy not much longer than he was, by a trio of Canadians with a raft of logs lashed together, by a man and his wife driving an amphibious jeep, by men in old lifeboats, small motorboats, and a folding canoe. Two men rowed across in a dory some years before Slocum sailed. In short, the North Atlantic has been crossed by just about everything except a boy in a bathtub or a man riding an aquatic bicycle. One hesitates to mention even these deficiencies, for fear some more than usually foolhardy optimist may feel inspired to set forth and remedy them.

It takes courage, and stamina, and good rugged individual qualities in abundance to make these small-boat crossings. I might have said that it took considerable ability, had it not been convincingly demonstrated by more than one ocean voyager that he sailed equipped with nothing of the kind—no special ability to navigate, little or no knowledge of seamanship in any of its branches, no experience of deep-sea cruising at all. The Lord has been very kind to some of these fellows. It is odd that it was, in the end, Captain Slocum that He drowned. The old Nova Scotiaman has been missing in the North Atlantic since 1909, when he sailed in the *Spray* from Bristol, Rhode Island, bound for the Orinoco River. Others have lost their lives, too, but few by comparison with the numbers who have successfully made their voyages. After all, if you leave Europe in the good weather season and sail west (from dawn to sunset) you are bound to fetch up somewhere in America, if you sail far enough, and all you have to avoid is foundering on the way and shipwreck at the other end.

The other way it is even easier, for the westbound little ship is wise to sail the long way round, down in the trade winds. The eastbound mariner, who likewise has a substantial landfall in front of him, also has a preponderance of westerly winds to assist him, to say nothing of the Gulf Stream Drift. More than one small ship has made that passage by herself, with no one aboard at all—ships like the Grand Banks fishing schooner *Marion J. Douglas* which, abandoned by her crew on the Banks because they thought her to be sinking, sailed off by herself and fetched up off the Scilly Islands some weeks later. Some dories, lost on the Banks, have drifted across to the Western Isles, too, but there has been nothing in them but the dead bodies of their dorymen. It is traditional for the dorymen, who face death daily, never to go prepared for long passages. To do so would be considered a poor outlook.

Now and again a well-found yacht like the *Spray* goes missing in the Atlantic. One such is the French *Mic*, which sailed to cross the Bay of Biscay a year ago and has not since been seen, though a piece of a yacht cabin later came ashore near Brigneau. Lashed to this was a camera bearing the name of Forin, which was the name of one of the six persons sailing in the *Mic*. The camera was loaded with film, some of which had been exposed. When this was developed it showed a part of the Irish coast, which was good evidence as to where the *Mic* had been, and another picture showed a group of the yacht's passengers smiling happily. The American yacht *Home, Sweet Home* is likewise missing, somewhere not far from Bermuda, and not even as much as a piece of the cabin top or an identifiable photograph has ever been washed up anywhere from her.

Now and again there is a grim little signal to Lloyd's such as this:

> LE TAIFUN (yacht).—Fortaleza, Sept. 13.—Vice-consul informs sailing boat *Le Taifun*, crewed by Canadian citizens Martin and Theodore Hudec, on voyage Santos for Panama, unreported since Aug. 21. Radio last night announced two bodies washed ashore on Pernambuco coast, identity unknown.

An odder mystery was reported on the arrival of a small yacht at Bridgetown, Barbados, from the Canary Islands, not long ago, with a German student named Hanner aboard. Hanner had sailed from Las Palmas with a Swiss couple. One night, when about half-way over, he was not called for his watch. The ship was very quiet. Waking, he went on deck. There was no one there. He searched the ship at once. There was no one anywhere. He had heard no cries. He went about and searched over the yacht's track all the following day, but his passengers had disappeared. The weather was not bad at the time.

Not all reports of tragedy end like that. There was, for instance, the case of a curious little vessel named *Orenda,* in which two young Canadians sailed from Canada to the English Channel in the fall of 1956. The *Orenda,* which from the look of photographs of her was a home-built and somewhat homely little vessel about 17 feet long, sailed from Montreal in mid-June, 1956, bound for Dartmouth, England. Their vessel leaked, so they put in at North Sydney, Nova Scotia, for repairs. Not daunted by the shaking-up their minute ship had already given them, the Canadians sailed again on September 1, which was a little late for an Atlantic crossing so far north in so small a vessel. They soon met with wind enough, and more than one hard gale.

In one of these gales their vessel was met by the liner *America.* From the liner no sign of life could be seen aboard the *Orenda.* Captain Fender, a kindly and most expert seaman who was in command of the *America,* stopped and had a good look. The *Orenda's* sails were dragging in the water. The tiller was lashed. The vessel looked an abandoned wreck. Captain Fender blew the *America's* great siren, for if there were people still aboard who needed rescuing, he meant to rescue them. No one showed. He blew again: still there was no sign of life. If there was no one to rescue, there was no point in remaining any longer, for the liner had a schedule to keep. Captain Fender continued his voyage, reporting the incident, and there were fears for the safety of the two young men.

But a fortnight or so later, another steamer—the tramp *Maribianca* —on her way across the North Atlantic, sighted the *Orenda* again, not in much better shape but this time with a human figure at the tiller. The yacht was very close and, the weather being good, she actually came right alongside, and the *Maribianca* handed over some provisions, and the wherewithal to do some sail repairs, which the *Orenda* needed. Then the ships parted, and the *Orenda* disappeared again. Fears were once more being felt for her safety (the North Atlantic weather was then extremely bad) but, in a week or two, along came the little *Orenda*, ambling upon a fine morning into the English Channel. A helicopter, going out with a radio reporter to get her story, dropped the reporter in the sea, which improved the story but not the reporter. A newspaperman, venturing out the same morning in a launch, boarded the vessel only to find her motion so excessive that he promptly became violently seasick. The *Orenda* had to divert from her intended port of arrival and run in to land this unhappy pair.

It seemed that, when the *America* blew her siren, the *Orenda's* crew had had such a hard night of it—not for the first time—that they were flaked out below, and not the Last Trump itself would have wakened them. But, apart from this tiredness and the sloppy way they had left their sails, there was nothing wrong with them.

They followed closely on the heels of yet another group of young Canadians, who had arrived about a month earlier at Falmouth in—rather, "on"—a craft made of lashed-up logs. The log-lashings, on which there were a bit of a small house, a tripod mast, a float for lifesaving, and a cat, was called *L'Egare II*. Like their compatriots in the *Orenda*, the French Canadians of *L'Egare* had made two attempts at the job. Their first was made from Canada in the summer of 1955, but their first raft broke up after drifting for 66 days. On the second attempt, they sailed from Halifax on May 24, 1956, and drifted into the Channel some three months later. Their vessel was fastened with cordage and wooden pegs. She was about 17 feet by 13 feet, and the house was 4 feet high. The original crew had been four men, but one suffered so constantly from seasickness that he was transferred to a Canadian schooner fishing on the Banks, and went home. Like the *Orenda, L'Egare II* met more than her share of bad weather, and was assisted by a chance meeting with a steamer in midocean. When she arrived at Falmouth her crew said they had had about "as much as they could stand," but they appeared fit and well. The cat got into trouble for landing in England without permission but, as is the way of cats, it promptly disappeared.

It was a Frenchman, Dr. Alain Bombard, who sailed the strangest raft, or rubber dinghy or whatever the thing might be called. He went the other way—down before the trade winds, to the westward, from the Mediterranean to Barbados. Dr. Bombard's was one of the few such voyages which had a really useful purpose, and that was to experiment with some new ideas for the survival of castaways at sea. It was the doctor's idea that a great many people died unnecessarily when shipwrecked, simply because they did not know how to survive at sea without what they imagined to be sufficient food and water. It was possible, he thought, to sustain life from the sea, sieving up the surface plankton for food and drinking moisture pressed from fish, and a little water from the sea. When he sailed, his *L'Hérétique* (which was the name of the dinghy) carried a sealed tin of emergency rations. When he landed in Barbados 65 days later, that tin was still sealed. Dr. Bombard had made his point. The only occasion when his physique was upset on the whole crossing, he said, was when a kindly steamship's captain, having taken him aboard for a shower and a yarn in midocean, insisted that he eat a light meal. He did, and it griped him.

Dr. Bombard's *L'Hérétique,* a "sort of horseshoe-shaped inflatable rubber sausage" 15 feet long and 6 feet wide, is now in the National Maritime Museum in Paris, and I have had a good look at its incredible fragility there. The bow is slightly raised, the stern quite open. The little vessel had a single light mast which could spread a pocket handkerchief of a sail, in good weather—rather like the tiny sails which fighter pilot's dinghies set when they had to ditch in the sea during the war. She had a couple of small leeboards, like a Dutch yacht, and she steered with a bit of an oar over the stern. When I saw her, *L'Hérétique* was not much battered, for all her 65 days in the North Atlantic, but I would hate to use the vessel for a summer's afternoon excursion on the Isis at Oxford. As for drinking sea water, which the doctor said he did, many seamen hold doggedly to the view that to do such a thing is fatal, no matter what any scientist may say. Even if he did use himself as a human guinea pig and spend 65 days in the North Atlantic to make his point, they are still not convinced. They remember grimly too many war experiences, when for a man to start drinking sea water was the beginning of the end.

Yet, during the war, there was the curious case of the Chinese steward from the torpedoed ship *Benlomond* who survived on a raft for 133 days, without any of the aids that Dr. Bombard took with him, and with no emergency rations in a sealed tin, or anything else. What did he live on? What did he eat and drink? Old-fashioned seafarers have a slight suspicion that it might have been some of his shipmates.

One after another—rafts (popular after the *Kon-Tiki* voyage, which was made in the Pacific), yachts, either homemade or the products of leading naval architects and sometimes sailed by the architects themselves; some built to provide seagoing wanderers with a home, or to make the reputation of a fresh idea in design—over the Atlantic they all go. Some sail east and some sail west. Some intend to continue round the world; some don't. A woman alone in a 23-foot sloop (Mrs. Ann Davison in her *Felicity Ann*); an outstanding yachtsman alone in an 18-footer (Patrick Ellam in his *Sopranino*); another famous yachtsman making almost a habit of Atlantic crossings in sundry small yachts (Edward Allcard in his *Temptress*, and assorted craft); Captain Romer in a Klepper foldboat; sixty-year-old Capt. Ludwig Schlimbach, retired from command in the Hamburg-America Line and crossing the Atlantic for a change in a slip of a yawl called the *Stoertebeker* (he was only 57 days sailing to New York from Lisbon, the trade-wind way); an American merchant seaman named Joffs in a 7-ton Bermuda cutter; a Coast Guard officer named Deal in a double-ended sloop; a Breton fisherman named Jacques-Yves de Toumelin in a home-built cutter called *Kurun;* a Finnish seaman named Givikoski in a little thing which he navigated, apparently, with an old sextant, an older watch, and a receiving radio set; a seventy-year-old Australian civil engineer named Sparkes in a 40-foot ketch which he and his wife had been sailing from Sydney, New South Wales, for *eight years;* a retired British admiral aged seventy-four in a 7-tonner with a crew of one girl; three little English yachts coming home from the Bermuda Race—there are hundreds more! Old lifeboats, new lifeboats (including a new Danish type enclosed like a submarine, which launches itself from sinking ships and is said to be unsinkable itself), old sloops, new yawls, catamarans of revolutionary design and ancient Bristol Channel pilot cutters, vessels sailed by lone men and lone women (but only one of the latter, and never one with a group that was wholly feminine), by family parties (these are rare birds), small groups and large groups, writers and artists, paying guests and professional adventurers, migrants and escapees—the crews are as varied as the ships.

They all share one thing in common, and that is the spirit of adventure. I would think they share one other feature, too, and that is stomachs of cast iron. I have tried those little ships on more passages than one and they always make me horribly seasick when there is any kind of a sea running—and that is the greatest hardship of all. I have made a couple of Atlantic Ocean races and a cruise or two, in yachts, though I prefer ships. Yacht racing in the open sea is a grand and exhilarating sport, but wet and tough, and sometimes it can be uncomfortable beyond imagining. There are extraordinarily grueling yacht races going on frequently in the North Atlantic—sometimes right across, as from Bermuda to Plymouth or from Newport, Rhode Island, to Marstrand in Sweden, a 3,500-mile course which seven yachts raced over in the summer of 1955, or from the United States to Spain: others from Newport to Bermuda (in which tough race there were 98 entrants in 1956), or round the Fastnet Rock off Eire from Cowes, or from England to Santander, or Corunna, or Lisbon, or Madeira; or from a convenient port in the southern United States to Havana in Cuba—which test the grit, the guts, the skill, and the all-round abilities of considerable numbers of volunteer yachtsmen in a way no landsman would ever dream of. Helping to crew a hard-run Yankee ocean racer, commanded by some competent and determined amateur mariner whose skill is matched only by his tremendous ability for doing without sleep and the inexhaustible energy with which he drives himself and the cheerful gang of fellow enthusiasts along with him, is a hard life! It has compensations—great compensations—but, speaking strictly for myself, I prefer my seagoing discomfort to be unavoidable, and I hate being sick. Cruising is a different thing and can be wholly delightful. By dint of grim experiment, I have discovered that 60 feet is my minimum waterline length for the open sea. I like a deck that I can walk on, and a ship that does not cavort and gyrate about the sea like a switchback car gone mad: but I greatly respect those yachtsmen and others who, knowing exactly what a really tough life they so cheerfully face, still go bravely out to sea and make their great little voyages.

As for the voyage-making in the Atlantic, there is nothing exceptionally difficult about that. There are good books of sailing directions, and charts, for the coastlines of the whole world, except those sections which are locked behind impenetrable ice. Yachts are good ships in these days, and there is no reason why a staunch and well-found little yacht should not go anywhere even if she be barely long enough to provide stretching-out room for the lone mariner who sails her (as the *Sopranino* is), or so small that her cabin top must be detachable and so shaped that in ports it can be her dinghy. Size has nothing whatever to do with seaworthiness. In some ways, little ships are safest. Their greatest risk, I'd say, was being run down by a steamship unable to see them, but they can avoid that hazard simply by keeping off the steamer lanes. Steamers make their ocean voyages along clearly defined routes nowadays: away from those sea lanes, the ocean is probably emptier than it has ever been since shortly after Columbus first crossed to the Indies.

The lone navigator is perfectly safe, turning into his tossing bunk night after night for a couple of months, if he likes, while his small ship runs before the trades which blow her quietly and slowly over the Atlantic. He can heave to at night if he feels like it, as the old East Indiamen used to do. Who is to stop him? Cooking, fishing, tending his vessel, a bit of navigation, and admiring the beauty of dawns and sunsets—he has plenty to occupy his time. It is better to go alone than to take a chance even on a known companion. A man ought to know how he can get on with himself: two is an awkward number, and three can be worse, for a mutual sharing of the spirit of adventure in the shape of a dimly comprehended and lengthy voyage, across what to the participants are unknown seas, can lead to mutual hatred and even murder (as it has done on more than one occasion). When the wanderer reaches the islands of his dreams, he does not have to pack his suitcase and march ashore. His suitcase is his ship, which travels with him. She is his hotel, his restaurant, his interest, and his home, and the real joys of travel can be his as they can rarely be to the wanderer who books himself by the orthodox routes and discovers the disadvantages after he has bought his ticket.

There was a time, lasting for three years and more immediately after World War II, when many strange little vessels, converted fishing boats, old trawlers, discarded minor war vessels, and the like, were pressed into service on long voyages, some transatlantic, some to South Africa or to Australia. Old Thames barges, old coasting schooners, and all kinds of craft were used for the purposes of reuniting scattered families, of getting migrants to new homes, or demobilized servicemen back to their own countries. There was a severe shortage of passenger ships at the time. Some of these small ships were used by fleeing refugees, coming from countries which had been overrun, where life was no longer possible for many. I saw one of these vessels at Dover once, in 1947. She was a Baltic-type, double-ended fishing boat, perhaps 35 feet long, and she was crowded with men, women, and children, little blond babies and all. There were, I think, twenty-three people aboard in five families, as well as a large crew. They were from Estonia and Latvia, and they seemed to be quiet, soft-spoken people. The crew were fishermen who were also escaping, and they knew their business. The little ship, which had no papers of any kind, was allowed to continue on her voyage in due course. She was bound, I think, toward Miami, or it may have been Buenos Aires. A few weeks later I read at Lloyd's that she had hit the coast of Portugal in a storm, and everyone aboard was drowned.

Most were luckier than that. In 1948, a party of twenty-three Estonians crossed successfully in another fishing boat from the

Baltic via Stornoway to Canada, where they were accepted as good migrants despite their lack of documents. Their ship was called the *Astrid*, and she, too, was about 30 feet long. At least three similar groups of refugees sailed themselves in small boats successfully to Miami, between 1947 and 1948. Two more such vessels, the *Elsa* and the *Olinda*, made Buenos Aires, packed with seventy refugees between them. Yet another was sailed from the Baltic across the Atlantic and made her landfall on Cape Cod, as the *Mayflower* had done. In something of the same spirit, the vessel went on to Plymouth hoping for a warm welcome there to the land of liberty. But—according to the story, at any rate—they were sent away, because Plymouth was not a legal port of entry for ships arriving from abroad, and they had to make for Boston. They found their liberty, for all that, and they have done very well.

Not all these escaping parties have been innocent. Immediately after the war, at least one party of staunch Quislings got out of Norway in a small yacht, said to be registered in the name of *Solbris*. A vessel of this name had touched at Weymouth, well filled with close-lipped Norwegians and flying no flag. She sailed allegedly for Vigo from there after a delay of twelve hours and, as far as I know, she was not traced again.

There were the inevitable swindlers, too, who exploited the ship shortage to their own temporary advantage. There was one fellow with an American accent who did very well out of arranging secret passages for war brides by fast motor torpedo boat which, he said, he had acquired from Admiralty. These boats, he declared to those foolish enough to listen, would reach New York within three days of leaving the west coast of England. The fare was $750. There were only two formalities—cash down, and strict secrecy. He explained that his enterprise was conducted without the usual inconveniences of exit permits, clearances, visas, and all that sort of bothersome thing. He did very well with the advance fares, for there was a large supply of brides. Then it occurred to someone, not having heard of any bride who had actually made the passage, to wonder just how so small a craft as an MTB could make the run to New York within three days. How could she carry the fuel and the passengers besides?

Or the fuel for so long a run at all? A very few inquiries served to blow that scheme sky-high; but there were others.

Most such schemes for cooperative voyages out of Europe were genuine, organized by servicemen anxious to return abroad, who financed old ships bought at top prices by inducing fellow optimists to put up some capital and share the other risks of the voyage. Many sailed, but the majority did not get very far. Freetown was about as far as most of those bound for South Africa ever reached, and several parties of cooperating migrants were stranded there. Some decrepit vessels did not even leave England. In the end, the British authorities stepped in and prevented such vessels from sailing. That was simple enough. After all, if anyone may buy a yacht and—provided the necessary documents are obtained—sail or try to sail it more or less anywhere in the free world, it is a straightforward matter for government departments to put a stop to such enterprises if they feel that they should do such a thing. All they have to do is to insist on strict compliance with the letter of the law in, say, the matter of safety appliances—fire-fighting, and lifeboats and the like, in size, equipment, and number sufficient to accommodate everyone aboard. In most small yachts, if any number of people is to be carried, this is impossible.

On the other side of the North Atlantic, the United States Coast Guard has more than enough work, at times, rescuing would-be voyagers who get outside, bound for Europe or more probably (according to themselves) round the world, and then promptly find their ships opening up or their sails blowing away and themselves otherwise in serious trouble, and call loudly for help. This they have been in the habit of doing by the dozen every summer, and the Coast Guard has pressed for supervision before sailing rather than rescue afterward. Its rescue facilities are for those who really need them.

Come to think of it, the old lads who sailed a hundred years ago and more were more like the real adventurers—fellows like Nat Palmer, who took a little 40-foot sloop called the *Hero* out of Stonington, Connecticut, one July day in 1820, and sailed off down both Atlantics to the Antarctic continent, where he celebrated his twenty-first birthday. Then he got himself a cargo of sealskins at the South Shetland Islands and, with a grand pioneering voyage behind him and a paying cargo in the hold, sailed cheerfully home again. And those indefatigable colonists who built themselves a couple of small vessels out of the wreck of a larger, and the local wood, at Bermuda in the early seventeenth century, and then sailed their handiwork over to Jamestown and thence back to Europe, made stirring voyages in craft which, in seaworthiness or anything else, could not compare with a well-built modern yacht.

In the early days of the Atlantic story, such little craft existed by the hundred, and got on with tough and necessary voyages as mere "routine." In a way they were fortunate, for the true spirit of adventure was with them always. Today our yachtsmen, ocean racers, and all others do their best to recapture that spirit, and they do magnificently.

TWO WORLD WARS

18

FIFTY THOUSAND merchant seamen lie dead on the Atlantic floor because of the two world wars—50,000 merchant seamen from 6,000 ships, to say nothing of the crews of war vessels, whereof 600 German U-boats were sunk in the 1939–1945 war alone, most of them with all hands. Fifty thousand merchant seamen! Burned to death, blown to death, frozen to death, starved to death, drowned: when the poor men's names from World War II were to be added to the already ghastly total on the British Merchant Navy War Memorial on Tower Hill in London, the memorial had to be doubled and then further extended, and the work of adding tablets enough to carry the new names caused the remodeling of the square. These were the names only of those lost at sea and still in the sea—not all the dead, by any means. No passengers, no naval men, no auxiliary gunners' names were there, no one who died subsequently ashore, from dreadful wounds.

In World War I enemy submarines sank 4,837 merchant vessels which grossed something over 11,000,000 tons, and they sank these ships at the average rate of 95 a month. In World War II the U-boats sank 2,775 merchant vessels of roughly 14½ million tons, at an average monthly rate of 40 ships, grossing 215,000 tons. The 40 World War II ships were of an average 5,200 tons, compared with an average 2,300 tons for the first war. If the U-boat fleet of

World War II had maintained the rate of sinkings which their less efficient and far shorter-ranged brethren did in the first, the Allies would have been defeated by that alone, but in the second war the convoy system was put into effect at once. More than that—aircraft, both long-range and carrier-based, took a very effective part in the Atlantic war from 1939 to 1945, and they made the U-boats' task much more difficult, as well as taking a considerable toll on their own. The second war was very much a scientists' war, too, and the Allied scientists, on the whole, stayed one jump ahead of the German.

It may have been a scientists' war at sea, looked at objectively, but that fact made no difference to the 50,000 dead seamen. Electric searching devices, "pinging" under the sea to echo upon the submerged U-boats' hulls or sweeping methodically either from aircraft or surface vessel to echo on a floating conning tower or even a raised periscope, wonderfully sensitive listening apparatus which could tune in on the electric intercommunication service of a closed-up U-boat's crew hundreds of miles away, new weapons which flung patterns of deadly high-explosive depth charges over the whole area where a submarine was known to be, and so made at least its damage certain—all these helped the Allied side.

The enemy replied with better, faster, bigger submarines, with better, faster, more dangerous torpedoes, with the device known as the schnorkel, a sort of tube by means of which a submarine could remain submerged for days on end, or weeks. Acoustic torpedoes which aimed themselves at the propeller noise of ships and "homed" on the ships, anti-asdic devices which allowed the submarines for a time to elude the searching ping of the surface hunters, an instrument which permitted the U-boats to detect radar search and so take avoiding action—these helped the submarines. But from a seaman's viewpoint, it was a cold-blooded, frightful, horrible war, this contest between the submarines and the merchantmen and their escorts. To them it was a war of sudden ghastly explosions in the middle of a gale-filled night and a great ship disintegrating in hellish fire and flames, slipping quickly—but never quickly enough—from the ranks of her convoy while horrified brother seamen watched, and the little escorts rushed to the attack; of stricken ships, mortally wounded, left behind the onward-moving convoy to die alone, for the convoys must go on. There was a dreadful inhumanity about it all. The ships looked as if there were no human beings aboard them as they steamed dispassionately along, or stumbled and sank. But it was flesh and blood that suffered and died.

I remember an old friend of mine, a fine seaman who had been master of the four-masted bark *Jordanhill*, in which he had raised a family. Retired when the war began, the old man went to sea again then, and shipped as master of a tanker. He was westbound in ballast in an early convoy in the war. Two tankers ahead of him in line, his eldest son was mate of another tanker. For a thousand miles they steamed in safety, zigzagging according to set pattern, steaming at best speed lightless at night, escaping collision with fellow steamers by a hair's breadth more often than enough, heart in mouth and great hulls all but grinding into one another as they pitched and rolled and wallowed across the ocean. The perils of a blacked-out convoy were very real, without the intervention of any U-boats. One dusk the attack came. The U-boats were picking off the tankers. First one, then another. The old man saw his son's tanker go up in flames. He saw a boat get away. It dropped back close by his own ship. He looked into it, peering from his high bridge. In it he saw his son, bloodstained from some dreadful wound. He had only an instant to see his son there before having to zigzag away; the son looked up, seeing him. Then his ship sped on, the boat dropped back, and the father never saw his son again.

Later there were rescue ships, which followed convoys to save their boats and offer succor to the distressed. But the U-boats sank them, too, for they were also targets. Nor were the U-boats the only menace. In home waters there were mines. In the nearer waters of the Channel and the North Sea, when the Germans held all Europe from the North Cape to the coast of Spain, there were attacks from fast torpedo boats which lurked near the swept channels by night, where the long lines of the convoys must pass, and dashed suddenly among them with gunfire and torpedo when the chance came. There was also attack from short-range aircraft. Farther at sea, long-range aircraft carried on the enemy offensive. The attacks from aircraft were a new menace. Merchantmen understood the U-boats, and hated them. But there was one case at least where some of those on the bridge actually waved cheerfully to an enemy aircraft which was about to attack them, because at that time seamen had not bothered to learn to distinguish one aircraft from another. It was a big Focke-Wulf 200 which was coming in to bomb, but the seamen saw that she had four engines, and that was sufficient for them. They thought the enemy to be a friendly flying boat, and waved. It seems incredible, but this incident occurred on the bridge of the 40,000-ton steamer *Empress of Britain,* and the Focke-Wulf put an end to her—not directly, for U-boats finished her off when she was in tow. But the airplane dropped the bombs which so damaged her that she was later a helpless target, and it summoned the U-boats to the final kill.

After that, the merchantmen, and too many of the naval escorts as well, opened up regardless on friendly aircraft sent to help escort them, for fear that these also might be enemies, and the seamen laid down stringent rules for the airmen to obey in order that they should always be known as friends. Friendly aircraft were not to approach any ship within less than a certain distance, to make their identity known to escort vessels, not to come suddenly out of cloud, and so forth and so on. The airmen also had their problems and had no control over clouds; minor battles between friendly aircraft and ships happened, now and again, almost until the end of the war.

The undersea battle against the merchantmen in World War I was bad enough, but the merchantmen had more of a chance then because submarines were comparatively slow when submerged, they had limited range, and they were compelled to surface at night in order to recharge their batteries. Because it was their habit to surface and destroy smaller vessels by gunfire, for a time there was some measure of success against them by the use of so-called Q-ships, decoy vessels which, while they looked like ordinary merchantmen, in fact bristled with guns hidden behind bulkheads, in false deckhouses, and that sort of thing. When attacked, the function of these decoys was first to lure the U-boats within fatal range and then, suddenly dropping the false bulkheads and the sides of the deckhouses, to open up a devastating fire in which the U-boat could not survive. But a U-boat did survive such an attack, and went home to report it as a most unfair proceeding. After that, merchantmen large and small were apt to be destroyed by underwater attack on sight. In World War II Q-ships had no future. Indeed, in the shape of converted merchantmen used as raiders, it was the Germans who made best use of auxiliary cruisers. The British were too often heroically lost, because (said the seamen) they were fighting the wrong war. The Germans used large, fast, long-range, and very well armed merchant vessels as surface raiders. One of these outfought and sank an Australian cruiser. Some carried their own torpedo boats and aircraft.

By August, 1943, Axis surface raiders, both warships and converted merchantmen but mainly the latter, had sunk at least 190 ships of a total tonnage of more than a million. They took good care to operate away from the North Atlantic, and their sinkings were mainly in the South Atlantic, the Indian, and South Pacific oceans. They were accustomed to shadow by day and attack by night. At least one of them was brutally used, the policy aboard being to sink without trace all merchantmen she met, even to the extent of machine-gunning any possible survivors. For her, dead men told no tales and reported the positions or manner of attack of no vessels, but most of the raiders did what they could to pick up survivors. I knew one of the raider captains, both before and after the war, a Capt. Carl Kircheiss, who was a mild sort of man who sailed small boats about the North Atlantic as a hobby and, in the end, was knocked down and killed by an automobile outside his home in Hamburg while trying to cross the road.

Captain Kircheiss would not have machine-gunned survivors; but there were others. One of the most remarkable of survivors' accounts, among many such stories, is the story of the men from the German raider known as Raider 16, which was sunk by the British cruiser *Dorsetshire*. The survivors took to rubber rafts and boats, in which they were towed by two U-boats several hundred miles across the South Atlantic to a rendezvous with a German supply ship. The supply ship, in her turn, was later sunk. Again the survivors took to rafts and boats. Again the two faithful U-boats, being aware of their fate, took the boats and rafts in tow until they met two more U-boats, when they shared the several hundred men among the four of them and began the long voyage back through both Atlantics toward France. Fifty men were taken below in each U-boat, and fifty lived on deck in their rafts in order that, whenever the U-boat had to dive, the rafts would float off. In this way the flotilla stood toward the area of the Azores, where they met some Italian U-boats, which took off the men in the rafts. Then the whole flotilla continued toward France and safely reached its destination in December, 1941, when these survivors promptly volunteered for service in raiders again.

Another raider, the *Komet* (known then as Raider B) made a circumnavigation of all Siberia, and so passed successfully from the Atlantic to the Pacific without being bothered by the Allied blockade. Disguised as the German merchantman *Donau*, the *Komet* sailed on the third of July, 1940, and passed from the Barents Sea to the Pacific in twenty-three days. Over most of the journey she had the assistance of Soviet icebreakers and Soviet ice information, but for the last 600 miles of the northern route she had no such assistance. The *Komet*, which was commanded at the time by Rear Admiral Eyssen, subsequently made a lengthy and far too successful cruise, returning in due course right down the Pacific and Indian oceans and round the Cape of Good Hope to a port in occupied France. She is one of the very few merchantmen or ships of any kind, therefore, which have really made a circumnavigation of the great continent system of Europe, Asia, and Africa. Indeed, I know of no other.

If the *Komet* distinguished herself in this way in World War II, it was also a German raider which was the best thing—to my mind at any rate—about World War I. This was the famous *Seeadler*, the auxiliary sailing ship commanded by Graf Felix von Luckner. What Count von Luckner did was to take an old sailing ship boldly through the Allied blockade and then use her as a raider against, mostly, other sailing ships. It was a brilliant idea, from the enemy's point of view. No one thought that such a thing was possible, and the poor sailing ships fell easy victims. There were plenty of them in those days, and they were doing their share of the world's work, as usual. Since Germany, being blockaded, could have little share in seaborne commerce, it followed that almost every ship trading to Europe, or engaging in trade which benefited the Allies in any way, was an enemy. By the old rules of privateering, she could be captured or sunk.

The *Seeadler* was no privateer but an auxiliary ship-of-war, and the Count knew where to find the ships. He had been a sailing-ship sailor himself, and he looked for them on the doldrums by the Equator (it is calms which bring sailing ships together), in the horse latitudes of the South Atlantic (another zone of calms and baffling winds) and of the North Atlantic too, but he got away from the North Atlantic as quickly as he could. It was too easy to be hunted himself there. He caused plenty of destruction but—and it is a very big "but"—he distinguished himself much more greatly, and uniquely, by being the only raider who destroyed so many ships without killing a single man of those who manned them. He did his best to look after his captured seamen (for whom he had a very real fellow feeling) and, from time to time, he let a captured sailer go with a load of his prisoners, first making sure that she would not be able to sail very fast.

I have known Count von Luckner for a good many years, and a benevolent old sea dog he is. He served his time, in part at least, in British sailing ships, including the four-masted bark *Pinmore*, which he had to sink during the war, though he hated to do it. I knew the Count first when he was living aboard his four-masted schooner *Mopelia* alongside the pier at 157th Street in the Hudson River, New York Harbor. He lived a lonely life there with his Swedish wife, a secretary, and his wonderful old bos'n, Charlie Muller, to look after the ship. I can see him now, seated in the spacious cabin of the big *Mopelia*, taking out his war medals and showing me, with pride, the cross given him by the Pope, not for war but for his humanity.

As a matter of fact, Count von Luckner should never have been able to break through the British blockade and to fool the boarding officers the way he did. Though he had done his best to be thorough, there was an error in the rigging of the ship *Pass of Balmaha* which he had converted to look exactly (he hoped) like a particular Norwegian full-rigged ship called *Irma.* There was a real *Irma,* then in existence, and the converted *Pass of Balmaha* differed very slightly from her but still sufficiently for an alert officer, the sort who took a real interest in sailing ships, to detect. In those days many, if not the majority of, British merchant service officers knew sailing ships, having been trained in them, and it was the custom for sailing-ship men to develop very observant eyes and exceptionally retentive memories for details of ships. It was a Royal Naval Reserve officer from the merchant service which the intercepting ship, the *Highland Scot,* sent aboard the *Seeadler;* but he noticed nothing strange. Von Luckner was ready for him, of course. The Count spoke excellent Norwegian and so did a sufficiency of his crew, while all the fighting men, and guns and such, were hidden down below. The fact that he had a seventeen-year-old boy dressed as his "wife," lying on a settee in the saloon, might have made the good-mannered British a little less suspicious than they might otherwise have been; the *Seeadler's* steward was dishing out large nips of best whisky in the ship's pantry, and that probably helped things, too.

The full-rigger was supposed to be outward-bound with a full cargo of sawed timber from Norway toward Melbourne, and some of this timber was stowed on deck. That fact should have made the boarding officer suspicious, if nothing else did. (If he had taken a good look below the water aft, he would have seen the propellers which had been added to give auxiliary power). Though sailing ships in the Pacific filled their decks high with lumber, as did those on short runs across the North Sea, it was not customary to load deck cargoes in ships that would have to run their easting down toward Melbourne, because such a practice would be dangerous. The *Seeadler's* deck cargo was good disguise for other unorthodox changes aboard, but they all passed unnoticed, and the *Highland Scot* signaled "happy voyage" when her boarding party returned.

Happy voyage, indeed! I like to think of the old Count, staring at his cross from the Pope. And, after all, the ships he sank—not all sailing ships, by any means—might have been destroyed later in their voyages by submarines, which could not afford to look after survivors. An offensive which had flared up with the brutal destruction of the Cunarder *Lusitania* was relieved a little, I think, by my friend the Count.

There were no sailing-ship raiders in World War II.

I was a child in Melbourne during World War I, and so I saw nothing of that, though I remember the big sailing ships lying at anchor in Port Phillip Bay waiting for crews to take them round the Horn to Europe. They were loaded with wheat, mostly, and they were lovely ships, painted white or pale gray, and many had large national flags painted on their sides, Norwegian, Danish, Swedish. Some of them waited weeks for crews, and I wondered that my parents would not let me apply to sail in them. They were lovely ships, and they offered £100 the run. But they offered a quick watery death, too, very often. Many of those beautiful ships never arrived, and it was not Felix von Luckner who got them.

In World War II, I managed to see some Atlantic service on various occasions, in mine sweepers, in a small destroyer, an aircraft carrier, and—most interesting—in command of a squadron of peculiar vessels assigned to amphibious warfare, which was then known as Combined Operations. These vessels had been built for no other purpose than to land armies on beachheads and so open up, in due course, what then was being clamored for, a second front. How there could be need for a second front when there was already a savage front wide open over the whole North Atlantic, a bloody battle raging up and down the coast of North Africa, and a hopeless (for the Germans) involvement in Russia, I didn't know. My business was simply to get on with bringing some queer landing ships across the North Atlantic, and then to land troops in them on enemy-held beaches as directed. It was early in 1943, and, being very short of troop-carrying vessels of any kind, it was imperative to get hold of these landing ships as quickly as possible. Without them, there could be no landings. So I assembled twenty-one LCI(L) as they were designated—Landing Craft for Infantry, Large, the craft being large, not the infantry—at Norfolk, Virginia, and hoped to get them all safely to the Mediterranean.

They were flat-bottomed, snub-nosed, businesslike little ships, welded together of steel plates so thin that the ribs looked through the sides, like a hungry dog's. They had been planned, fabricated, and assembled in a hurry in various parts of the United States, and their engines were as odd as they were. They were driven by two propellers each geared to four diesel bus engines, and they went astern in negative pitch, and steered with a little electric gadget like a streetcar's driving handle. As far as I could find out, no one in any of the twenty-one ships had ever been to sea, except to cross the North Atlantic when drafted to my squadron.

A British admiral from the staff in Washington came down to inspect us before leaving. I remember how the poor old man's face fell as he searched through my hundreds of optimists, looking for a man who had been to sea. Rating after rating, motor mechanic after motor mechanic, sublieutenant after sublieutenant, the story was the same—green hands. Alongside us, jammed into a little basin at Berkeley in Norfolk, were the twenty-one ships, puffing and grunting as their generators exhausted through elbows above the surface, their masts off center, their decks of steel so thin that it sprang as one walked upon it, their antisubmarine defense a few old depth charges which, whatever harm they might have done to U-boats, would certainly have put any of us out of commission if we dropped them; their "guns" four 20-mm. cannon apiece and nothing else, not a lifeboat among the lot—nothing but one dinghy, for my ship, and a couple of small rafts per vessel. Some stout young women, even then, were rewelding the decks and sides of many of the vessels where they had cracked. Forward, great whisker booms to carry the ramp outhauls protruded from both bows, a menace in collision and coming alongside; aft the cutoff counters were razor-sharp; underneath the ramps a ramlike protuberance had been built up, which acted like an outsize can opener when the ships hit one another or somebody else, which they often did.

The admiral gave up his inspection before reaching the end of the parade (it was a trying Norfolk day), and turned to me and wished me luck. He looked as if he meant it, and he sent me five experienced naval officers when he got back to Washington. I suppose these were all he could find.

To make things more difficult, just before we sailed the whole signal code was changed. The officers and signalmen had been trained in the naval code of signals, so there was a sudden switch to the merchant service code—the international code, which was used by the United States Navy. This suited me as it was the only code I knew, anyway; but it suited no one else in the squadron. There were more important things to worry over—navigation, for example. It had been decided, when turning out young fellows to be officers in a hurry for amphibious warfare, that they should learn what were called air methods of navigation, as this was thought to be fast, and heavy casualties were expected. Fast it might be but effective it was not. What had been learned fast was forgotten with an even greater haste, and many of the young gentlemen in command of the LCI(L) could not navigate at all. No matter; after all, neither could Drake. We had only to leave the Atlantic seaboard of the United States, head east, and thread the ships, some time afterward, through the Straits of Gibraltar. But I took the precaution, in the few days I had available, of giving a course in the simple elements of practical astronomical navigation.

Because some LCI(L) had already made the Atlantic crossing successfully, someone decided to load us down with cargo. Every bit of food and war supplies that could be got across the North Atlantic was vital then; LCI(L) had big troop spaces. So we loaded every vessel with all the food she could carry. (When we finally reached our destination it was only with great difficulty that we could induce any authority to take delivery of this stuff.) With full stocks of water and fuel, with all our engine spares aboard, the maintenance staff dispersed among the ships to best advantage, and every man jack with his quota and more than his quota of gifts for his folk in the United Kingdom (he had to land the stuff on the Sicily beaches first, but he didn't know that), the little snub-nosed ships were so deep loaded on sailing that the sea began to break aboard, even before we were out of Chesapeake Bay.

We went by way of Bermuda, which can be a nasty place to find from a small vessel. To get there, we had to bash our way across the Gulf Stream, and eleven of my twenty-one vessels arrived with serious hull cracks. No matter, they were quickly welded together again. A look at the plot of the Atlantic before we sailed showed ninety-four hostile U-boats between us and Europe, any one of which could have sat among us on the surface and picked us off one by one, by gunfire, without wasting a single torpedo. I rigged a big "gun" out of a piece of telegraph post, in order that we would at least look as if we were armed, and hoped for the best.

From Bermuda we were bound toward Gibraltar. We had a fixed route, and were supposed to stick to it, for there was much other shipping in the ocean and friendly operations staffs had to know where we were.

"In the distance, you fellows look just like submarines, you know," said the briefing officer. "So whatever you do, keep out of the way of other vessels. You're very likely to be fired on by your own side, if they see you. Most ships won't know about LCI's, or care. But they know about submarines."

This was a blow. In fact, we were fired on by our own side more often than enough, though not on that crossing. I took good care to keep my LCI(L) out of the way of other vessels. And I also took good care to stick strictly to the route laid down and to the speed of advance, so that I should at all times be where I was supposed to be, to give the operations officers ashore a chance to route stuff clear of me.

We advanced in a wide group of five columns, each of four ships except the central column, which was of five. This gave me a wide and shallow group, which I could see. It was difficult to see all the ships in the bad weather of the North Atlantic, and many a worried counting of masts and tiny bridges went on, evening after evening, dawn after dawn. Sometimes I had to turn the whole lot round and go back to hunt for stragglers. In the blacked-out nights nothing could be seen beyond the nearest ships, sometimes not even them. Narrow escapes from collision were commonplace. I hoped no U-boat would turn up, looking for a little gunnery practice. My telegraph-post "gun" was washed over the side in a blow.

Morning after morning I counted the ships in sight—sometimes fifteen, sometimes twelve. Once there were only seven. The others had straggled and I had to find them. Somehow I always did. Day after day we stumbled along. Sometimes the North Atlantic rose in small mountains about us; sometimes hulls cracked a little; there were alarms hourly about this or that ship, careering wildly with electric steering failed and her rudder jammed hard astarboard or hard aport, and the others scurrying to avoid her. But the U-boats, for some peculiar reason, kept out of our way.

One nasty night I had a radio message from Admiralty informing me that a wolf pack was on our tracks, but they left us alone. About that time, many U-boat commanders were worried at the increasing rate of loss among their kind; maybe they thought us a new sort of hunter, and after them. A wolf pack of U-boats could have sat on the surface there and murdered the lot of us at their convenience. I knew that, but they didn't. There were eight of them, Admiralty said—eight U-boats, skulking below the surface somewhere close by, discussing among themselves whether to attack us or not. I saw nothing. It was eerie, thinking of some back-room experts maybe a thousand miles away—girls, probably—listening intently by secret device to the discussions being carried on electronically among those U-boat commanders as to whether we all died or not, there and then, while I could do nothing whatever except maintain my course, formation, and speed. I would not even have known the U-boats were there if Admiralty had not wirelessed the information.

I thought of those U-boat captains, hastily thumbing through the latest amendments to their recognition manuals, looking for something that resembled our silhouettes. No, nothing there—we were too new, too secret. Those queer booms at all our bows, now—what were they? Could they be rigged there to support some kind of antennae, a detecting device against cruising submarines? Maybe! If so, the submarines had better make themselves scarce! I looked at the cold sea, so near by, and hoped it was not soon to close over all my ships. I had no sending radio (except for emergency use), nor electronic means of intercommunication: nobody was listening to me. We were expendable. What was it the man in the Second Sea Lord's office had said? Ah yes, I remember. If I got 60 per cent across, it would be all right. Their Lordships were planning for 40 per cent casualties. Well, if those U-boats surfaced, they were going to get 100 per cent casualties from me, unless a bit of smoke saved one or two of us. That sea looked a cold place to drown in.

But no attack came. Nothing happened. I thought, for a moment, perhaps of scattering, or of making smoke (if our smokemaking apparatus worked: it had been put aboard at the last moment). But if I did these things I should be telling those U-boats both that I knew of them, and was afraid of them. Therefore I could be no danger to them, and that would be final. If I knew where they were, I could turn toward them, and put up a show, but I had not the slightest idea in which direction they bore from me. I knew only that they were very close, and we were in their periscopes. I had neither asdic nor radar.

That February, U-boats had sunk 63 ships in the North Atlantic of over 350,000 tons, but 20 of the U-boats had paid for it with their lives—that was about one in five of the U-boats then at sea. One in five in a month is a heavy rate of loss. Though still competent, fearless, and very much on the offensive, most U-boat commanders were getting somewhat wary by then. In that business, the aces die young. By the grace of God there were no aces, apparently, among the U-boat captains shadowing me. They left me alone and I steamed on, and in due course came to Gibraltar and, after that, to the landings from Sicily onward—Sicily, Salerno, Anzio, side issues in the Adriatic; then Normandy, the greatest of them all. That is a story of the Narrow Seas: we had done with the open Atlantic then, except for having to pass through once afterward, bound for the campaign in Burma. With the beachheads thoroughly established in France our work there was done, and we moved on to another ocean where there were enemy-held beaches in plenty.

It was a grim and dreadful war indeed, in the North Atlantic and elsewhere. Sometimes I ponder on its complete and murderous futility, pointed up by that incident of the annihilation that was not, when the U-boats allowed me to pass by. My ships were manned by all kinds of chaps—clerks, policemen, schoolmasters, parsons, farmers, and butchers' boys—doing their best to help keep the Atlantic lifeline open, and the whole purpose of our being was to lead the way in pouring so vast a concourse of troops (most of them drawn also from the ranks of the clerks, policemen, schoolmasters, farmers, and butchers' boys) into Europe that the ability of the enemy to send further U-boats to sea would be destroyed, and yet another unnecessary war would be ended. And a pack of those U-boats, armed to the teeth, bewildered by lack of recognition data on my vessels and worried by the increasing rate of loss among their kind, had allowed me to pass by, after my only sizable gun (the wooden one) had been washed over the side.

CONQUEST BY AIR

19

ALMOST since the Wright brothers first induced a controllable flying machine to stagger into the air and stay there a moment or two one day at Kitty Hawk on the windy coast of North Carolina, the airplane has made greater and more rapid progress than any other form of transport man ever invented. First a freak, then a stunt, and always a menace, in far less than a half century the airplane has become a form of transport almost of preeminent importance. Kitty Hawk is close by Roanoke, where Raleigh's first colonists made their tragic attempt at a settlement; maybe the Wright biplane whirred above their long-lost bones. As soon as the military mind realized the tremendous powers for destruction latent in this new form of transport (which took a little time, for the military mind is not given to fast working), the airplane's progress was spectacular and assured.

Never in the history of human endeavor had there been anything like this in transport before—a new kind of vehicle which could cover oceans and continents in a matter of hours where all other forms had taken days, weeks, months. Even before World War I, there were attempts at Atlantic crossings by air, and it is possible that one or two might soon have succeeded had the war not come along to upset things. There was the dirigible *America*, for example—no airplane, for sure—a bit of an airship with a couple of weak engines, which an optimist named Wellman took off from Atlantic City bound by way of Newfoundland and the Azores toward Europe somewhere, one day in the fall of 1910. The *America*, as might be expected, didn't get very far, but it was a brave attempt. One of her troubles was a so-called "equilibrator," which was an arrangement of floating cylinders in the sea attached to the airship by cable, and supposed to steady her in flight. Actually, their drag was impossible in a seaway, and it was just as well the ship had not gone far when the thing broke down. A steamer was able to pick up Mr. Wellman and his crew.

Wellman's effort promoted interest in flying the Atlantic, and substantial prizes were offered, on both sides, for the first aircraft across. In America department-store owner John Wanamaker said he would pay for any reliable aircraft—not an airship—which could fly across, and the London *Daily Mail* offered a prize of £10,000, which was a lot of money in those days. In the war, aviation progressed by leaps and bounds (sometimes literally). The United States Navy developed some useful flying boats which probably could have flown across without great difficulty, by stages, and it was intended to deliver them in that way, rather than to rig them down and ship them. Though they were not ready in time to take part in the war, the idea was persevered with. Three navy Curtiss flying boats, big brutes of things with wing spans of 126 feet and four Liberty engines, took off from Long Island Sound, one day in the early summer of 1919, with the intention, well planned and thoroughly well organized (at the public expense), of being first to fly across the North Atlantic. These machines had a maximum range of 1,500 miles, but they were large enough to offer accommodation of a sort for fifty passengers, had they been converted for that purpose. With their comparatively short range, they had to fly the Atlantic by the shortest hops possible, and the shortest way is from Newfoundland first to the Azores and then on to Europe. A little more range makes it possible to fly direct from Newfoundland to Ireland, which is easier to find, though the Azorian islands are high and most of them are large.

The three Curtiss flying boats, known as NC1, NC3, and NC4,

had fifty naval vessels strung out along their route to assist in navigation (like marks along an enormous runway) and, perhaps, to fish out downed crews. NC4 had to put down in the sea but rescued herself by taxiing back to the United States coast again, for she was only a hundred miles out at the time. However, she taxied the hundred miles, which in itself was quite a feat: but aircraft were not invented to taxi across oceans. NC3 also came down in the sea but she was not far from the island of St. Michael in the Azores, toward which she immediately began to taxi, despite the fact that the hull had been seriously damaged in the landing on a bumpy, high ocean swell. NC3 safely taxied into harbor, which was a very good show. NC1 also came down at sea, and her crew were taken off by a passing steamer.

In the meantime, NC4 had made good the engine defects which had given her that 100-mile taxi ride back to the American coast, and then flew successfully from Trepassey Harbor in Newfoundland to Flores in the Azores, which she made in 15 hours 18 minutes. A week or so later, NC4 flew on to Lisbon, where she arrived safely after a ten-hour flight. This naval Curtiss flying boat was therefore the first heavier-than-air machine ever to fly across the North Atlantic—a fact which seems to be fairly generally forgotten today on both sides of the ocean.

One odd reason for this oversight is the fact that, while NC4 was on her way or waiting for good weather to continue from the Azores, there had been a more spectacular attempt—and failure—made by a couple of cheerful fellows flying a bit of a biplane, also from the coast of Newfoundland but, in their case, toward Ireland. These were Harry Hawker and Mackenzie Grieve, and when their engine failed and they had to put down in the sea fourteen hours out, they had the great good fortune to be picked up at once by a little Danish steamer called the *Mary*. The *Mary* had no radio and could send in no report. All the world knew was that Hawker and Grieve were missing, and when the *Mary* came chugging along off the coast of Scotland a week or more later and signaled the Butt of Lewis that she had the two missing aviators aboard, that was the big news story of the year. Hawker and Grieve's failure made the story; the poor NC4 had only successfully made the flight. The Hawker machine was a sturdy little biplane which not only withstood the ditching in the open sea but survived to be salvaged there a week later, when it was brought to London and exhibited to delighted crowds. Those low-powered little biplanes landed slowly and did not disintegrate when they hit the water. After all, there was not a great deal to come to pieces and what there was would float, except the engine.

After the Hawker-Grieve triumphant failure came the Alcock and Brown success, but, being a success, in due course it was also forgotten. It was still 1919 when Alcock and Whitten Brown took off from Newfoundland on June 14, in a twin-engined Vickers Vimy bomber almost as big and bulky as the Curtiss flying boats. Alcock and Brown also were professional airmen, service-trained as the crews of the U.S. naval flying boats had all been—Alcock the pilot and Brown the navigator. They flew safely across to the Irish coast with one pretty bad scare when (because they were flying blind and had no adequate instruments for the job) the clumsy big biplane came out of cloud close to the water and almost upside down, and Alcock had barely time to right her. They landed in a bog near Clifden; they were the first to make the transatlantic flight nonstop.

After a brief notoriety this was regarded as little more than a stunt, and no one paid much attention. It was left to a young Swedish-American named Charles Lindbergh, who flew the Atlantic alone in a single-engined monoplane eight years later, really to jolt the world into paying more than a little brief and hysterical attention to the long-range merits of the airplane. Lindbergh had been an airline pilot, a professional who had chosen to make flying his business. His nonstop New York–to–Paris flight did more than make the headlines: it kept them, and it has kept them ever since almost to the entire exclusion of the other pioneers. The others had been fly-by-night affairs, literally: in due course, the Lindbergh success was to lead to the opening up of regular transatlantic airlines. The public took Lindbergh and his feat to heart, especially on the American side of the ocean. At the time there were others waiting to take off for the first nonstop flight originating in New York, well-publicized and well-organized fellows who had big aircraft and big backers and, in one or two cases, already had transoceanic experience. Along came this fair-headed young fellow of whom no one (outside aviation) had ever heard, with a bit of a monoplane built by the Ryan Company at St. Louis—with no public-relations experts, no build-up, no powerful backers, no stunts—and he took off and made the flight as if he had been making such 3,600-mile hops every day for weeks, and intended to go on making them. The public loves a plain man who gets on with the job.

After Lindbergh came the stunters, whose name was legion, whose usefulness was nil, and whose effect, even when successful, was to make the transatlantic flight into a source of personal publicity and profit if possible and, when unsuccessful, to give themselves death without burial. There was one fellow who found his way across by flying low over the liners that he met, identifying them and working out roughly (from a sailing list in a copy of that day's *New York Times* which he had with him) their approximate distances from New York. This optimist reached the far side: others did not. If the first eastbound flight had already been made (three times), there remained the first westbound, and it took some time to dispose of that. The westbound flight was a very different proposition, and still is. Then there were the first woman passenger to fly across, the first woman to fly solo, the first Frenchman, the first one-armed Finn or cross-eyed Swede, and a hundred more flights or attempted flights just for the hell of it. The death roll climbed not because of the hazards of the flight, for it was the same flying over the ocean as over the land except that there was more ocean and there were no wayside stops. Any good air frame with an engine that could hold out for thirty hours or so, and a pilot of the same caliber, could make the journey. The trouble was to get the finance, and the public became a little tired, after a while, of the more flamboyant efforts to do this.

Airships flew the Atlantic successfully after the war, so much so that they might have made a regular service of it—indeed, had begun to do so, when the dreadful accident to the German passenger airship *Hindenburg* put an end to that kind of flying. The unfortunate *Hindenburg*, if one overlooks her unwieldiness, had only one serious disqualification. That was enough to kill her, for it was her misfortune that she had no helium gas; and so she blew up, and those who had come to the mooring field in New Jersey one day in early May, 1937, to watch her come in to land watched instead a holocaust. It was final: the airship, as things turned out, could never be in the same race as the faster, more maneuverable and—then—less costly airplane.

It took the airlines to remove the stunt from transatlantic flying and turn it from adventure into routine. While they were quietly getting on with this job which, a few years earlier, would have seemed a matter of utter impossibility, World War II came along, and the utterly impossible was done every day, for aircraft of all kinds then flew across by the thousand.

It was as early as October, 1927, when fringe flying began across part of the North Atlantic. That month, a three-engined Fokker monoplane, a wooden machine with a large fixed undercarriage, splashed and roared its way across a rain-swept field in Florida, became slowly airborne, and headed toward Cuba. This was the first scheduled flight by Pan American World Airways, which has specialized from its inception in overseas flying of the highest standard. The Caribbean was the proving ground, but there was a long way to go before the Atlantic was conquered. British, French, Germans, Portuguese all shared in the pioneering efforts. As early as 1922, the Portuguese Admiral Gago Coutinho, with one companion, had made a remarkable flight from Lisbon toward Brazil. As they had been the greatest of all pioneers at sea, the enterprising Portuguese now took to the air.

The Germans developed some remarkable flying boats, among which the enormous twelve-engined DOX was a sort of flying *Great Eastern*, and their eaglelike Blohm and Voss diesel-engined seaplanes were pioneer oceanic flyers in their own field. Germans, French, British, and Americans all developed the flying boat for oceanic (and sometimes also world) routes, at first. The flying boat could be put down on quiet water anywhere and so was independent of the expensive flying field. Pan American, Deutsch Lufthansa, Imperial Airways, Air France all used big boats. By 1939, Yankee Clippers of Pan American were flying from New York to Lisbon, and BOAC were flying the Atlantic from England. A year later, a great four-engined British flying boat surprised New Yorkers by dropping out of the skies into the East River after flying from Poole Harbor in Dorset, war or no war. Among that flying boat's cargo was a bundle of London newspapers from the previous day, telling of the blitz on London by Göring's Luftwaffe. The transatlantic flights begun in that way have continued, until today they are commonplace.

The boats have gone, for they had serious disadvantages as well as advantages (slower speed and more costly operation were the worst). In their stead have come the marvelous four-engined giants from Douglas, Lockheed, Boeing, de Havilland, and the Bristol Aircraft Company—Constellations and Super-Constellations, DC7's, double-decked Stratocruisers, the new Comet, the turbo-prop Britannia—which fly nightly from Paris, London, and New York with the regularity and absence of fuss of express trains. In 1954, aircraft (which did not include some of the more modern of these) flew 578,000 people safely across the North Atlantic; in 1955, the figure had climbed to 652,000 and aircraft were handling 47 per cent of all transatlantic passenger traffic. By 1956, even these figures were exceeded. In the first nine months of this year, aircraft had flown 613,000 transatlantic passengers, and there was no sign of any fall in the traffic. These figures are staggering. The total for 1956 averages well over 2,000 air passengers a day.

Not only the pioneers—Pan American, British Overseas Airways, Air France, and now again Deutsche Lufthansa—share in this harvest. Scandinavian airliners fly a special route almost over the Pole, continuing some schedules directly thence to Los Angeles in California. Canadians, Icelanders, Hollanders (of long experience and expert skill), Swiss, Belgians, Spanish crews and aircraft all fly the Atlantic regularly, as well as other great American airlines such as TWA, which began as an internal United States airline and now has spread round the world. As I write this, Pan American is flying its 60,000th schedule between Europe and America. This line alone now operates a fleet of more than fifty huge aircraft on its various transatlantic services, seven of them Douglas DC7C "Super Sevens," comfortable great airborne limousines which hurtle along at 400 miles an hour or so through the Atlantic skies, with the ease of a perfect automobile on a perfect road. BOAC, TWA, Air France, KLM, SAS, TCA—today's passenger may take his choice from their abundant schedules, any day, and, leaving Europe in the evening, find himself after resting comfortably in a reclining chair overnight, in New York in the morning. The latest machines, when they come into service, will fly so fast that at least one plans a schedule which will reach New York—in terms of clock time—before it left London. There is five hours' difference of longitude between New York and London, and the fastest Comet will span the distance in less than this. The great Boeing 707 jet airliner will do as well, when it comes into service in 1958.

Just who wants to arrive in New York before he left London I wouldn't know, but so far there has always been an avid public for faster flights. Good facilities have, apparently, created their own traffic. While the aircraft's greatest disability—its fantastic cost—is disguised or hidden in various ways for one reason and another, it looks as if this state of affairs will continue, and there will be traffic to support the fantastic industry. The British Comet IV and the American Boeing 707, each of which has the annual carrying capacity of a 40,000-ton liner, may bring a new picture to the North Atlantic service. Twelve such aircraft could handle existing North Atlantic passenger traffic. Three hundred of them could just about handle all the air business now done in the whole world (outside Russia), but only long flights where reasonably larger passenger loads could constantly be assured could carry such expensive aircraft—expensive not only in their capital outlay and operational costs, but in airport facilities, and every other item. Only a few great airports have runways long enough to accept them, and it is an expensive business to extend runways. But air traffic is expected to double by 1958 or 1959, and operators are optimistic.

As shipowners have pointed out, however, they would not be so optimistic if they had to meet all the real costs of the form of transport they are selling, or had had to finance its rapid and extraordinary development in the way that shipping men have had to finance ships. Who thought of stringing out fifty Spanish warships along Columbus's course to help him on his way toward America? Looked at in cold blood, air transport is seen to be very much a pampered business, compared with shipping which (in Britain and most other European countries, at any rate) has always had to develop sensibly on its own merits and at its own cost. If aircraft had been forced to develop in the same way, perhaps we would just be getting round to thinking of the first transatlantic service now—and perhaps not. A ship, for instance, carries a ton of freight for one penny a distance of six miles. For the same penny, the average railroad could carry the same ton about a quarter of a mile, road transport would shift it a furlong, and the subsidized airplane would lift it thirty yards. A ship can anchor, and can use barges and tenders, and a ship can stop. The airplane must get safely out of the air onto an expensive runway, thoughtfully provided at the public expense and to the annoyance of the neighbors, who have to put up with the noise.

As taxpayers, they have also to share the burden of the airport costs, the cost of training airliner crews (who can gain their expensive multiengined flying experience in one way only, by joining an air force and learning to fly there at the public expense), and ease the burden of the aircraft's high operational cost, which is covered by subsidy of one sort or another. Not the least of these subsidies is the immense amount of public money poured ceaselessly into the development of better, bigger, faster aircraft, and better, bigger, and more economical aircraft engines. If the airline companies had themselves to meet this colossal expense from which they draw so great a benefit, they would have to go out of business. But they do not, and so they remain very nicely in business. It is the ships which have withdrawn from passenger trades here and there (the interisland trade in Hawaii, some of the transpacific trade, the trade between New York and the West Indies, for example) and suffered on others, though the extent to which they may be losing business has so far been disguised by the remarkable increase in *all* travel. (Up to the end of September, 1956, shipping had carried 55,000 more transatlantic passengers than for the same period of 1955, for example, but the figures for air travel were even better.)

Again, as shipowners have pointed out, air transport is unique in having been developed for the sake of its strength alone (which is speed) and totally regardless of its weakness (which is cost). That has been pushed onto the taxpayers. If shipowners were similarly treated, there is no doubt that they could get the steaming time between New York and Plymouth, say, down to three days. If they gave an outsize destroyer hull power enough and did not have to earn any money, on a properly competitive commercial basis, there is no reason why they should not be able to carry two or three thousand passengers in such a ship very comfortably from New York to Plymouth inside three days. The ship, however, would cost at least a hundred million pounds. Who is going to stake shipowners to such a sum, or subsidize the running costs of so impossibly expensive a vessel? It is true that she would carry some people to Europe as fast as some airliners now manage, especially on winter schedules, for a night's delay at such salubrious spots as Sydney, Nova Scotia, Gander, Goose Bay, or Keflavik very quickly adds wearisome days to flight time. So can diversions at either end; but such delays are becoming increasingly things of the past.

It would, in fact, be of little use for shipping to fight the airliner so expensively, on its own ground, with just the one vessel. Shipowners have not the comforting reflection, either, that some revolutionary new form of power is going to increase ships' efficiency by 30 to 40 per cent, as the jet engine did for aircraft. Atomic power may come for merchant ships, but it looks as if it is going to take some time—a long time.

The passenger service across the North Atlantic is the very heart of the air-sea "war" which, quiet as it is, is steadily going on today. In the 44 per cent total traffic increase which was recorded on the Atlantic between the years 1951 and 1954, the airliners secured half the increase, although they were still carrying only about a third of the whole. While the dominant thought among airline operators is to reduce their fares and in that way to increase their business, rather than to operate on a true commercial basis and reduce their dependence on the taxpayers, shipping on the North Atlantic routes may continue to lose some traffic. Shipping men have no fear of the airlines' power to provide more lovely air hostesses (a very expendable commodity) or more luscious meals served aloft with more free champagne (which would be difficult, for such trimmings are running at capacity now). What they fear is one thing only, and that is lower fares. Already the airlines' tourist-class fares for winter round-trip excursions are below the cost of good liner accommodation. Tourist class is crowded a bit, it is true, and the unfortunate occupant of the central seat of three would be better off in a bus. But it is only for one night. There are no extras (provided one's luggage is light enough); he can probably stretch his legs at Shannon and Gander, on the way to New York, and the interval between is remarkably short. If he does not get these breaks, he has the comforting reflection that the longer nonstop flights at least reduce the possibility of delays. An hour of Gander is enough, and half an hour of Keflavik. If there is discomfort and sitting up becomes irksome, it is worthwhile for one night, and if the traveler also finds that he is left with a spare pound or two in his pocket which he would not have had if he had gone by sea, it is so much the easier to convince himself that time is of the essence.

At the moment, there are still plenty of travelers who prefer ships, but if the airlines can seriously undercut ship costs (which show no sign of decreasing) there will undoubtedly be yet a further increase in the number of travelers who will find themselves in the flying machine. Transatlantic flights, nowadays, are just routine. You go aboard at Idlewild, say, and in a little while the four-engined monster, whirring and purring, takes its place in the take-off queue. Then, with a deafening roar of four great engines at full throttle, it rushes down the expensive tarmac and soon is air-borne. The pressurized cabin takes the discomfort out of height. The hostess no longer bothers, usually, even to come round with bits of chewing gum. You must look quickly (if you have the unusual good fortune of having anything like a clear view out of the aircraft at all) if you are to see anything of the distant Manhattan skyline, or anything else.

Your flight soon becomes a dull business, even sitting in the most wonderfully upholstered "slumber seat." It is still a seat and not a bed. Splendid service, luxurious meals, constant attention, books and magazines to read while away the time. Cruising at great height, the engine noise becomes a purr, loud or soft depending on where you sit in the airplane, lulling you to sleep. You forget that you are staring at a bulkhead and little else, or that the bald head of the passenger immediately in front of you is uncomfortably close to your lap. The airplane purrs on through the night, lights flashing at either wingtip, flames issuing from the exhausts of all four engines. Above are the stars, below is nothing. Steadily the airplane flies toward the dawn, and when the dawn comes, you are over England. In a few moments then, the machine is descending. Odd noises indicate the lowering of landing flaps and undercarriage. You see nothing of the airport. Only the pilots have a clear view out. What matter? In a little while you are touching down smoothly and then rumbling to the disembarking tarmac, to go through the formalities of immigration and customs. It is all very smooth and very wonderful. On my last two such flights, I didn't see the Atlantic at all—nor, if the truth be told, miss it. When the shipping man is convinced that time is of the essence, he takes to the air too.

But he knows as he flies that ships are not obsolete, nor likely to be. He may reflect that the advantages of the aircraft depend upon some very tenuous threads, any one of which could snap at any time. One snapped thread could be enough to change all those aircraft into heaps of expensive scrap, almost overnight. As for ships, they can be with us always.

TODAY

20

TODAY the North Atlantic Ocean is a safer place for ships, aircraft, seamen, and passengers than it has ever been before, though it is still the most dangerous and the roughest of oceans—most dangerous because of the ice which drifts into it spring after spring, summer after summer; roughest because of the hurricanes which blow across with deadly strength from the Caribbean, and the heavy winter gales which lash the ocean to a torment during at least three months of the year and sometimes five. Ever since the loss of the liner *Titanic* on an April night in 1912, there has been an International Ice Patrol whose purpose is to plot the positions of icebergs and other dangerous drifting ice in the North Atlantic, and to see that this information reaches all ships using that ocean. Largely the responsibility of that quietly efficient service, the United States Coast Guard, today the main work of the ice patrol is carried out by air.

If ships do get into trouble, powerful salvage tugs are stationed at the four corners of the Atlantic to rush out and bring them in from sea. At Falmouth in Cornwall and Brest in France, at Ponta Delgada in the Azores, at St. John's in Newfoundland, at Halifax in Nova Scotia, at Lisbon, at New York, and in a convenient port in the West Indies, ocean-going tugs, which are each marvels both as tugs and salvage vessels, are stationed during all the bad months of the year with one purpose only, to rescue ships. There are still ships enough which call for rescue—some too late, like the Isbrandtsen cargo ship *Flying Enterprise*, which went over on her side and finally slipped beneath the surface when in tow not far from a port of refuge.

It was in the *Flying Enterprise* that Danish-American Capt. Kurt Carlsen gave the world a quiet and inspiring picture of a shipmaster going about his duties with steadfast courage and indefatigable skill and then, when he had so bravely lost, gave an even greater example by refusing absolutely to have the least thing to do with all the blatant efforts to exploit the position thrust on him through the blare and glare of world publicity. The *Flying Enterprise* was so beset by a vile and continued gale, while bound with a heavy cargo from Germany toward the United States during Christmas week, 1951, that she took in water and began to list—at first a little, then heavily.

Because he thought there was some chance of saving her if one of those salvage tugs could arrive in time, Captain Carlsen refused to leave his ship. Because he feared that the chance was slim, he stayed alone, ordering the rest of the ship's company to abandon ship, which they did in safety. Then, when the tug *Turmoil* had been towing him for some days while the ship slowly listed farther and farther over, and the weather did not let up at all, with the whole world waiting, watching, and hoping, finally the *Flying Enterprise* rolled right over and slipped beneath the sea. It was a great effort. Today Captain Carlsen continues to exercise his profession as a shipmaster, with thousands more, conducting great ships of ever-growing complexity and expense over the sea lanes of the North Atlantic, mindful of the great advances which have been made, yet fully aware, too, of the undying enmity of the deceitful sea, and prepared at all times to do battle with it until the last.

In weather information, the advance has been tremendous, brought about not only by the increasing use of selected ships which send in reports according to a prepared program, but by stationing a fleet of ships at selected places in the sea whose duty it is to provide weather information constantly. These weather ships are internationally financed, like the ice patrol. They are British, American, Canadian, French, Dutch; the majority is provided by the United States Coast Guard. Their job is grim, to sit there bouncing and rolling on the stormy sea, not going anywhere until each tour on station is done, just sitting there, taking the howling gales and wet, gloomy misery of high latitudes, month after month, year after year. Theirs is a fine service, and the weather forecasts and plots of today are excellent. If there had been such information so freely available in the days of the packet ships, they could have clipped days off the run both eastbound and westbound. But the occasional gale still whips in with swift savagery and catches ships out, drowning the fishermen, smashing little ships and sometimes the odd big ship, too.

With electronic means of fixing the positions of all ships which bother to equip themselves with the necessary apparatus to receive the beams and the simple skill to plot them, with radar to decrease collision and grounding risks, and electronic sounding machines further to ensure safe navigation, the well-found steamer's way is made much simpler—or it ought to be. Sometimes not radar itself but the failure to plot its findings properly or to act upon them when they are observed has caused serious collisions, or helped to cause them—so much so that at least one great line scrapped the aid altogether, preferring that its shipmasters should be without it rather than be misled by it. In the view of other seamen, this was overdoing a temporary dissatisfaction with some defects of a new and not thoroughly developed device, the uses of which far outweigh any possible disadvantages.

Nevertheless, very recently there was a wholly unnecessary collision between two of the newest and finest liners on the North Atlantic service, when the Swedish 12,000-ton *Stockholm* and the Italian 29,000-tonner *Andrea Doria* smashed into each other on a quiet night in the summer of 1956, not far from Nantucket. The *Stockholm* was eastbound out of New York, and the Italian was approaching New York from the Mediterranean. Both ships were equipped with every possible modern aid to navigation. There was some fog, noticeable aboard the *Andrea Doria;* the Swedish ship had not then encountered bad visibility. The two ships should have passed each other safely, as a thousand other ships do every night. There is an international rule of the road, agreed to and enforced by all nations, the whole purpose of which is to prevent the possibility of collision arising. Yet suddenly the *Andrea Doria* was across the *Stockholm's* bows, and she suffered such vital injury that she sank. Over forty people died; the tragedy would have been much greater had the weather not remained so quiet, for the lifeboats on the Italian's lifted side were useless and she would possibly not have been able to get all her people off by herself.

One of the shocks of this accident was just that fact of the inadequacy of the most modern lifeboat, even when provided with the profusion now required by law—a profusion insisted upon since that awful night when the *Titanic's* sophisticated and hitherto complacent passengers in the ship which "God Himself couldn't sink" slowly realized that, along with all the other luxuries, there were boats enough only for one-third of the ship's complement. The *Titanic* affair shocked the world; the *Stockholm–Andrea Doria* collision shocked the shipping world. Those dance bands playing hymns, the great ship in her final agony rearing herself vertically for the final plunge, the millionaires struggling in icy seas—these things in the *Titanic* story became legendary. Though no one claimed again that ships were "unsinkable," it was a shock to realize that human error, in a fleeting moment, could still bring a fine liner to the bottom of the sea. Man will never be infallible, that is certain, and no invention upon earth will ever relieve him from his personal responsibilities or decrease his need for complete integrity and skill, upon the bridge of an Atlantic liner or anywhere else. The consequences can be terrible when the aberration occurs upon the bridge of a liner in the shipping lanes.

Yet the loss of that lovely Italian ship, one of the most luxurious vessels in the world, was an extraordinary accident. Ship losses everywhere are lower today than they ever were. In 1955, the official record shows that the casualty percentage among ships of over 100 tons was the lowest on record. Of all the thousands upon thousands of voyages made by the thousands upon thousands of ships of all kinds throughout the world, only 178 ships were lost that year through casualty—sinking, grounding, fire, collision, and so on. That is an extremely small percentage of the whole. These ships included trawlers fishing in wintry Arctic seas, sealers, and other vessels called upon to accept unusual hazards either by their employment, the seas they work in, or the cargoes they carry. Today's great liners and little ships—the 50,000-ton oil tankers and the 80,000-ton ore carriers, the *Queens* and the *United States*, the *Liberté*, the *Mauretania*, and all the vast fleet of ships ranging down to the little summer Great Lakes traders coming up the St. Lawrence from Europe—go about their business, voyage after voyage, with a risk of loss so minute that the occasional accident is news indeed.

Modern wireless installations permit the vast majority of ships to keep in constant touch with the land, and even the smallest vessels carry efficient radio telephones. Among other amenities, instant medical care is available for all ships, which have only to ask for it —either from the United States Coast Guard, or from any of the specially equipped shore stations on either side of the North Atlantic. Instead of the old privateering spirit when to sight another vessel was to be at once suspicious and alert, today any ship will go to the aid of any other ship, in emergency. On a December crossing in 1956, for instance, one of the great *Queens* diverted from her course in order to take off a man from a Panamanian steamer who was urgently in need of medical attention, though to do so upset her schedule. To the deep-draft *Queens*, their schedule is of more importance than to most other ships, for they must enter and leave their ports only at certain states of the tide. What the great Cunarders do, every ship is prepared to do. The public hears only of these incidents, usually, when some well-known ship is involved in them.

While France is building a new huge liner to cost at least $80,000,000 and America is planning a nuclear-powered consort for the wonder ship *United States*, a hotel man is attempting to organize a couple of 90,000-tonners to carry transatlantic tourists to Europe at $40 a head. Aircraft are taking their share of traffic, but the ships continue to prosper too. Recently, for example, the *United*

States completed her 200th Atlantic crossing, and a reclearing showed that during her four and one-half years' service she had carried 95 per cent of her total capacity; and, incidentally, she had then steamed 734,482 statute miles at an average speed of 35.28 miles an hour. Passenger aircraft flew a daily average of eighty-six flights across the North Atlantic for two months during the height of the season in 1956; but forty new liners have entered the North Atlantic service since the end of World War II, and today's passenger may take his choice of twenty-eight steamship lines. There is a catch in all this at the moment, unfortunately. Too much Atlantic travel is a one-way traffic, or the comings and goings of those whose journeys originate on the American side of the ocean. Few Europeans, other than migrants, businessmen, and politicians, get the chance to go because, ever since the war, their governments have forbidden them to buy or to have any dollars to go with. No British tourist, as such, has been able to visit the United States, for example, for the past seventeen years. It seems a pity, when so much is talked of the need for Anglo-American solidarity and understanding, and the facilities for transatlantic travel are better than they have ever been.

As for the aircraft, they bring their own new problems which have yet to be settled internationally. Since little Oceanus Hopkins was born aboard the *Mayflower* in 1620, it has been common for pregnant mothers to travel by sea and to increase the ship's complement while doing so. But what is the status of their babies born in the air? Under British law, for instance, a child born aboard a British aircraft is of British nationality. But if the aircraft were passing over a piece of France at the time, the child would be considered by French law also to have French nationality. If the father chanced to be a national of yet another country whose laws required that the child take the nationality of its legitimate father, then the poor baby would be given a third nationality. Again, if the baby were born in an airliner belonging to Air France, the baby's legal status would be quite different, for there is no present uniformity in these matters.

The same thing applies to crimes committed in the air—happily rare as yet: at least those which are detected—and marriages, contracts concluded, or wills signed in international flight. The same problem arises in all these cases, the determination of the applicable national law, and a learned subcommittee of ICAO (the International Civil Aviation Organization) is at work on that and other problems now. It took a long time to work out international law for shipping; for aircraft, there has not been much time. These problems can be important.

The stateless man, however, is far worse off than the babe with too many nationalities, and far more common. At least two such unfortunates, unable to prove any specific nationality, have been wandering the Atlantic for years in ships which, once having accepted them, find that they can never again get rid of them, for neither the country which they left (since they cannot prove their allegiance to it), nor any other country at which the ships call will permit them to land, except into jail, and in jail they remain at the ship's expense. Two such wanderers have served the best part of twenty years between them. It is true that both began as stowaways—and yet, it seems somewhat inhuman. It is hard on the shipping companies, for they have to bear the expense.

One wonders why they did not simply provide their unwelcome guests with a slip of a yacht to share under a flag of their own, for then surely they could at least sail at will, though they still could not stop anywhere permanently. It would have been more economic to buy them a raft or something, like the Canadian *L'Egare II* or Dr. Bombard's; but perhaps there is a law against this, too.

Those tragic, unwanted wanderers perhaps sum up the negative side of man's wonderful advances materially in the North Atlantic. Sometimes one gets to thinking about it all, of the incredible pace of advance during the past century, accelerating always, and yet with complications—the whole wonderful creation dependent upon the well-being and the confident progress of the one world, with its diverse lands, its populous continents and all their problems, on both sides of the ocean. One world, but how divided still!

Christopher Columbus started something when he set out in the old *Santa María* to sail toward the New World—the New World whose existence neither he nor any other had then imagined possible, a New World which now leads the Old. The Atlantic—now violent with its winter gales, now lost beneath a pall of gray and wretched fog, or calm and smiling beneath the summer sun—is at any rate no longer a dividing and fearsome gulf, but a bridge between.

Man made the bridge. Now his hope of progress and of peace lies in its better maintenance, and the assured continuity of its ever-expanding existence.

INDEX

Acadia, 238
Adventurers in sailing, 265–277
Africa, 36, 59, 98
  circumnavigation of, 37–41, 53, 74
Agamemnon, 246
Agriculture, 130, 171
Agulhas Current, 39
Air France, 299–300
Aircraft, laws applying to, 310–311
  ocean crossings by, 293–304
  patrol service by, 305
  vs. ships, 301–304, 310–311
  used in ocean research, 28–29, 33
  in world wars, 280–281
Alabama, 208–209
Albermarle, H.M.S., 182–183
Alcock, Mr., 296
Alfred, 176
Allcard, Edward, 271
Allen, W. H., 196
Amazon, 256–257
America, discovery of, 69–70
  naming of, 88–90
  (*See also* North America; South America)
America, dirigible, 293–294
America, liner, 268–269
American Revolution, 172–174, 179–180, 185, 190
American Taxation Act, 174
Amidas, Captain, 107, 109
Amundsen, Roald, 99
Anderson, Capt. Magnus, 48
Anderson, R. C., 161–162
Andrea Doria, 307–308
Anglo-Australian, 248
Antarctic, 91, 229, 276
Antarctic Pole, 89
Antilia, 11, 42
Anti-Slavery Society, 202
Antitrade winds, 80, 93
Arabs, 37–39, 64
Archives, of Columbus, 85
  Portuguese, 57, 59–60
Arctic, 242
Arctic Current, 25
Arctic Ocean, 24, 33
Argus, schooner, 63, 213
Argus, sloop, 196
Asia, 69–70, 73, 82–83, 87, 98
Astrid, 275
Atlantic Royal Mail Steam Navigation Company, 243
Atlantis, lost continent, 6, 10–11, 42, 99
Atlantis, ketch, 28, 30
Atlas of Benincasa, 60
Atomic power, 302
Aud, Queen, 43
Australia, 229–230
Avalon, 11
Azores, 9–10, 16, 102, 116, 227, 250, 265, 283, 294–295
  Columbus in, 72, 94
  history, 12, 42, 55
  whaling and fisheries, 32, 59, 205–207, 211
Aztecs, 91

Baffin Island, 18
Baggala, 7
Bahamas, 80, 138

Baker, Peter, 191–192
Baker, William A., 162
Balboa, 91
Baltic Sea, 19, 56
Baltimore, Maryland, 189–190, 248–249
Barbados, 248–249, 268, 270
Barbary Coast, 197
Barcelos, Pedro de, 58
Barkentines, 55–56
Barlowe, Captain, 107, 109
Barnacles, 8, 14
Bart, Jean, 194
Bathythermograph, 29
Battle of the Saints, 183
Battleships, sailing, 204
Belgium, 247
Belle Isle, Straits of, 96
Benguela Current, 39
Benincasa, atlas of, 60
Benlomond, 271
Bermuda, 9–10, 33, 139, 272, 277, 289
Bermuda yacht race, 272
Bianco, Andrea, 60
Biplanes, 295–296
Bird migrations, 47, 53, 78
Biscay, Bay of, 4, 6, 13, 37, 111
Black Ball Line, 222–223
Black Prince, 193
Black Sea, 33
Black Star Line, 222
Black X Line, 222
Blackett, P. M. S., 2
Blackwall, England, 124
Blessing, 137
Blessing of the Bay, 170
Blockades, wartime, 283–285
Bobadilla, 84
Bombard, Dr., 37, 86, 270–271
Bonhomme Richard, 177, 179–180
Bonney, Anne, 198–199
Boston, Massachusetts, 170–171, 229, 233, 238, 275
Boston Tea Party, 173–174
Bradford, Governor, 143, 146, 150
  quoted, 151–152, 161
Bradford, Mrs., 153–154
Brave, 113
Brazil, 98–100, 202, 248, 298
  discovery of, 61
Brazil Island, 6, 9, 43, 94–95
Brigantines, 256
Briggs, Capt. Benjamin S., 250, 252–253, 257–259, 263–264
Briggs, Mrs., 253, 258–259, 264
Bristol, England, 94–96, 98, 150, 185–186, 243
Bristol, Rhode Island, 266
Bristol Channel, 196
Britannia, 238
British Association, 2
British Isles, climate of, 18, 27
  ocean trade of, 31–32
  research in, 33
  (*See also* England)
British Merchant Navy War Memorial, London, 278
British Overseas Airways (BOAC), 299–300
Brixham, England, 165
Brooks, slaver, 200–201
Brown, Whitten, 296
Brunel, Isambard Kingdom, 237, 243–244
Buenos Aires, 274–275

Cable, transatlantic, 245–246
Cabot, John, 95–96
Cabot, Sebastian, 96
Cabral, 61
Cadamosto, 55–56, 60
Caledonia, 238
California, 175, 229, 299
Calms, 8
  equatorial, 12–15
Canada, 26–27, 46, 94, 97, 99, 268–269, 275
  Viking relics in, 43–44
Canada, liner, 225
Canary Current, 23, 39, 41
Canary Islands, 9, 42, 60, 76–77, 107, 114, 123, 268
Cape Breton Island, 96
Cape Horners, 166–167
Cape Verde Islands, 9, 60, 206–207, 231

Caravels, 55–56, 64
Cardiff Museum, 42
Caribbean Sea, 22–24, 90–91, 100, 104, 110–111, 197–198, 298
Carlsen, Capt. Kurt, 306
Carnatic, 190
Carolina coast, 198
Caroline, 237
Carthaginians, 12
Cartier, Jacques, 97
Cartographers, 9, 31, 54
Carver, Nat, 183
Caspian Sea, 33
Catherine of Russia, 181
Central America, 84, 91
Champion, H.M.S., 193
Chancellor, Richard, 98
Channel Islands, 94
Charles, Cape, 129
Charles W. Morgan, 210
Charlton, Warwick, 162
Charnock, Henry, quoted, 27–28
Charts, 9, 11, 31, 57–60, 183
Chesapeake Bay, 128–130
Chicago Exhibition of 1893, 48–49, 163
Chronometers, 65, 226
City of Boston, 242
Civil War, 202, 208
Clarke, Thomas, 200
Climate, British, 18
  changing, 24–26
  Gulf Stream system and, 18–19, 22–28, 30
Climatology, 27
Clippers, 12, 48, 92, 224, 229–230
Clouds, 28
Coale, Comdr. Griffith Baily, 141
Coastlines of North Atlantic, 1–2
Cobb, Rev. Leander, 258
Cochrane, Lord, 237
Cod, 50, 57–59, 93–95, 212–215
Cod, Cape, 123, 153, 182–183, 205, 275
Collins, Edward Knight, 236, 242
Collins Line, 237, 241–242, 247
Colombo, Domenico, 71
Colonists, Massachusetts (*see* Pilgrims)
Colonists, Plymouth, 123, 137
  Spanish, 83–84
  Virginia, 105, 107–116, 119, 121, 125, 128–141
Columbia, 238
Columbus, Christopher, 20, 42, 48, 57, 61, 69–87, 96, 98–99
  crews sailing with, 75–76, 78–79, 84
  death of, 85
  education of, 71–72
  first voyage of, 69–81, 85–86
  fourth voyage of, 84
  old age of, 84–85
  personality of, 69–71, 73, 75, 82–83, 86–87
  third voyage of, 83–84
  and Vespucci, 88–90
Columbus, Ferdinand, 69, 71
Comoro Islands, 39
Compass, 217
Compasses, sailing by, 62, 64, 78
Confederate ships, 208–209
Connaught, 243
Connecticut, 170, 276
Constitution, 204
Convoys, 279–280
Copeland, Robert, 112
Cornwall, 4, 19
Corte Real, Gaspar, 58
Corte Real, João Vaz, 58, 66
Corte Real, Miguel, 58
Cortes, 91
Cortesão, Armando, quoted, 51
Corvo Island, 12
Cosa, Juan de la, 75, 89
Costa, Captain, 217
Coutinho, Admiral Gago, 298
Cowes, 272
Crest of the Wave, clipper, 229
Crews, 191–192, 250, 253, 258–260
  for Mayflower II, 166–167
  packet, 227
  racing, 272–273
  steamship, 239–241
  whaling, 210–211
Crisis, packet, 229
Croatan Island, 114–115

Crusades, 52
Cuba, 80, 272, 298
Cunard, Samuel, 237–240, 247
Cunard Line, 225–226, 236, 239–242, 245
Curaçao, 237
Curtiss flying boats, 294–295
Cutoff eddies, 30–31
Cutty Sark, 225
Cyclops, U.S.S., 248–249

Dampier, William, 31
Danes, 55
Dare, Virginia, 111
D'Arfet, Anna, 54–55
Davis, John, 98
Davis Straits, 50, 55, 98
Davison, Mrs. Ann, 271
Dawson, master of privateer, 191–192
Deal, Mr., 271
Dei Gratia, 250–251, 253–254, 256, 260
Delano, Capt. Amasa, 13–14
Delaware, 171
Deliverance, sloop, 140
Denmark, 48, 247
Depth of North Atlantic, 2
Derelict ships, 15
Deutsche Lufthansa, 299
Deveau, Oliver, 250–253, 255, 260–262
Devon, 4, 19, 99–101, 113, 165
Dewis, Joshua, 256
Dhows, Arab, 37–39, 41, 156–159
Diamond, 137
Dias, Bartolomeo, 7, 56, 61, 74
Dias, Diniz, 56
Dickens, Charles, 223
Diesel engines, 231, 287
Dinghys, 266
Dirigibles, 293–294
Discipline, shipboard, 92–93, 239–240, 247
Discourses on the Trade Winds, Dampier, 31
Discovery, 124, 130, 140
Disease, 133, 154, 223
Doldrums, 12–14, 284
Dominica, 83, 128
Donau, 283
Dories, 211–218, 265, 267
Dorsetshire, cruiser, 282
Doyle, Conan, 263
Drake, 177
Drake, Sir Francis, 100–101, 103, 109–110
Dreadnought, packet, 224–228
Drift bottles, 28
Droughts, 27, 30
Duras, 177
Dutch, 97, 101, 107, 136, 144–145, 147, 174, 186
  in New World, 169, 172
  (*See also* Netherlands)
"Dutchman's log," 66

Eagle, U.S.C.G. bark, 231
Eannes, Gil, 56
Earth, crustal movement of, 2–3, 10
East, trade routes to, 5, 50–51, 53, 55–56, 58–59, 90, 97–98
East Indiamen, 190, 192, 219
East winds (easterlies), 7
Eels, 32–33
Egypt, 53
Electronic devices, 279, 307
Elizabeth I of England, 67, 100–101, 106–107, 109–110, 113, 117–118
Ellam, Patrick, 271
Elsa, 275
Empress of Britain, 281
England, in American Civil War, 209–210
  in American Revolution, 177–179, 185–187, 190
  colonization by, 101–102, 105, 107–116, 118–155
  discovery and exploration by, 94–100, 116–117
  packet ships, 222, 231
  sea supremacy of, 235–237
  war with Spain, 103–104, 116
  (*See also* British Isles)
England, packet, 229
English, 94, 97–103, 195, 298
  (*See also* England)

English Channel, 103, 146–149, 268–269, 281
Equator, 1–2, 13, 20, 284
Eric the Red, 45–46
Eskimos, 46, 50
Esmeraldo de Situ Orbis, 65
Essex, 207
Estonians, 274–275
Europe, climate of, 19, 21, 26
  droughts in, 27, 30
  Northern, 24
  northwest, 26
  overpopulation of, 35–36
  and shipping, 221–223
  tobacco brought to, 116
  Vikings in, 44–45
  Western, 18, 24–26
Exports, American, 171–172
Eyssen, Rear Admiral, 283

Factory ships, 208
Facy, Capt. Arthur, 112–113
Fagundes, João Alvares, 58
Falcon, 137
Falmouth postal packets, 188
Fame, 195
Farewell, Cape, 21, 45, 150
Faroe Islands, 10, 19, 45
Favorite, 209
Felicity Ann, sloop, 271
Felix, Brother, quoted, 62–63
Fender, Captain, 268
Ferdinand, King, 74–75, 82
Findlay, A. G., 18, 20
  quoted, 21
Fish and fishing, 4, 6–7, 24–25, 34, 37, 39, 50, 56, 59, 67, 93–95, 123, 130, 168, 170–171, 174, 183, 211–218
Flattery, Cape, 105
Flood, Frederick, 260–263
Flores, Azores, 16, 116, 295
Florida, 100, 107, 169
Florida, Straits of, 20, 22, 249
Florida Current, 22–23, 25
Florida Stream (*see* Gulf Stream)
Flying boats, 298–299
Flying Cloud, clipper, 229
Flying Enterprise, 306
Flying fish, 86
Fog, 21, 307
Foldboats, 271
Folger, whaleman, 31–32
Food, shipboard, 14, 66–68, 126–127, 157–159, 223
Forest King, schooner, 258
Fox, 195
France, 94, 174, 177, 180–181, 190, 212, 231, 247, 283, 289
  colonization by, 169
  trade with, 174
  (*See also* French)
Franklin, Benjamin, 31, 195
French, 97, 99–101, 108, 177, 182–184, 192–194, 242, 298
  (*See also* France)
French Huguenots, 108, 110
Frobisher, Martin, 98
Fructuosa, 57
Fuglister, F. C., 31*n.*, 33
Furnas Island, 10

Gales, 4–5, 150–152, 268, 305–306
Galleons, 8, 14, 91–92
Galway Line, 243
Gama, Vasco de, 7, 56, 61
Gates, Sir Thomas, 137, 139–140
Gazela Primeiro, barkentine, 56
Genoa, Italy, 71, 95, 257
Geomagnetic electrokinetograph, 29
George III of England, 172
George Washington, packet, 223
Germany, 231, 247, 298
Gibbs, Charles, 197
Gibraltar, 250–253, 256, 259–260, 262, 265, 288–289
Gil Eannes, 213, 215–216
Gilbert, Sir Humphrey, 98
  quoted, 67, 99, 101–102, 106–107, 115–116
Givikoske, seaman, 271
Gjoa, sloop, 99
  replica of, 162
Glaciers, 27
Glory of the Seas, clipper, 229

Gloucester, Massachusetts, 211, 265
God Speed, 124, 140
Gokstad ship, 47–48
Gold, 119, 123, 136, 145
  in California, 229–230
Gold Coast, 201
Gomes, Diego, 56
Good Hope, Cape of, 37, 39, 41, 56, 59, 74, 91, 94, 98, 105, 230, 283
Goodschall, Gottlieb, 260
Gosnold, Bartholomew, 123–124, 126, 128, 149–150
Gourock Ropework, 165
Grand Banks (*see* Newfoundland)
Grasse, Count de, 174, 183
Great Britain, 243
Great Eastern, 243–247
Great Western, 237–238, 243
Greece, 247
Greeks, 41
Greenland, 9–10, 27, 43, 45–47, 150, 206, 213
Greenland ice cap, 27
Greenwich, England, 106
Grenville, Sir Richard, 108–110, 115–116
Grieve, Mackenzie, 295–296
Guadaloupe, 83
Guanahani, 79–80
Guardafui, Cape, 37–38
Guiana, 118–119, 145
Guinea, 60, 97, 99
Guinea Current, 39
Gulf Stream, 15, 19–34, 78, 96, 150, 289
  course of, 24, 28
    changes in, 26
    tracing of, 28–33
  heat energy of, 24, 28
  whales and, 32
  width of, 31
Gulf Stream Drift, 15, 19–20, 23, 32–33, 80, 93, 267
Gulf Stream system, 19–20, 23
  complexity of, 30
Gunnbjorn, 45
Haiti, 80
Hakluyt, Richard, 118
Hakluyt Society, 65*n.*, 115, 118
Half Moon, 136
  replica of, 163–164
Halifax, Nova Scotia, 237–238
Hamner, Mr., 268
Hanno, 41
Harald Harfagre, 44–45
Harmony, schooner, 183
Hatteras, Cape, 24, 29–30, 105, 107–108, 110, 114–115
Havre, Le, 222, 234
Hawker, Harry, 295–296
Hawkins, John, 99–100, 103
Hawkins, William, 99
Head, Edward William, 259
Head winds, 40
Helluland, 46–47
Henry, Cape, 128–129
Henry the Navigator, Prince, 41–42, 51–52, 55–56, 58, 66–67, 71
Hero, Guineaman, 193–194
Hero, sloop, 276
Herodotus, 40
  quoted, 36
Herring, 24–25
Hibernia, 243
Highland Scot, 285
Hilgendorf, Robert, 225
Hindenburg, airship, 298
Hispaniola, 80
History of Merchant Shipping, Lindsay, 220
History of Plimoth Plantation, Bradford, 143
Hojeda, 89
Holland (*see* Netherlands)
Home, Sweet Home, yacht, 267
Homem, Alvaro Martins, 58
Hopestar, 248
Hopkins, Oceanus, 152, 310–311
Horn, Cape, 91, 98, 105, 152, 160, 175, 222, 229–230
Hornblower family, 164
Horse latitudes, 283

Howland, John, 144, 152
Hudson, Henry, 107, 136
Hudson River, 136, 153
Hughes, Messrs. Kelvin, 166
Hunt, preacher, 134–135
Hurricanes, 8, 26–27, 30, 76–77, 79, 104, 138–139

Ice Age, 24
Icebergs, 45, 216, 305
Icebreakers, 99, 283
Iceland, 9–10, 19, 21, 42–43, 45–46, 94
Idrisi, 11–12
Immigrants, 222–223, 228
Imperial Airways, 299
Imrama, 43
India, 55–56, 59, 80
Indian massacres, 115, 133
Indian Ocean, 4–5, 7, 23, 41, 50, 53, 60, 206, 282–283
Indians, 82
  American, 35, 117, 122–123, 130–133, 139, 154, 205
Industrial revolution, 235
Infante de Sagres, schooner, 218
Inland seas, 1, 3
International Civil Aviation Organization (ICAO), 311
International Geophysical Year, 33
International Ice Patrol, 305
Ireland, 94, 104, 116, 195–196, 228, 237, 243, 294–296
  early voyages from, 42–45
Ires, William, 76
Irish, 42–43, 227
Irish Sea, 186, 192, 196
Irma, 285
Isabella, Queen, 74–75, 82, 84
Iselin, Mr., 33
"Island of the Seven Cities," 11, 57, 94
Islands, "lost," 6, 10–11
  mythical, 11, 42–43, 54
  North Atlantic, 6, 9, 55
"Islands of the Blest," 11, 42
Italians, 71, 88, 95, 97
Italy, 71, 90, 95, 212, 231, 247

Jacobus Rex, 1607, cross, 130
Jacome, Master, 54
Jamaica, 83–84, 201
James I of England, 118–119
James Baines, clipper, 229
James River, 129, 132, 136, 138
Jamestown, Virginia, 105, 119, 121, 129–141, 277
  reconstruction of, 140–141
Jamestown fire, 134–135
Japan, 27, 83, 87
Jet airliners, 300
Joffs, seaman, 271
John and Francis, 133–135
Jones, Capt. Christopher, 144, 148–151, 153
Jones, John Paul, 175–182
Jordanhill, bark, 280
Joseph Conrad, 166–167, 234

Kearsarge, U.S.S., 209
Kennings, measurement by, 112
Kidd, Captain, 198
Kimble, George H. T., 65*n.*
Kircheiss, Capt. Carl, 282
KLM, 300
Komet, raider, 283
Kon-Tiki, raft, 271
Kurum, cutter, 271

Labrador, 18, 45, 47, 59, 96–97, 174
Labrador Current, 18, 45, 96, 214
Lajes, Tallarte de, 76
La Navidad, 80
Landing Craft for Infantry, Large (LCI[L]), 286–292
Lane, Rafe, 108, 116
Las Casas, Bishop, 69, 88–89
Latitude, 65
Lavrador, João Fagundes, 57–58
L'Egare II, 269
Le Havre, 222, 234
Leif Ericson, 46, 48–49
León, Ponce de, 20
Le Taifun, yacht, 267
Letters of marque, 193, 195–196

Leyden, Netherlands, 144–145, 147, 149
Leyland, Thomas, 202
L'Hérétique, raft, 37, 270
Lightning, clipper, 229
Lindbergh, Charles, 296–297
Lindsay, W. S., quoted, 220
Liners, 16, 222
(*See also* Steamships)
Lion, 137
Lisbon, 72, 80–82, 168, 271, 295, 298
Little Powhatan, 130
Lively, 193
Liverpool, 178–179, 185–186, 189–192, 195–196, 201–202, 222, 225, 227, 230, 238–239
Liverpool, packet, 229
Lloyd's, 267
London, 106, 121–123, 134–135, 137, 186, 222, 274, 278, 300
London company, 134, 145, 147
London General Steam Navigation Company, 236
Longboats, 146–147, 157, 166
Longitude, 65
Loran, 29
Lorenzen brothers, 260
Lottery, 202
Louis XVI of France, 180–181
Louisiana, 169
Lousado, schooner, 218
Luckner, Count Felix von, 283–286
Lyonesse, 6

Machin, Robert, 54–55
McKay, Donald, 229, 237
Madalan, brigantine, 231
Madeira, 9–10, 54–55, 60, 72–73, 86, 94, 113, 205–207, 211
Magellan, Ferdinand, 61, 91
Magellan, Straits of, 91, 98
Mail contracts, 233, 238–239
Maine, 47, 124, 138
Maldive Islands, 50, 231
Maps (*see* Charts)
Maria das Flores, schooner, 218
Maribianca, tramp, 268–269
Mariners, 194
early, 4–5
European, 5–8, 31
Marion J. Douglas, schooner, 267
Markham, Sir Clements, 115
Markland, 46–47
Marquess, Lionheart, 217
Martens, Arian, 260
Martha's Vineyard, 123
Martyr, Peter, 20
Mary, Queen, 100
Mary, steamer, 295
Mary Celeste, 249–264
Mary Margaret, 136
Maryland, 173
Massachusetts, 25, 47, 142, 153–155, 171–172
Massasoit, 154
Mathematics, navigation and, 53, 65
Matthew, 95–96
Mauro, Fra, 60
Mayflower, 142–144, 146–154
life aboard, 156–161
Mayflower II, 161–168
Mediterranean Sea, 4–5, 37–38, 72, 183
Melanie Schulte, 248
Melbourne, Australia, 285–286
Melgueiro, David, 58, 66
Mentor, 191–192
Merchant seaman in world wars, 278
Merchantmen, 283
sailing, 204
sinking of, in wars, 278–282, 291
Merrimac, 204
Mexico, 91, 100
Mexico, Gulf of, 8, 22–23
Miami, Florida, 274–275
Mic, yacht, 267
Mines, 280
Minnesota, runic stone of, 44
Mocha Dick, 207
Monitor, 204
Monks, Irish, 42–43
Monoplanes, 296–298
Monsoons, 39
Moonshine, 98
Moors, 52–53, 58–59, 197

Mopelia, schooner, 284
Morales, Pedro, 55
Morehouse, Captain, 250, 253–254, 260, 262
Moslems, 52
Motor torpedo boats, 275
Mozambique Current, 39
M'Quie, Capt. Peter, 200
Muller, Charlie, 284
Mutiny, 200, 239
Mystic River, 170, 210

Nantucket, Massachusetts, 206–208
Nationality, determination of, 310–311
Nautical instruments, 62, 64, 78, 166
Naval architecture, 53
Naval stores, 170–171
Navidad, La, 80
Navigation, astronomical, 28, 47, 53–54, 64
  by Columbus, 80–81
  by compass, 62, 64, 78
  electronic, 29, 279, 307
  Gulf Stream current and, 31–32
  science of, 9, 51, 53–54, 59–62, 64–66
  sixteenth century, 112–113
  (*See also* Sailing)
Navigation Acts, 173
Navs, 92
Necho, Pharaoh, 36, 38, 40
Negroes (*see* Slave trade)
Nelson, Lord, 175, 182–184
Netherlands, 103, 144–146, 190
  trade with, 174
  (*See also* Dutch)
Nevis, 128
New Amsterdam, 169, 172
New Bedford, Massachusetts, 206–208, 210
New Brunswick, 231
New England, 94, 169–170, 172, 175, 189–190, 195
  founding of, 142–155
  shipping and, 220–221, 229–230
  whaling and, 205–211
New Jersey, 171
New South Wales, 272
New York City, 171–172, 221–222, 225, 228, 233–234, 237–238, 257, 271, 275, 284, 296–297, 299–300
New York State, 171, 175
Newfoundland, 9–10, 47–48, 55–60, 67, 93–97, 101–102, 243, 294–296
  Grand Banks, 29–30, 57, 67, 95–97
    fisheries, 57–58, 93, 95, 97, 149, 150, 168, 174, 211–218, 267
Newport, Capt. Christopher, 124, 130, 133–136
Newport, Rhode Island, 33, 43, 272
Newport News, Virginia, 141
Niagara, 245–246
Niña, 75, 78, 80–81
  replica of, 75, 163
Noble, Captain, 200–201
Norfolk, Virginia, 171, 287
Normandie, 247
Normandy, 44
North Africa, 52
North America, 32, 46, 56, 98
  climate of, 18, 26
  colonization of, 101–102, 105–107, 118–155, 170
  first British colony in, 101–102
  first ship built in, 170
  first white child born in, 111
  (*See also* United States)
North Atlantic, 1, 12, 16–17
  age of, 2–3
  air service across, 293–304
  charts of, early, 9
  climate around, 18–19, 22–27
  coastline of, 1–2
  discoveries of, early, 36
  islands of, 6, 9–11, 16
  myths about, 6, 42–43, 54
  present-day, 305–312
  size of, 2–3
  weather pattern of, 4–5
North Atlantic Drift (*see* Gulf Stream Drift)
North Atlantic Memoir, Findlay, 21
North Cape, 4, 18, 280
North Carolina, 105, 119
North Equatorial Drift, 23

North Pacific, 23
North Pole, 1–2, 299
North Sea, 19, 24–25, 58, 103, 179, 280
Northeast Passage, 98–99
Northwest Passage, 58, 61
Norway, 4, 18–19, 21, 35, 43–46, 48, 94, 247, 275
Norwegian Sea, 19
Norwegians, 99
(*See also* Vikings)
Nova Scotia, 47, 94–96, 101, 174, 211, 231, 237, 250, 256, 268

Oarsmen, 38
Ocean currents, 7, 23, 25–28, 30, 39
recording of, 33
Ocean lanes, 239, 273
Ocean Passages of the World, 22
Oceanographers, 25, 27, 33, 220–221
Olinda, 275
Oluf the White, 43
Operation Cabot, 29–31, 34
Orenda, 268
Orinoco River, 119
Oseberg ship, 47
Oysters, 130

Pacheco, Duarte, 61, 65
Pacific, 242
Pacific Ocean, 56, 91, 206–207, 271, 283
North, 23
South, 23, 282
Packet ships, 188, 219–231
Painted-port ships, 187
Palmas, Cape, 3
Palmer, Nat, 176
Palos, 75–76
Pan American World Airways, 298–299
Panama, Isthmus of, 83, 91, 229
Panama Canal, 230
Papal Bulls, 97
Paris, 296
Parma, 166–167
Pass of Balmaha, 285
Passenger service, 222–230, 232–237
air vs. sea, 301–304, 310–311
Patience, sloop, 140
Pearson, Captain, 179–180
Pelican, H.M. sloop, 196
Pennsylvania, 171
Percy, George, 130–131
Peru, 91
Peter, cartographer, 54
Petroleum, whaling and, 208, 210
Philadelphia, 171, 220
Philip II of Spain, 100, 102
Phillips, Sir Thomas, 57
Phoenicians, 36–42
Pilgrims, 143–145, 147–155, 157–160
Pillars of Hercules, 10, 12, 40
Pilots, 78, 182–183
Portuguese, 60
Pinmore, bark, 284
Pinta, 75–76, 78, 82
replica of, 75, 163
Pinzón, Martín Alonzo, 78, 82
Pinzón brothers, 75, 81
Piracy, 101–102, 112–113, 119, 193, 197–199
Pizarro, 91
Planetary air current, 26–27
Plankton, 270
Plato, 10–11
Plymouth, England, 101, 109, 114, 148–150, 165, 272
Plymouth, Massachusetts, 142, 154–155, 161, 196, 275
Plymouth Company, 123, 145
Plymouth Plantation, 164
Pocahontas, 132–133, 141
Polar ice, 99
Polar routes, pioneering of, 98
scheduled flights over, 299
Populations, pressure of, 35–36
shift in, 26
Porto Santo, 54, 72
Portugal, 6, 52, 247
archives of, 57, 59–60
Columbus in, 72–74, 80–82
discovery and exploration by, 52–68, 90, 97, 100
fisheries, 58–59, 94–95, 168, 211–213

Portuguese, 7, 36–37, 42, 51–68, 71, 90, 298
in the Americas, 91, 98–100, 207
fishermen, 94–95, 168, 211–218
Portuguese Pioneers, The, Prestage, 67*n.*
Potatoes, 116
Powhatan, 131–132, 136, 141
Little, 130
Preble, Mr., 195
Prediction of the Unpredictable, A, 34
Prestage, Edgar, 67
Privateering, 107, 112, 172, 174, 176–179, 185–197
Providence, Rhode Island, 171, 231
Provincetown, Massachusetts, 153
Prussia, 195
Puerto Rico, 83
Purdy, J., 9
Puritans, 170, 210
Pyramid of Khufu, 53–54

Q-ships, 281–282
Queen Elizabeth, 247
Queens, the, 245, 309

Race, Cape, 59
Radar, 279, 307
Radiation thermometers, airborne, 29
Radio, 309
Radio beams, 29
Radioactive waste, disposal of, 33
Rafts, 37, 86, 269–271, 311
Raiders, 282–285
Raleigh, Sir Walter, 101, 106–113, 116–119
Ranger, 176–177
Read, Captain, 220
Read, Mary, 198–199
Red Cross Line, 224
Red Sea, 37, 40
Red Star Line, 222
Refugees, 274–275
Revenge, 116
Rhadamanthus, 237
Richardson, Albert G., 259, 264
Richmond, Virginia, 130, 136
Rigging, 38, 49, 61
barkentine, 55–56
Rio Lima, schooner, 218
Rising Star, 237
Roanoke adventure, 105–116
Roanoke Island, 105, 109
Roberts, Bartholomew, 197
Rockefeller, John D., Jr., 141
Rodney, Admiral, 183
Roe, 113
Romans, 41
Romer, Captain, 271
Route Books, 64–65, 112
Royal Mail Line, 238
Royal William, 237
Rudders, side, 49
Russians, 98–99
Rut, John, 97
Ryan Company, 297

Sagas, 46
Sagres, Navigation School at, 54, 60, 64
Observatory of, 54
Sagres, Point of, 4, 52
Sailing, fair-wind, 86
modern, 166–168
problems of, 37–38
in small boats, 265–277
to windward, 37–38
(*See also* Navigation)
Sailing ships, 12–17, 35–50
British, 64
disadvantages of, 232–233
Norwegian, 47–50
Phoenician, 36–37, 41
Portuguese, 7, 55–56, 61–68
reckoning for, 65–66
rigging of, 38
Spanish, 63
Sails, 49–50, 61–62, 166
number of, 38
packet ship, 224
St. Augustine, Florida, 108
St. Brandan, 42–43
St. Brandan's Isle, 42

St. George's Bank, 182–183
St. George's Channel, 195
St. John's, Newfoundland, 101, 211, 216–218, 243
St. Lawrence River, 97
St. Malo, France, 97
St. Michael Island, 10
St. Nazaire, 16
St. Paul Rocks, 9, 13–14
St. Vincent, Cape, 4, 81
Salem, Massachusetts, 171
Salt, 3, 19, 25
Salvage awards, 260, 262
Salvage tugs, 305–306
Samkey, 248
Samuels, Samuel, 224–227, 239
San Domingo, 83
San Salvador, 79
Sandglasses, 63–64
Santa María, 71, 75–78, 80–81
  replica of, 75, 163–164
São Paulo, 248
São Roque, Cape, 3
Sargasso Sea, 8, 13–15, 32–33, 168
Savannah, 234
Scandinavian airliners, 299–300
Schlimbach, Capt. Ludwig, 271
Schmidt, Johannes, 32
Schnorkels, 279
Schooners, 63
  derelict, 15
Scilly Islands, 11, 37, 267
Scotland, 4, 16, 19, 44, 103–104, 165–166, 175–176, 196, 235, 295
Scurvy, 68
Sea horses, 14
Sea serpents, 8–9
Sea surveyors, 28–29
Sea Venture, 137, 139
Sea Witch, clipper, 229
Seamen (*see* Crews; Mariners)
Seaplanes, 298
Seasickness, 269
Seaweed, 8, 14–15, 21, 168
Seaworthiness, size and, 273
Seeadler, 283–285
Semmes, Comdr. Raphael, 208
Senhora da Saude, schooner, 218
Serapis, 179–180
Seven seas, the, 1
Shallops, 130, 146, 153
Sharks, 16
Shenandoah, 208–210
Shetland Islands, 10
Ship losses, 308–309
Shipbuilding, 161–168, 172, 191, 220
Shipping (*see* Trade)
Ships, 4–5, 12
  vs. aircraft, 301–304, 310–311
  derelict, 15
  sailing (*see* Sailing ships)
  seaworthy, 37–38, 43
  steam (*see* Steamships)
Shipwrecks, 21, 217–218, 227–229, 241–242, 248–264, 270, 274, 306–308
Shufeldt, Capt. R. W., 252
Siberia, 26, 283
Silver, 173
Sintra, Pedro de, 60
Sirius, 237–238
Slave trade, 99, 171, 176, 186, 194, 199–203
Slocum, Capt. Joshua, 265–267
Smith, Captain John, 119–141, 205
  quoted, 130
Somers, Sir George, 137, 139–140
Sopranino, yacht, 271, 273
South, the, 199
South Africa, 276
South America, 83, 89, 91
  (*See also* Brazil)
South Atlantic, 3, 23, 220, 282, 284
  coastline of, 3
  size of, 3
  winds of, 39
South Pacific, 23, 282
South Pole, 89
South Sea Islands, 207
South Shetland Islands, 277
Southampton, England, 146–148
Spain, 48, 57, 61, 247, 272
  Columbus in, 61, 73–74, 80–82, 84–85
  conflict with England, 100–104, 116
  discovery and exploration by, 88, 90–94, 97–99
  fisheries, 91–92, 212

Spanish, 90, 94–95, 102–103, 186
in the Americas, 91, 98–101, 105, 107–109, 111, 116, 119, 121, 123, 145
Spanish Armada, 102–104, 113
Spanish Main, 88–104
Sparkes, Mr. and Mrs., 271
Speed of ships, 65–66
Speedwell, 146–149
Spice Islands, 55
Sprague, Horatio, 259–260
Spray, yacht, 265–267
Squanto, 154
Square-riggers, 222, 224–225, 231
Stamp Act of 1765, 173–174
Standish, Miles, 154
Starvation, 133–134, 139, 223
Steam engines, 235–236, 244
Steamships, 229–230, 232–247
first, 233–234, 237
Stephen Whitney, packet, 228
Stockholm, 307–308
Stoertebeker, yawl, 271
Stop watches, 66
Strommel, Mr., 33
Submarines, 196
German, 278–281, 289–292
Italian, 283
Suez Canal, 230
old, 40, 42
Sumter, 208
Sun, radiation of, 27–28
Sunshine, 98
Supercargoes, 72
Superstition, 77–78
Surcouf, Robert, 194
Susan Constant, 122–125, 130, 140
Swallow, 138
Swallow, J. C., 33
Swallowtail Line, 222
Sweden, 247, 272

Tagus River, 80–81
Taifun, Le, yacht, 267
Tampa, cutter, 25
Tarshish, 42
Tasman Sea, 56
Tea trade, 230
Teach, Blackbeard, 197–198
Teive, Diogo de, 57–58, 66
Temperature, subsurface, 29
Tempest, 242
Temptress, yacht, 271
Terra Nova (*see* Newfoundland)
Thomas, 200
Thorfinn Karlsefni, 46
Thorne, Robert, 98
Tiger, 108–109
Time, measurement of, 63–64, 66
Titanic, 305, 308
Tobacco, 116–117, 119, 170–171, 173, 189
Tobago, 83
Tordesillas, Treaty of, 61
Torpedo boats, 275
Torpedoes, 279
Toumelin, Jacques-Ives de, 271
Trade, 6, 12, 41
American, 93, 170–174, 234–235
Australian, 229, 243
British, 235–237
Caribbean, 90
Eastern, 5, 53, 56, 58–59
Guinea, 60, 97
West Indian, 83, 91–92
(*See also* Privateering)
Trade winds, 6–7, 23, 41, 61, 93, 267, 271
northeast, 39, 77, 80
Train, Enoch, 229
Trans-Canada Air Lines (TCA), 300
Trans World Airlines (TWA), 299–300
Transatlantic cable, 245–246
Transatlantic flights, 293–304, 310–311
Transatlantic yacht races, 265, 272
Treasure, sunken, 198
Trinidad, 83, 119
Tristán, Nuño, 56
Trouin, Duguay, 194
True Blooded Yankee, 195
Turks, 122–123
Turmoil, tug, 306
Typhoons, 27

U-boats (*see* Submarines)
United Kingdom, 242
United States, beginning of, 105
climate of, 25–27
droughts in, 27, 30
Viking relics in, 43
United States, frigate, 196
United States, liner, 309–310
United States, packet, 229
United States Coast Guard, 276, 305, 307, 309
United States Navy, 294
Unity, 137–138
Upham, Stuart, 165

Van Keulen, 9
Verde, Cape, 60
Verrazano, 97
Vespucci, Amerigo, 88
Vickers Vimy bombers, 296
Vikings, 7, 35, 42–50
Vinland, 44, 46–48
Virgin Islands, 83, 128
Virginia, 47
colonies in, 101–102, 105–120, 145–146, 169–170, 173
first map of, 135
Jamestown settlement, 121–141
Virginia, 138

Waddell, Captain, 208–209
Wales, 4, 11, 94
War of 1812, 195
Warr, Lord de la, 137, 139–140
Watchkeeping, 62–63
Water, fresh, 39, 66, 68
salt, 270–271
velocity of, 29
Waters, Comdr. D. W., 63*n.*
Watling Island, 79, 86
Watt, James, and Company, 244
Weather, 3–5
(*See also* Climate)
Weather information service, 306–307
Websters, sailmakers, 166
Wellman, Mr., 294
West Africa, 39, 42, 52, 196, 201–202
West Indiamen, 190
West Indies, 128, 182, 183, 197, 238
discovery and exploration, 9–10, 71, 79–80, 83–84, 89–91, 99–100
slave trade in, 199–202
trade with, 169, 172–173, 188, 189
West winds (westerlies), 7, 43, 52
Western Isles, 267
Western Ocean (*see* North Atlantic)
Whale oil, 206
Whalebone, 205–206
Whales and whaling, 32, 205–211
White, John, 111–112, 114–115
Whitehaven, England, 177
Wilke, Leopold, 163
Williamsburg, Virginia, 141
Winchester, James H., 253, 257, 262
Winds, circulatory movements of, 26, 39
continental, 25–26
easterlies, 7
system of, 23, 27–28, 38
trade (*see* Trade winds)
westerlies, 7, 43, 52
Wine, 68
Wingfield, President, 129, 132–133
Winthrop, Governor, 170
Women pirates, 198–199
Woods Hole Oceanographic Institution, 25, 31*n.*, 33–34
Wool trade, 230
World War I, 278, 281, 283–286
World War II, 278–283, 286–292
Worthington, L. V., 31*n.*, 33

Yacht races, Gulf Stream and, 33–34
Yachts, 265–268, 271–273, 277
Yankee, 196
Young, Captain, 209

Zacuto, 54
Zarco, João Gonçalves, 54–55

ABOUT THE AUTHOR

Alan Villiers, born in Australia, went to sea at the age of fifteen, and one year later got his first glimpse of the Atlantic, when as an ordinary seaman in a lime-juice four-masted bark, he sailed from Australia to France. He has sailed throughout the world, and has crossed the Atlantic as many times as any man alive, in a great variety of vessels.

Included in *Wild Ocean* is a description of the new *Mayflower*, made in England as a replica of the original—"58 feet in the keel, 24 feet odd in the beam, some 12 feet deep, and 90 feet from stem to stern." The new *Mayflower*, commanded by Alan Villiers, set sail in the spring of 1957 to make the same voyage to Plymouth that was made in 1620.

Alan Villiers is the author of some twenty books about the sea and his seagoing adventures, including *Posted Missing*, *Quest of the Schooner Argus*, *By Way of Cape Horn*, and *Cruise of the Conrad*. This is Mr. Villier's third book in the "Oceans of the World" series, the others being *The Coral Sea* and *Monsoon Seas.*